Second Language Lexical Processes

SECOND LANGUAGE ACQUISITION
Series Editor: Professor David Singleton, *Trinity College, Dublin, Ireland*

This series brings together titles dealing with a variety of aspects of language acquisition and processing in situations where a language or languages other than the native language is involved. Second language is thus interpreted in its broadest possible sense. The volumes included in the series all offer in their different ways, on the one hand, exposition and discussion of empirical findings and, on the other, some degree of theoretical reflection. In this latter connection, no particular theoretical stance is privileged in the series; nor is any relevant perspective – sociolinguistic, psycholinguistic, neurolinguistic, etc. – deemed out of place. The intended readership of the series includes final-year undergraduates working on second language acquisition projects, postgraduate students involved in second language acquisition research, and researchers and teachers in general whose interests include a second language acquisition component.

Other Books in the Series
Studying Speaking to Inform Second Language Learning
   Diana Boxer and Andrew D. Cohen (eds)
Language Acquisition: The Age Factor (2nd edn)
   David Singleton and Lisa Ryan
Focus on French as a Foreign Language: Multidisciplinary Approaches
   Jean-Marc Dewaele (ed.)
Second Language Writing Systems
   Vivian Cook and Benedetta Bassetti (eds)
Third Language Learners: Pragmatic Production and Awareness
   Maria Pilar Safont Jordà
Artificial Intelligence in Second Language Learning: Raising Error Awareness
   Marina Dodigovic
Studies of Fossilization in Second Language Acquisition
   ZhaoHong Han and Terence Odlin (eds)
Language Learners in Study Abroad Contexts
   Margaret A. DuFon and Eton Churchill (eds)
Early Trilingualism: A Focus on Questions
   Julia D. Barnes
Cross-linguistic Influences in the Second Language Lexicon
   Janusz Arabski (ed.)
Motivation, Language Attitudes and Globalisation: A Hungarian Perspective
   Zoltán Dörnyei, Kata Csizér and Nóra Németh
Age and the Rate of Foreign Language Learning
   Carmen Muñoz (ed.)
Investigating Tasks in Formal Language Learning
   María del Pilar García Mayo (ed.)
Input for Instructed L2 Learners: The Relevance of Relevance
   Anna Nizegorodcew
Cross-linguistic Similarity in Foreign Language Learning
   Håkan Ringbom

For more details of these or any other of our publications, please contact:
Multilingual Matters, Frankfurt Lodge, Clevedon Hall,
Victoria Road, Clevedon, BS21 7HH, England
http://www.multilingual-matters.com

SECOND LANGUAGE ACQUISITION 23
Series Editor: David Singleton, *Trinity College, Dublin, Ireland*

Second Language Lexical Processes
Applied Linguistic and Psycholinguistic Perspectives

Edited by
Zsolt Lengyel and Judit Navracsics

MULTILINGUAL MATTERS LTD
Clevedon • Buffalo • Toronto

Library of Congress Cataloging in Publication Data
Second Language Lexical Processes: Applied Linguistic and Psycholinguistic
Perspectives/Edited by Zsolt Lengyel and Judit Navracsics.
Second Language Acquisition: 23
Includes bibliographical references and index.
1. Second language acquisition. 2. Lexicology–Psycological aspects. I. Lengyel, Zsolt.
II. Navracsics, Judith
P118.2.S4356 2007
401'.93–dc22   2007000093

British Library Cataloguing in Publication Data
A catalogue entry for this book is available from the British Library.

ISBN-13: 978-1-85359-967-5 (hbk)
ISBN-13: 978-1-85359-966-8 (pbk)

Multilingual Matters Ltd
UK: Frankfurt Lodge, Clevedon Hall, Victoria Road, Clevedon BS21 7HH.
USA: UTP, 2250 Military Road, Tonawanda, NY 14150, USA.
Canada: UTP, 5201 Dufferin Street, North York, Ontario M3H 5T8, Canada.

Copyright © 2007 Zsolt Lengyel, Judit Navracsics and the authors of individual chapters.

All rights reserved. No part of this work may be reproduced in any form or by any means without permission in writing from the publisher.

The policy of Multilingual Matters/Channel View Publications is to use papers that are natural, renewable and recyclable products, made from wood grown in sustainable forests. In the manufacturing process of our books, and to further support our policy, preference is given to printers that have FSC and PEFC Chain of Custody certification. The FSC and/or PEFC logos will appear on those books where full certification has been granted to the printer concerned.

Typeset by Techset Composition Ltd.

Contents

The Contributors vii

Preface xi
Zsolt Lengyel and Judit Navracsics

Part 1: The Nature of the L2 Mental Lexicon
1 How Integrated is the Integrated Mental Lexicon?
   David Singleton 3
2 Word Classes and the Bilingual Mental Lexicon
   Judit Navracsics 17

Part 2: L2 Lexical Perception and Production
3 Speech Perception Processing in First and Second Language
   in Bilinguals and L2 Learners
   Mária Gósy 39
4 A Comparative Study of Mother-Tongue and Foreign
   Language Speech Perception, Lexical Access and Speech
   Comprehension Processes
   Orsolya Simon 60
5 Slip of the Doctor's Eye: Recognising English Contact
   Induced Features in Hungarian Medical Texts
   Csilla Keresztes 83

Part 3: The Lexicon in L2 Writing
6 Vocabulary Assessment in Writing: Lexical Statistics
   Ewa Witalisz 101
7 The Use of High- and Low-Frequency Verbs in
   English Native and Non-Native Student Writing
   Katalin Doró 117

Part 4: The Lexicon in Second Language Acquisition
8 Selection of Grammatical Morphemes in Early Bilingual Development
  Zsuzsanna Gergely 133
9 The Importance of Language Specific Features for Vocabulary Acquisition: An Example of Croatian
  Lidija Cvikić 146
10 Analysing L2 Lexical Processes Via C Test
  Zsolt Lengyel, Judit Navracsics, and Anikó Szilágyi 166

Index 186

The Contributors

Cvikić, Lidija (University of Zagreb, Croatia)

Lidija Cvikić took her BA in Croatian language and literature and she is a PhD student of linguistics at the same University. She is a research fellow at the University of Zagreb, Department of Croatian language and literature. Her research focuses on Croatian as a second and foreign language, second language grammar and vocabulary acquisition. She has been teaching Croatian as L2 in the University School of Croatian Language and Culture, University of Zagreb for many years. She also spent two academic years at the Indiana University, Bloomington, USA, as a visiting instructor for the Croatian language.

Doró, Katalin (University of Szeged, Hungary)

Katalin Doró took her MA in Italian, American Studies and Russian at the University of Szeged, Hungary, where she is an assistant professor in applied linguistics. She has been carrying out research in the field of English and Italian as a second/foreign language. She has published academic papers and teaching materials in Hungarian, English and Italian. She is also involved in the university's English Applied Linguistics PhD programme researching the receptive and productive vocabulary of Hungarian EFL students.

Gergely, Zsuzsanna (University of Pécs, Hungary)

Zsuzsanna Gergely took her MA in English and General and Applied Linguistics at the University of Pécs. She taught at Klára Leőwey Grammar School, and she has been teaching full-time at the English Department of Pécs University since 1988, specialising in bilingualism, partly as a result of her marriage to an Englishman and the subsequent birth of a child. She has been the author of several papers on language development. Recently she has begun to publish her findings in bilingual acquisition. At present she is writing her PhD dissertation: "Linguistic Theory in the Light of Bilingual Acquisition."

Gósy, Mária (Research Institute for Linguistics, Hungarian Academy of Sciences and Eötvös Loránd University, Budapest, Hungary)

Mária Gósy took her MA and PhD in phonetics at ELTE, Budapest, the DSc academic doctoral degree, and she undertook her habilitation. She has been member of the Chief Scientific Board of the Presidency of the Hungarian Academy of Sciences, Secretary General of the International Society of Phonetic Sciences. She was a board member of ESCA European Speech Communication Association in 1997–2000. She was given the Brassai Sámuel Award for applied phonetic research in 2004. Mária Gósy is the author and editor of many books and papers on experimental and applied phonetics, psycholinguistics and speech disorders.

Keresztes, Csilla (University of Szeged, Hungary)

Csilla Keresztes (Rapoltine) took her MA in English, General and Applied Linguistics and Philosophy at the University of Szeged, Hungary. She worked at the Department of Social Medicine as an assistant lecturer, and wrote her dissertation in Social Medicine (Patient Information). She works for the English-Hungarian Medical Translator Group at the Faculty of General Medicine (Szeged, Hungary) as a teacher and coordinator of the Medical and Pharmaceutical Translator Courses. She attends the English Applied Linguistics PhD Programme researching English contact induced features in Hungarian medical texts, especially hospital discharge reports from the field of Cardiology.

Lengyel, Zsolt (University of Pannonia, Veszprém, Hungary)

Zsolt Lengyel is Professor at the University of Pannonia, Veszprém, part time Professor at the University of Pécs and visiting Professor at Zagreb University, Croatia. He took his MA in Hungarian, Russian philology and Applied linguistics at Debrecen University, Hungary. He received his PhD in developmental psycholinguistics. He was given the Brassai Sámuel Award in 2002. His research interests include language development of Hungarian children, development of literacy before schooling, bilingual education in the kindergarten, word associations of 10- 14-year-old children and students of 18–24 years of age. He has written numerous articles, books on the mentioned topics. He is editor, member of editorial boards of several applied linguistics journals both in Hungary and abroad.

Navracsics, Judit (University of Pannonia, Veszprém, Hungary)

Judit Navracsics took her MA degree in Russian at Eötvös Loránd University, Budapest, in English at the University of Pannonia, Veszprém, her PhD degree at Pécs University and her habilitation at Eötvös Loránd University, Budapest. She is Associate Professor in the Department of Applied Linguistics at the University of Pannonia. She is Secretary of the Applied Linguistics Branch of the Hungarian Academy of Sciences, and her habilitation is under way. She does research into bi- and multilingualism. She is the author and editor of books and papers on childhood bi- and trilingualism, the psycholinguistic aspects of multilingualism, early second language acquisition and the bilingual mental lexicon.

Simon, Orsolya (University of Pannonia, Veszprém, Hungary)

Orsolya Simon is Assistant Professor in the Department of Applied Linguistics, University of Pannonia, Veszprém, Hungary. She took her MA in English and Portuguese at Eötvös Loránd University, Budapest. She has been working for the Department of Applied Linguistics since 1996 and has taught subjects mainly in the fields of Psycholinguistics and Neurolinguistics. She has been involved in the projects of the Centre for Language Examinations (University of Pannonia, Veszprém). She focuses her research on speech perception and comprehension from a psycholinguistic aspect. Her PhD dissertation (2006) is a comparative analysis of mother-tongue and foreign language speech perception, lexical access and speech comprehension processes of 11- and 12-year-old schoolchildren.

Singleton, David (Trinity College Dublin)

David Singleton took his BA at Trinity College Dublin and his PhD at the University of Cambridge. He is a Fellow of Trinity College Dublin, where he is Associate Professor of Applied Linguistics and Head of Discipline at the Centre for Language and Communication Studies. He has served as President of the Irish Association for Applied Linguistics, as Secretary General of the International Association of Applied Linguistics and as President of the European Second Language Association. He has published books and articles across a wide range of topics in the areas of language learning and teaching – including syllabus design and pedagogical grammar – but in recent years his principal domains of interest have been cross-linguistic influence, the age factor in language acquisition, multilingualism and the mental lexicon.

Szilágyi, Anikó (University of Pannonia, Veszprém, Hungary)

Anikó Szilágyi is Assistant Professor in the Department of Applied Linguistics, Pannon University, Veszprém, Hungary. She took her MA in Hungarian and German at Eötvös Loránd University, Budapest. She has been working for the Department of Applied Linguistics since 1999 and has taught subjects mainly in the fields of sociolinguistics and minority studies. She has been involved in the projects of the Centre for Language Examinations (Pannon University, Veszprém). She focuses her research on the acquisition of German among Hungarians and the linguistic questions of German minorities in Hungary.

Witalisz, Ewa (Jagiellonian University, Kraków, Poland)

Ewa Witalisz took her MA in English, and PhD in Applied Linguistics at Jagiellonian University, Kraków, Poland, where she has been lecturer at the English Department since 1988. Her research area embraces L2 writing, process writing, teaching writing to advanced EFL learners, transfer in L2 writing, error analysis in written English and lexical statistics. Her publications concern various aspects of L2 writing such as teaching writing to advanced EFL learners, introducing process writing into a Polish setting, developing writing expertise, analysing written English produced by poor EFL learners (vocabulary assessment, error analysis, writing assessment, evaluation of content and organisation).

Preface

ZSOLT LENGYEL and JUDIT NAVRACSICS

This book provides a multidisciplinary perspective on processes in the L2 mental lexicon, including insights from psycholinguistics, corpus linguistics and educational linguistics. The novelty of the book is that the studies make reference not only to English but also to a Finno-Ugric language (namely Hungarian).

The four parts provide different perspectives of the lexicon and lexical processing. In Part 1, the two papers discuss the nature of the bilingual lexicon. David Singleton, in his paper, critically reviews evidence from various strands of research bearing on cross-lexical interaction and argues that, at some level, and in some sense, there is separation between the lexicons associated with the different languages known to an individual.

The structure and the build up of the bilingual mental lexicon are the focus of attention in the paper written by Judit Navracsics. Her goal is to find out whether the bilingual mental lexicon works the same way as the monolingual one or whether there are differences between the storages of lexemes.

In Part 2, the three papers highlight the questions of speech perception and production in second language lexical processing. In Mária Gósy's paper, monolingual and bilingual children's speech perception processing is compared in their two languages with the aim of finding specific similarities and differences in their perceptual mechanisms. The actual goal of this study is to investigate the speech perception subprocesses of Hungarian-speaking children, both in their first language (Hungarian) and in their second language (English), and to compare their data with that of Hungarian-English bilingual children whose dominant language is claimed to be Hungarian. In her study, Orsolya Simon summarises research findings on the relationship between L1 and L2 perception and comprehension processes of a hundred 11-year-old and a hundred 12-year-old Hungarian schoolchildren. Eight standardised subtests on perception, lexical access and comprehension of both Hungarian and English (as a foreign language) were used for the research. Csilla Keresztes, in her project, controlled processing of visual stimuli and carried out an investigation by making medical professionals proof-read Hungarian medical texts. Hungarians in the field of medicine are significantly under the influence of the English language and tend to use various types of Anglicism.

Part 3 describes second language writing. In the first of the two papers, Ewa Witalisz discusses vocabulary assessment in writing with the focus on quantitative measures of learner production, that is, lexical richness, such as lexical variation (type-token ratio), lexical sophistication (the ratio of sophisticated word families to all word families) and lexical density (the ratio of content to grammatical words). Katalin Doró, in her contribution, investigates the lexical complexity of verbs in English narratives written by Hungarian high-school students and American children on the basis of four pictures. Authentic learner and native speaker data are compared using linguistic software tools to facilitate the initial stage of the linguistic analysis.

Part 4 introduces the lexicon in second language acquisition, both under natural circumstances and in the classroom environment. The paper, written by Zsuzsanna Gergely, contributes data to refute the idea of an initial single system of vocabulary and grammar. The data are drawn from the observation of the early utterances of a Hungarian-English bilingual child. Mixing happens in both directions. In her paper, Lidija Cvikić deals with intralexical factors that influence vocabulary acquisition in Croatian as a second language. The data were collected by using a vocabulary translation test. The same types of incorrect answers made by the speakers of two different L1 (English and Italian) confirm the intralexical nature of errors. In the study undertaken by Zsolt Lengyel, Judit Navracsics and Anikó Szilágyi, L2 lexical processes are analysed with the help of cloze tests administered to Hungarians with English and German as target languages. The study provides the reader with valuable information and conclusions about the lexical processes deployed by subjects at different stages in their acquisition of their L2.

Research into the lexicon has always been hard to conduct; descriptions of cognitive and linguistic development are always subject to inference and uncertainty. These difficulties are compounded when two languages occupy the linguistic domain of mind. Questions of integration, storage, vocabulary acquisition and assessment, word retrieval and lexical access are the focus of the studies reported in this volume, which includes reference to language users from a Finno-Ugric (Hungarian) and a Slavic language background.

The book is intended for the use of undergraduate and graduate university and college students majoring in any kind of second language studies, psycholinguistics and/or bilingualism researchers. It is also for the use of teachers and academics whose interests include a second language acquisition component.

Part 1
The Nature of the L2 Mental Lexicon

Chapter 1
How Integrated is the Integrated Mental Lexicon?

DAVID SINGLETON

Separation or Integration?

The L2 mental lexicon has sometimes been represented as qualitatively different and, by implication, separate and distinct from the L1 mental lexicon (e.g. Meara, 1984). Arguments against such a qualitative difference are not hard to find (Joannopoulou, 2002; Singleton, 1999; Singleton & Little, 1991; Wolter, 2001), and indeed have sometimes gone to the opposite extreme (Cook, 1992; Dijkstra, 2001, 2003; Franceschini *et al.*, 2003 – all discussed below). This chapter critically reviews evidence from various strands of research bearing on cross-lexical interaction and argues on the basis of this review that at some level, and in some sense, there must be separation between the lexicons associated with the different languages known to an individual.

The Integrationist Perspective

There is, of course, plenty of evidence – from a wide range of research domains (cf. Singleton, 1999: chap. 4) – that the L2 and the L1 mental lexicons dynamically interact (cf. Herdina & Jessner, 2001), and such evidence clearly indicates a high degree of L1–L2 connectivity. Whether, however, it points to integration in the strongest sense of the term is another matter. We shall explore, in the following, three representative sets of proposals espousing the integrationist perspective and see how far in fact they take us in the integrationist direction.

Evidence cited by Cook (1992) in respect of lexical aspects of his 'multicompetence' model includes the following:

- Reaction time to a word in one language is related to the frequency of its cognate in another known language (Caramazza & Brones, 1979).

- Morphemic similarities between two known languages influence translation performance (Cristoffanini *et al.*, 1986).
- When processing an interlingual homograph, bilinguals access its meanings in both their languages rather than just the meaning specific to the language being used (Beauvillain & Grainger, 1987).

Clearly, such evidence suggests extremely high levels of interaction between the L1 and L2 mental lexicons, but it does not amount to a convincing case for the idea of a fully unitary mental lexicon. Cook, recognizing this, goes no further than talking about 'intricate links between the two language systems in multicompetence' (Cook, 1999: 193). He notes (2003: 7f.) that 'total separation is impossible since both languages are in the same mind' but also that 'total integration is impossible since L2 users can keep the languages apart', going on to suggest that 'between these two extreme, and probably untenable positions of total separation and total integration, there are many different degrees and types of interconnection'.

Dijkstra (2001, 2003) cites experimental findings that, according to him, indicate that when a particular word form is activated, similar lexemes known to the individual are activated also, whatever the language affiliation of the forms in question. The findings to which he refers largely derive from studies where the stimulus words were decontextualized and often presented in written form. Such conditions may particularly favour the activation of formal 'neighbours' across languages. The question of whether constraining contexts in normal linguistic interaction impede the activation of one language or another has not to date been explored with any rigour. It may be worth recalling that, although early research on the activation of meanings of polysemous/homonymous words suggested that contextual factors did not inhibit context-unrelated meanings (e.g. Swinney, 1979), more recent research indicates that when contexts are *strongly* constraining only contextually relevant meanings are activated (Moss & Gaskell, 1999; Simpson & Krueger, 1991; Tabossi *et al.*, 1987). However, even if parallel activation does occur in contextualized language use, this does not of itself confirm the proposition of unitariness in the bilingual/multilingual lexicon; it can be explained simply in terms of a high level of connectivity between lexicons. Dijkstra himself accepts that individual languages as sets can be at different levels of activation, and, indeed, proposes a model in which 'language nodes' are operative, thus acknowledging that the lexical items and processes associated with each of the languages known to an individual may be activated and/or deactivated as a set.

Franceschini *et al.* (2003) interpret recent brain-imaging research as indicating that lexical-semantic aspects of the processing of all languages known to an individual make use of the same areas of the cerebral cortex. This again suggests very close connections between lexical operations relating to the languages in question, but does not justify the inference of Franceschini *et al.* that lexical-semantic processing draws on a common system across languages. For one thing, there are (Fabbro 2002: 209f.) important limitations to the current methodology of neuro-imaging. For another, 'cortical topography is at best the surface component of a multidimensional set of systems – cortical linked with subcortical – that enable us to use language' (Obler & Gjerlow, 1999: 168), which implies that we need to beware of over-interpreting topographical evidence. Finally, we need to remind ourselves that every language articulates the world differently in terms of its lexical structure, and that the concepts and configurations of concepts that are lexicalized vary from language to language. What this signifies is that, to the extent that L2 learners make use of the lexico-semantic system specific to their L2, they must be drawing on a system that is differentiated from that of the L1.

Arguments for Separation

One argument against L1–L2 lexical integration – at least in respect of adolescent/adult L2 learners – derives from the modularity hypothesis (e.g. Singleton, 1998), which sees the mind as comprising (perhaps in addition to some general-purpose structures) of 'a number of distinct, specialized, structurally idiosyncratic modules' (Garfield, 1987: 1), one of which is devoted to language (e.g. Fodor, 1983). Some modularists suggest that a substantial part of the functioning of the L1 mental lexicon is intramodular (e.g. Emmorey & Fromkin, 1988; Smith & Wilson, 1979), and some hold that any L2 competence acquired beyond the childhood years is extramodular (Bley-Vroman, 1989). Taken together, these two positions imply that, in the case of a post-pubertal learner of additional languages, the lexical operations of these languages are isolated from those of the L1.

A perhaps more persuasive argument against total integration relates to the fact that languages differ widely in formal terms. An individual faced with the task of coming to grips with the morphological structure of an unfamiliar word will refer to the phonological structure of more familiar items and then analogize (Bybee, 1988; Stemberger & MacWhinney, 1988). To take an example from English, someone encountering *adeptness* for the first time will refer to the structure of such words as *cleverness* and *sweetness*.

As the languages known to such an individual may have highly divergent phonological systems (e.g. /nəs/ would not be a possible syllable in Chinese), the implication is that the search on which such analogizing depends runs through the lexicon of each language separately.

Other evidence pointing to separation comes from reports of the selective recovery of languages lost in the wake of brain damage and of aphasia affecting only one of a multilingual's languages (e.g. Fabbro, 1999: chaps. 12–16). Thus, Whitaker (1978: 27) discusses the case of an English classics scholar who recovered Greek, Latin, French and English (his L1) in that order, and Grosjean (1982: 260) refers to the instance of a native speaker of Swiss German who recovered first French and subsequently Standard High German, but who never recovered his native variety. With regard to aphasia, Paradis and Goldblum (1989) report the case of a trilingual subject who, following a brain operation, evidenced disorders typical of Broca's aphasia in Gujarati (his L1), but no deficits in his other languages, Malagasi and French.

Noteworthy also is the fact that individuals who have more than one language at their disposal typically keep their languages apart, to the extent that where the expectation is that language x is being spoken but, in fact, language y is being used, comprehension may be blocked, even where both languages are known to the individual in question. This is shown in the following example (from Elisabet Service):

> My sister, while studying in France was once addressed on the street in Finnish. Only after several attempts by the speaker did she understand her own native language, the point being that she was expecting French. I have had a very similar experience trying to make Finnish out of something that was easy enough to understand when I realized it was English. (Service: personal communication)

We should perhaps recall that the demise of the Contrastive Analysis Hypothesis was occasioned by the discovery that many L2 errors 'seem to have little, if any, connection with the mother tongue' (Dušková, 1969: 19). Cross-linguistic influence admittedly increases when the languages involved are perceived as close (Kellerman, 1977, 1979, 1983; Ringbom, 1987); however, the very fact of this 'psychotypological' dimension runs counter to the notion of total lexical integration, as it implies a degree of selectivity in relation to consultation of the languages represented (cf. Singleton, 2003, and discussion below).

With regard to cases where languages are not kept apart – that is, cases of code-switching – these have been seen (De Bot & Schreuder, 1993) as evidence in favour of the notion that both languages are continuously activated, although each to a different level (cf. Green 1986, 1993; Paradis, 1981). For De Bot and Schreuder (1993: 212), activation models allow for the possibility that 'words from the non-intended language may always slip in' – a very different concept, let it be said, from the notion of lexical unitariness, presupposing as it does intention, selection and separability (even if it also presupposes that the system sometimes breaks down). One might add that the manner in which code-switching proceeds appears to be sensitive to the particularities of the languages involved. For example, Myers-Scotton (2003) notes that code-switching between Arabic and English exhibits a very high proportion of embedded English inflectional phrases (i.e. phrases including a tensed verb) where Arabic is the matrix language. Myers-Scotton argues that the reason for this atypically large number of embedded language 'islands' is the essential incongruity between the Arabic frame and the nature of English verbs. Such sensitivity to cross-linguistic incongruities constitutes further evidence of the separation of languages in the mind.

Let us return, as a coda to this section, to the question of language loss. We saw earlier that languages may be lost as a result of brain damage. However, languages may also be lost in other circumstances. Where, for example, a child migrating to a particular community has an L1 that is different from that of the majority of members of the host community, where his/her home language receives little or no support from the community in question and where his/her parents make little or no effort to support it either, the language in question may attrite to the point of virtual disappearance. A number of case studies of such L1 attrition are reported by Kouritzin (1999). One such case (Kouritzin 1999: 75–96) is that of Lara, who had migrated with her family from Finland to Canada at age two, and had subsequently lived for four years in a small town within a tight-knit Finnish community. Lara was thus, until the age of six, a Finnish speaker with very little English. From age six onwards, however, having moved to a large city, and under the influence of her parents' decision that the time had come to integrate with English-speaking Canada, her development in Finnish came to a halt and English progressively took over. Lara reports that the last time she tried (and failed) to converse in Finnish had been when she was eighteen years old. Her current perception is that she has lost her L1. Here, then, we have an instance of a family taking a decision to favour one language and effectively to abandon another, with the result that the latter language was lost, which clearly implies choice, which in turn implies separation.

A more extreme case of this phenomenon is that of the subjects studied by Schmid (2002), namely 54 German Jews who emigrated from Nazi

Germany between 1933 and 1939 and who subsequently spent their lives in Anglophone countries (either England or the United States of America). When Schmid analysed the attitudes of her subjects towards the German language she found that, essentially, the later in the 1930s they had left, and the more intense the persecution they had accordingly experienced, the more negative their attitudes towards German tended to be, and the less inclined they were to continue using German. Those who had turned away from German in this way were found to have lost more of their German than those who had not. For such deliberate rejection of a particular language in favour of another to be able to take place, the languages in question clearly must have separate identities in the individual's mind. Competence in the rejected language may remain at a high level even decades after the rejection, as Schmid's study also shows, and it may continue to have a strong influence on the processing and use of the replacement language. Nevertheless, the language user is clear which language is which and which language he/she is attempting to use and which language he/she does not wish to use.

Degrees of Integration

The most widely cited model of the relationship between the L1 and the L2 mental lexicon is Weinreich's (1953) account in terms of 'subordinative', 'compound' and 'co-ordinate' categories. In subordinative bilingualism, L2 word forms are represented as connected to L1 meanings via primary connections to L1 forms. In compound bilingualism the L1 and L2 forms are seen as connected at the meaning level. In co-ordinate bilingualism separate systems of form-meaning links are assumed to exist for each language. Weinreich sees these different types of bilingualism as associated with different types of learning experience, but he acknowledges (1953: 10) that a person's bilingualism need not be of a single kind. One notes also that all of Weinreich's categories are predicated upon some degree of separateness.

More recent research suggests that different types of L1–L2 relationship may co-exist in the same mind-brain. Thus, De Groot (1993, 1995) proposes a mixed representational system, where concrete words and words perceived as cognates across the two languages are stored in a 'compound' manner, whereas abstract words and noncognates in the respective languages are stored in a 'co-ordinate' manner. Kirsner *et al.* (1993: 228) go further, suggesting that, as far as cognates are concerned, there may be integration at the formal level – that 'some fraction of the second language vocabulary is represented and stored as variants of the first language vocabulary'. The suggestion seems to be that, for example, Anglophone learners of French store French *table* as a 'variant' of English *table*. However, *variant* implies that the French version is stored with its specifically French pronunciation and also that it is tagged to be deployed whenever the active language is French, which in turn implies selectivity rather than full integration.

Some research indicates a proficiency effect on bilingual lexical organization, subordinative structure being associated with low proficiency, and compound and co-ordinate structure with higher proficiency (De Groot, 1995; Jiang, 2000; Kroll & De Groot, 1997; Kroll & Tokowicz, 2001; Woutersen, 1997). Cieślicka (2000), for her part, takes the line that formal-associative and conceptual links exist in some measure between the L1 and L2 mental lexicons in all learners, but that 'associative links linking various nodes will vary in strength according to the type of a bilingual person's experience in his or her L2' (Cieślicka, 2000: 33). Again, however, it is clear that none of the above researchers is proposing that the L1 and L2 lexicons are completely undifferentiated at any proficiency stage.

Cook (2003) posits an 'Integration Continuum' that 'favours a single mental system within which a balance can be struck between elements of a particular aspect of language in a particular situation' (p. 10) and which 'implies that the relationship of integration versus separation varies from component to component' (p. 11). There is, of course, no contradiction between arguing for a 'single mental system' while not postulating integration. The former need only imply that L1 knowledge and L2 knowledge are in intimate contact with each other and may affect each other in language learning and use; the latter, on the other hand, would imply that L1 and L2 knowledge are completely undifferentiated by the language user – an idea that Cook, for good reasons, discards.

Some Relevant Findings (Old and New) from Ireland

To return to the psychotypological dimension of cross-lexical interaction, a number of studies carried out in Ireland since the 1980s have yielded evidence of such a dimension. Brief summaries of six of these studies follow.

Study I (Singleton & Little, 1984/2005)

Study I investigated the degree to which Anglophone subjects with no previous experience of Dutch could make sense of a Dutch text. It also collected introspective data on the process of dealing with the text (via immediate retrospection). The participants were university students, all of whom had learned other languages; some had learned German and the rest had no knowledge of any Germanic language other than English. The findings of the study were as follows:

- Participants with knowledge of German outscored those without German by on average about 30%.
- Participants with German found the task easier than those without.
- A large majority of participants in both categories mentioned the strategy of looking for clues from other languages.
- Most who mentioned this strategy referred only to the language that was typologically closer to Dutch than their other languages (German in the case of subjects with German, English in the case of the others).

Study II (Singleton, 1987)

Study II focused on a beginning adult learner of French whose native language was English and who had some knowledge of Irish, Latin and Spanish. Irish and Latin he had learned at school, his Spanish had been acquired during a three-year working visit to Spain, and his French had been picked up during three very brief visits to France. He was recorded conversing in French and performing short narration/description and translation tasks. Some introspective data were also gathered. The relevant findings were as follows:

- When trying to produce French, this learner privileged Spanish as a source of transfer over English, Irish and Latin, English being the second most often drawn-upon transfer source.
- He knew Spanish to be typologically related to French.
- He was aware this relatedness had practical value when he was communicating in French.

A neater result might have been for Latin to have outstripped English as a transfer source. On the other hand, this learner's competence in English was incomparably broader, deeper and more active than his knowledge of Latin. It is worth adding too that in lexical terms English can be regarded as, to a considerable degree, a Romance language like Spanish (cf. below).

Study III (Singleton and Little, 1991; Singleton, 1999: chap. 7)

Study III analysed responses from English-speaking university students of French and German to C-tests in their respective target languages. Of particular relevance here are instances where participants had produced coinages drawing on their L1. Examples include, in French, *fanaticisme* (required word: *fanatisme*; cf. English *fanaticism*) and, in German, *Army* (required word: *Armee*; cf. English *army*). English–German coinages were very markedly less frequent than English–French coinages, which Singleton and Little ascribe to psychotypological factors. They point out that, whereas English is in its basic structure a Germanic language, in lexical terms it can plausibly regarded as a Romance language. English-speaking learners of French soon realize that large numbers of English words can – after a relatively straightforward 'conversion' process – readily be deployed in French. With regard to German, on the other hand, apart from loan-words and a few cases where English and German share virtually identical descendants of Proto-Germanic forms, 'converting' English words into their German cognates is more complicated, requiring one to put into reverse at least two sound shifts.

Study IV (Herwig, 2004)

Study IV was based on an empirical investigation involving subjects in the composition of a story in their L1 and the subsequent translation of the same story into another language. The translation task required subjects to provide concurrent think-aloud data. Of particular interest here is that part of the study which had a plurilingual dimension. The subjects in this case were four university students of Germanic languages – three of whom had English as L1 and the fourth, Norwegian. Their programme included courses in German, which they had learned at school, and *ab initio* instruction in Dutch and Swedish. These subjects were asked to translate their L1 story not only into German but also into Dutch and Swedish. What emerged was that English was used when subjects were exploring the semantics of different aspects of the translation tasks – formulating approximation strategies, and so on – but that actual cross-lexical borrowing drew predominantly on 'pure' Germanic sources (Dutch and Swedish when the translation was into German, Dutch and German when the translation was into Dutch, and so on). The fact that the Norwegian student also used English at the semantic exploration level is explained by Herwig in terms of the fact that this student lived in an English-speaking environment and studied her target languages through the medium of English.

Study V (Singleton and Ó Laoire, 2006a, b)

Study V was a two-part investigation that involved Anglophone learners of French (L3) in providing French synonyms and antonyms for underlined words in French sentences, as well as introspecting on this task. The first part of the study focused on learners of French as an L3 who had considerable experience of Irish as an L2. English rather than Irish influence predominated in these participants' errors, which was interpreted as reflective of a psychotypological factor, because English is lexically much closer to French than is Irish. However, as the privileged transfer source in this case was English, one explanation that had to be entertained was that English was simply more firmly entrenched than Irish. The study was therefore replicated with informants who had both English and Irish as L1s. English continued to emerge as a privileged source of cross-lexical borrowing, which, for the researchers established the notion of psychotypological causation more firmly.

All five of the above studies, in keeping with a wealth of other research findings (see references cited earlier), point to a strong psychotypological factor in the operation of cross-lexical influence. As has already been argued, psychotypology undermines the notion of a unitary mental lexicon, because it implies a degree of selectivity with respect to the consultation of the languages known to an individual. A possible integrationist explanation of the data underpinning psychotypological perspectives might be that a given form simply triggers all similar forms available to the subject. Such parallel activation, as we have seen, certainly occurs. However, there is evidence that selectivity of consultation occurs at a level well above that of the individual word. A sixth study conducted in Ireland, summarised below, yields evidence in precisely this direction.

Study VI (Soufra, 2001)

Study VI investigated English–Greek cross-lexical influence affecting beginning English-speaking learners of Modern Greek. The elicitation instrument comprised Greek–English written translation tasks and a multiple-choice collocation recognition task (again written). Although the study found abundant evidence of cross-lexical influence, it also found that in some instances where the formal and semantic relationship between the Greek and English terms was very close indeed – for example, γαλαξίας: *galaxy*, αυθεντικός: *authentic* – learners failed to make the connection. Soufra's explanation is that Anglophone learners of Greek perceive the distance between Greek and English as being relatively large and do not therefore pay as much attention to similarities between Greek and English forms as one might expect.

The kind of psychotypological assessment – in this instance of a negative kind – plausibly posited by Soufra implies that there is a dimension to the process of lexical activation that has to do with attributes and perceptions at the language level rather than at the level of lexical items; this in turn implies a degree of psychological differentiation and therefore separation between different languages and their associated lexicons.

Conclusion

There are clearly many persuasive arguments favouring the idea of a high degree of cross-lexical connectivity, but such arguments do not license the notion of a complete absence of differentiation. The proposition that the lexis associated with various languages known to an individual are stored and processed without any regard for their language affiliation does not appear to be sustainable in the light of the full range of empirical evidence.

The findings from the Irish studies reviewed above suggest (along with many other studies) that when we encounter new languages we make judgements about their relationship to languages we already know and in processing terms exploit our lexical resources accordingly, prioritising those of our established languages that we judge to be most useful and making less use of those that we see as less relevant. Such judgements and prioritisation would seem to be incompatible with any suggestion that multilingual lexical knowledge is radically unitary.

References

Beauvillain, C. and Grainger, J. (1987) Accessing interlexical homographs: Some limitations of a language-selective access. *Journal of Memory and Language* 26, 658–672.

Bley-Vroman, R. (1989) What is the logical nature of foreign language learning? In S. Gass and J. Schachter (eds) *Linguistic Perspectives on Second Language Acquisition*. Cambridge: Cambridge University Press.

Bybee, J. (1988) Morphology as lexical organization. In M. Hammond and M. Noonan (eds) *Theoretical Morphology*. London: Academic Press.

Caramazza, A. and Brones, I. (1979) Lexical access in bilinguals. *Bulletin of the Psychonomic Society* 13, 212–214.

Cenoz, J., Jessner, U. and Hufeisen, B. (eds) (2003) *The Multilingual Lexicon*. Dordrecht: Kluwer.

Cieślicka, A. (2000) The effect of language proficiency and L2 vocabulary learning strategies on patterns of bilingual lexical processing. *Poznań Studies in Contemporary Linguistics* 36, 27–53.

Cook, V. (1992) Evidence for multicompetence. *Language Learning* 42, 557–591.

Cook, V. (1999) Going beyond the native speaker in language teaching. *TESOL Quarterly* 33 (2), 185–209.

Cook, V. (2003) Introduction: the changing L1 in the L2 user's mind. In V. Cook (ed.) *Effects of the Second Language on the First*. Clevedon: Multilingual Matters.

Cristoffanini, P., Kirsner, K. and Milech, D. (1986) Bilingual lexical representation: The status of Spanish–English cognates. *Quarterly Journal of Experimental Psychology* 38A, 367–393.

De Bot, K. and Schreuder, R. (1993) Word production and the bilingual lexicon. In R. Schreuder and B. Weltens (eds) *The Bilingual Lexicon*. Amsterdam: Benjamins.

De Groot, A. (1993) Word-type effects in bilingual processing tasks: Support for a mixed-representational system. In R. Schreuder and B. Weltens (eds) *The Bilingual Lexicon*. Amsterdam: Benjamins.

De Groot, A. (1995) Determinants of bilingual lexicosemantic organisation. *Computer Assisted Language Learning* 8, 151–180.

Dijkstra, T. (2001) What we know about bilingual word recognition: A review of studies and models. Paper presented at the Third International Symposium on Bilingualism, Bristol.

Dijkstra, T. (2003) Lexical processing in bilinguals and multilinguals. In J. Cenoz, U. Jessner and B. Hufeisen (eds) *The Multilingual Lexicon*. Dordrecht: Kluwer.

Dušková, L. (1969) On sources of errors in foreign language learning. *IRAL* 7, 11–36.

Emmorey, K. and Fromkin, V. (1988) The mental lexicon. In F. Newmeyer (ed.) *Linguistics: The Cambridge Survey. Volume III. Language: Psychological and Biological Aspects*. Cambridge: Cambridge University Press.

Fabbro, F. (1999) *The Neurolinguistics of Bilingualism: An Introduction*. Hove: Psychology Press.

Fabbro, F. (2002) The neurolinguistics of L2 users. In V. Cook (ed.) *Portraits of the L2 User*. Clevedon: Multilingual Matters.

Fodor, J. (1983) *The Modularity of Mind: An Essay on Faculty Psychology*. Cambridge, MA: MIT Press.

Franceschini, R., Zappatore, D. and Nitsch, C. (2003) Lexicon in the brain: What neurobiology has to say about languages. In J. Cenoz, U. Jessner and B. Hufeisen (eds) *The Multilingual Lexicon*. Dordrecht: Kluwer.

Garfield, J. (1987) Introduction: Carving the mind at its joints. In J. Garfield (ed.) *Modularity in Knowledge Representation and Natural-Language Understanding*. Cambridge, MA: MIT Press.

Green, D. (1986) Control, activation and resource: A framework and a model for the control of speech in bilinguals. *Brain and Language* 27, 210–223.

Green, D. (1993) Towards a model of L2 comprehension and production. In R. Schreuder and B. Weltens (eds) *The Bilingual Lexicon*. Amsterdam: John Benjamins, 249–277.

Grosjean, F. (1982) *Life with Two Languages: An Introduction to Bilingualism*. Cambridge, MA: Harvard University Press.

Hammond, M. and Noonan, M. (eds) (1988) *Theoretical Morphology*. London: Academic Press.

Herdina, P. and Jessner, U. (2001) *A Dynamic Model of Multilingualism*. Clevedon: Multilingual Matters.

Herwig, A. (2004) *Aspects of Linguistic Organization: Evidence from Lexical Processing in L1–L2 Translation*. Vasa: Faculty of Education, Åbo Akademi.

Jiang, N. (2000) Lexical representation and development in a second language. *Applied Linguistics* 21, 47–77.

Joannopoulou, M. (2002) Form and meaning in the second language lexicon: Some evidence from Greek advanced learners of English. *Journal of Applied Linguistics* 18, 29–42.
Kellerman, E. (1977) Towards a characterization of the strategy of transfer in second language learning. *Interlanguage Studies Bulletin* 2, 58–145.
Kellerman, E. (1979) Transfer and non-transfer: Where are we now? *Studies in Second Language Acquisition* 2, 37–57.
Kellerman, E. (1983) Now you see it, now you don't. In S. Gass and L. Selinker (eds) *Language Transfer in Language Learning*. Rowley, MA: Newbury House.
Kirsner, K., Lalor, E. and Hird, K. (1993) The bilingual lexicon: Exercise, meaning and morphology. In R. Schreuder and B. Weltens (eds) *The Bilingual Lexicon*. Amsterdam: Benjamins.
Kouritzin, S.G. (1999) *Face[t]s of First Language Loss*. Mahwah, NJ: Lawrence Erlbaum Associates.
Kroll, J.F. and De Groot, A.M.B. (1997) Lexical and conceptual memory in the bilingual: mapping form to meaning in two languages. In A.M.B. De Groot and J.F. Kroll (eds) *Tutorials in Bilingualism: Psycholinguistic Perspectives*. Mahwah, NJ: Lawrence Erlbaum.
Kroll, J.F. and Tokowicz, N. (2001) The development of conceptual representation for words in a second language. In J.L. Nicol (ed.) *One Mind, Two Languages: Bilingual Language Processing*. Oxford: Blackwell.
Meara, P. (1984) The study of lexis in interlanguage. In A. Davies, C. Criper and A.P.R. Howatt (eds) *Interlanguage*. Edinburgh: Edinburgh University Press.
Moss, H.E. and Gaskell, M.G. (1999) Lexical semantic processing during speech comprehension. In S. Garrod and M. Pickering (eds) *Language Processing*. Hove: Psychology Press.
Myers-Scotton, C. (2003) Code-switching: Evidence of both flexibility and rigidity in language. In J.-M. Dewaele, A. Housen and L. Wei (eds) *Bilingualism: Beyond Basic Principle*s. Clevedon: Multilingual Matters.
Obler, K. and Gjerlow, K. (1999) *Language and the Brain*. Cambridge: Cambridge University Press.
Paradis, M. (1981) Neurolinguistic organization of a bilingual's two languages. In J. Copeland and P. Davis (eds) *The Seventh LACUS Forum*. Columbia, SC: Hornbeam Press.
Paradis, M. and Goldblum, M.C. (1989) Selective crossed aphasia in a trilingual aphasic patient followed by reciprocal antagonism. *Brain and Language* 36, 62–75.
Ringbom, H. (1987) *The Role of the First Language in Foreign Language Learning*. Clevedon: Multilingual Matters.
Schmid, M.S. (2002) *First Language Attrition, Use and Maintenance: The Case of German Jews in Anglophone Countries*. Amsterdam: John Benjamins.
Schreuder, R. and Weltens, B. (eds) (1993) *The Bilingual Lexicon*. Amsterdam: Benjamins.
Simpson, G.B. and Krueger, M.A. (1991) Selective access of homograph meanings in sentence context. *Journal of Memory and Language* 30, 627–643.
Singleton, D. and Ó Laoire, M. (2006a) Psychotypologie et facteur L2 dans l'influence translexicale. Une analyse de l'influence de l'anglais et de l'irlandais sur le

français L3 de l'apprenant. *Acquisition et Interaction en Langue Étrangère* 24, 101–117.
Singleton, D. and Ó Laoire, M. (2006b) Psychotypology and the 'L2 factor' in cross-lexical interaction: an analysis of English and Irish influence in learner French. In M. Bendtsen, M. Björklund, C. Fant and L. Forsman (eds) *Språk, lärande och utbildning i sikte*. Vasa, Faculty of Education, Åbo Akademi, 191–205.
Singleton, D. (1987) Mother and other tongue influence on learner French. *Studies in Second Language Acquisition* 9, 327–346.
Singleton, D. (1998) *Lexical Processing and the 'Language Module'*. Dublin: Trinity College, Centre for Language and Communication Studies (*CLCS Occasional Paper* 53), and Alexandria,Virginia (*ERIC Reports* ED 421 856).
Singleton, D. (1999) *Exploring the Second Language Mental Lexicon*. Cambridge: Cambridge University Press.
Singleton, D. (2003) Perspectives on the multilingual lexicon: A critical synthesis. In J. Cenoz, U. Jessner and B. Hufeisen (eds) *The Multilingual Lexicon*. Dordrecht: Kluwer.
Singleton, D. and Little, D. (1984) A first encounter with Dutch: Perceived language distance and language transfer as factors in comprehension. In L. Mac Mathúna and D. Singleton (eds) *Language Across Cultures* (pp. 259–269). Dublin: Irish Association for Applied Linguistics. Republished in B. Hufeisen and R.J. Fouser (eds) *Introductory Readings in L3*. Tübingen: Stauffenberg Verlag, 2005, 101–109.
Singleton, D. and Little, D. (1991) The second language lexicon: Some evidence from university-level learners of French and German. *Second Language Research* 7, 61–82.
Singleton, D. and Little, D. (2005) A first encounter with Dutch: Perceived language distance and language transfer as factors in comprehension. In B. Hufeisen and R.J. Fouser (eds) *Introductory Readings in L3* (pp. 101–109). Tübingen, Stauffenberg Verlag. First published in L. Mac Mathuna and D. Singleton (eds) *Language Across Cultures*. Dublin: Irish Association for Applied Linguistics, 1984, 259–269.
Smith, N. and Wilson, D. (1979) *Modern Linguistics: The Results of Chomsky's Revolution*. Harmondsworth: Penguin.
Soufra, M.-H. (2001) *Crosslinguistic Influence in the Acquisition of Greek as a Foreign Language*. Unpublished M. Phil. dissertation. University of Dublin, Trinity College.
Stemberger, J. and MacWhinney, B. (1988) Are inflected forms stored in the lexicon? In M. Hammond and M. Noonan (eds) *Theoretical Morphology*. London: Academic Press.
Swinney, D. (1979) Lexical access during sentence comprehension: (Re)consideration of context effects, *Journal of Verbal Learning and Verbal Behavior* 18, 645–660.
Tabossi, P., Colombo, L. and Job, R. (1987) Accessing lexical ambiguity: Effects of context and dominance. *Psychological Research* 49, 161–167.
Weinreich, U. (1953) *Languages in Contact*. New York: Linguistic Circle of New York.
Whitaker, H. (1978) Bilingualism: A neurolinguistics perspective. In W. Ritchie (ed.) *Second Language Acquisition Research: Issues and Implications*. New York: Academic Press.
Wolter, B. (2001) Comparing the L1 and L2 mental lexicon: A depth of individual word knowledge model. *Studies in Second Language Acquisition* 23, 41–69.
Woutersen, M. 1997. *Bilingual Word Perception*. Nijmegen: Katholieke Universiteit Nijmegen.

Chapter 2
Word Classes and the Bilingual Mental Lexicon

JUDIT NAVRACSICS

Introduction

The mental lexicon is a kind of internal dictionary that contains not only the 'entries' for each word a speaker knows but also all the linguistic information about the word: its semantic content, syntactic properties, phonological shape, and so on. The semantic memory, which is reflected in the lexicon, is not strictly linguistic as it also contains the mental representation of the individual's knowledge of the world. This knowledge is represented in concepts and relations between these concepts (Appel & Muysken, 1987). When studying the semantic representation of bilinguals, the structure of the bilingual mental lexicon and the connections of language, thought and culture must also be taken into consideration. Studies of mental structure have never been easy to conduct and descriptions of cognitive and linguistic development are always subject to inference and uncertainty. These difficulties are compounded when two languages occupy the linguistic domain of mind (Bialystok, 1998).

In language/speech processes, it is the cerebral hemispheres and the subcerebral structures, in particular including the cerebellum, that are mostly concerned (Lamb, 1999; Gósy, 2005). The temporal, parietal regions of the cortex are responsible for the declarative memory, that is, the mental lexicon. The mental lexicon stores semantic (facts) and episodic (events) knowledge. The procedural memory is an implicit memory that stores learning skills and enables us to learn new skills, to create sequences and to use grammar. The procedural memory stems from the frontal/basal ganglia structures of the subcortical white matter. Ganglia structures, which are responsible for learning rules and serve grammatical processing, morphological and syntactic structuring, are connected to the frontal region through the thalamus and thus have an extraordinarily significant role in the unbelievably complex processes of speech production and perception (Ullmann, 2001). This memory is especially important in the creation and acquisition of sequential and hierarchical structures. The sequences having been learned may depend on the temporal-parietal regions, which then may be the points of convergence of declarative and procedural memories.

The same memories serve the language processes of bilinguals. The question arises, how can the brain cope with more than one language – or rather – is the memory store common or is it separated for each language the bilingual speaks?

There has been no consensus concerning the presumed storage theories so far. Attempts have been made to clarify whether bilinguals store information about a word and its associations separately for each language, that is, do they establish distinct types of system, or do they process words in terms of their semantic meanings and represent them in one memory store, that is, they can function as monolinguals in some aspects.

Some neurolinguists presuppose that all languages of a bilingual or a polyglot subject are localized in common language areas (cf. Paradis, 1989, 2001; Fabbro, 1999). They also claim that differences in age and manner of learning a language may influence the way languages are stored in the brain. If a second language is learnt in an instructed way at school, it is represented in the cerebral cortex more widely than the first language, but it is more likely to involve subcortical structures (basal ganglia and cerebellum) if it is acquired informally as is the case with the first language (Fabbro & Paradis, 1995; Fabbro, 2000). Event-related potentials (ERPs) reveal possible differences in the cerebral cortical organization of languages according to the age of acquisition and learning strategies, whereas there is a difference between the cerebral representation of closed-class and open-class words in L1. This difference cannot be observed in L2 if the second language was acquired after the critical age (about 7 years of age) (Weber-Fox & Neville, 1997). However, Chee et al. (1999) found that cortical representation of words in bilinguals involved the same cortical areas regardless of the age of acquisition of L2 and that cerebral asymmetries were the same for both languages and identical to those of monolinguals. Positron emission tomography (PET) and functional magnetic resonance imaging (fMRI) studies found no difference in the activation of the two languages in the basal ganglia (Fabbro, 2001). Illes et al., (1999) and Hernandez et al., (2000) used fMRI to investigate brain activation during a naming task and found no evidence that each language was represented in different macroanatomical areas of the brain. In contrast, Kim *et al.*, (1997) reported differential activation of left frontal regions for L1 and L2 for subjects with varying native languages who acquired the second language at a later age ($M = 11.2$ years) but not for childhood learners of various L1 and L2 combinations. However, there were no differences for either group in the left temporal areas. There have been findings concerning different cortical activation depending on word classes (Gósy, 2005).

In summary, neuroimaging studies on differences of activation between first and second language production have so far led to controversial results (cf. De Bleser *et al.*, 2003). Evidence both supporting and contradicting the role of age and manner of language acquisition has been found so far.

In the psycholinguistic approach to the study of bilingual speech processing, language fluency has also been taken into account when considering the question of storage. According to Kroll and Stewart's hierarchical model of bilingual memory representation (Kroll & Stewart, 1994), less fluent bilinguals appear to have a dual-store, and the more fluent ones a single-store conceptual representation. This model proposes that the conceptual store is connected to both L1 and L2 lexicons. However, the connections between the L1 lexicon and the conceptual store are strong and direct, whereas the connections between the L2 lexicon and the conceptual store are weak. Thus, the subject's L1 is more likely to access the conceptual store directly than the subject's L2. Heredia, in his Second Revision (R-2) Hierarchical Model (1996), suggests using the terms MDL (more dominant language) and LDL (less dominant language) instead of L1 and L2, based on the simple fact that in many cases L2 becomes more dominant than the earlier acquired L1. In this way, MDL has a stronger and more direct connection to the conceptual store regardless of whether it is L1 or L2.

As language proficiency increases, the connection between the word and its meaning becomes more direct, relying less on a mediating connection through the L1 lexicon. The degree of meaning similarity between the words within a translation pair may ultimately determine the bilingual representational form. The more similar the meanings of the translations, the more likely they are to be stored compoundly in the mental lexicon. For many words in one language, a truly equivalent term does not exist in the other language (De Groot, 1993). Singleton (1999) claims that the relationship between a given L2 word and a given L1 word in the mental lexicon will vary from individual to individual, depending on how the words have been acquired and how well they are known, and also on the degree to which formal and/or semantic similarity is perceived between the L2 word and the L1 word in question.

Models of speech production distinguishing thought from verbal formulation carry two immediate implications for models of bilingual performance as follows:

- There must be a mapping between the conceptual representation and the specification of word meanings.
- Such a mapping might differ between languages because languages differ in terms of how concepts are lexicalized. Macroplanning is language-independent, microplanning is language-specific (Green, 1993).

Results of recent word association tests show that words are stored according to their meaning relations. The closest link that can be observed in information storage is the semantic one, which means we prefer to build our mental lexicon either in strings of synonyms or in antonym pairs, but we very often put together hyponyms and meronyms (Jackson & Zé Amvela, 2000). Sometimes, meaning relations can be observed only because words belong to the same semantic field. However, apart from the semantic links, syntagmatic structures are also built and are present as set expressions in the mental lexicon. There is a third kind of relation which could be called miscellaneous when, due to the activation of the associative memory, which can be based either on similar sounding or on random memories from the past, words seemingly having linguistically nothing in common are retrieved. According to Cook (1996), age plays a crucial role in storage as in the first language children go through a regular progression called the syntagmatic/paradigmatic shift, that is, they start with syntagmatic responses and move on to paradigmatic responses. In L2, a similar shift seems apparent except that there are more of the paradigmatic miscellaneous responses (mostly as a result of similar sounding). In L2, a choice of alternative words has to be built up but the available choice will probably never be the same as in the L1.

In this study, the role of word classes in lexical storage is in focus. As languages differ in terms of how concepts are lexicalized, we wonder to what extent word classes determine the structure of the mental lexicon. In what follows, we will examine the results of a word association test carried out among bilinguals, and see whether word classes play a role in word retrieval in one language and across languages. Results of early and late bilinguals will be compared to see whether there is a difference in the structure of the mental lexicon according to the age of becoming bilingual.

Subjects and Method

There were 90 bilinguals participating in the experiment. All of them had Hungarian (a Finno-Ugric, mostly agglutinative language) as

L1 or L2. The following languages were their other language: Arabic, Chinese, Croatian, Czech, English, French, German, Greek, Italian, Latvian, Polish, Romanian, Russian, Serbian, Slovak, Swahili, Swedish and Vietnamese. The participants became bilingual at different ages: 50 of them belong to the bilingual first language category (Meisel, 1989) and 40 to the category of late bilinguals, that is, they became bilingual well after age three. Although their language competences differ, they all meet the requirements of Grosjean's definition concerning bilingualism. They use both their languages on a regular basis in their everyday life with different people, in different situations and for different purposes (Grosjean, 1997, 1998).

The subjects were given the task of saying the very first word that came into their minds after hearing 188 Hungarian prime words one after the other. The words were identical with those enumerated in the 'Hungarian Verbal Associations' edited by Balló (1983) and Jagusztinné (1985) and carried out among Hungarian monolinguals in 1979 and 1981 in the Debrecen region. The test was oral and audio-taped. The responses (16,920 items) were categorised according to the links between the prime words and the activated words. For the present analysis, we determined the word classes of both the prime and the activated words. We examined

(1) to what extent the word class of the prime word determined that of the retrieved word;
(2) whether the proportion of the same word classes was identical in words retrieved from Hungarian and in L2;
(3) the most frequent meaning relations in responses from L2 according to the word classes; and
(4) whether the results for the two age groups (that is, early and late bilinguals) were different in terms of proportion of word classes in responses.

Results

Data Analysis

The number of prime words was altogether 16,920; their word class distribution was as follows:

- nouns: 53%
- verbs: 18%
- infinitives: 6%
- adjectives: 23%.

The word class distribution of responses was somewhat different. There was a wide range of word classes in addition to the four mentioned above:

- nouns: 50%;
- verbs: 15%;
- infinitives: 2%;
- adjectives: 22%;
- adverbs, modifiers, pronouns and cardinal numbers: 5%.

There were no answers in 4%, and in 2% of the responses the subjects made up whole phrases with the prime words.

Analysing the word classes of the prime words one by one, the following can be stated: There were responses from many more kinds of word class in the retrieval from Hungarian than from L2. In the case of nouns, there were four kinds of word class, and in a lot of cases subjects made up phrases. In addition, in even more cases there were no answers. However, when subjects recalled words from their L2, they used only three word classes: nouns, adjectives, verbs.

In the verb class, seven different word classes appeared in the answers, as well as the phrases and the no answer category. In L2 responses, there were only three word classes involved: verbs, nouns and adjectives. However, phrases also appeared.

With adjectives, the same phenomenon could be observed: six word classes in Hungarian together with the phrases and the no answers; whereas in L2, again, only three word classes were involved: verbs, nouns and adjectives.

Nouns

The majority, that is 67%, of the Hungarian answers given to nouns maintained their word class. However, 18% of the answers were adjectives, 6% verbs, 1% pronouns and 1% cardinal numbers, and 2% of subjects made up phrases with the prime nouns. Thus, the ratio of paradigmatic and syntagmatic relations is 67:28 with 5% no answers. In L2 responses, the vast majority of answers preserved their word class: 95% of the answers were of paradigmatic character, that is nouns; 3% adjectives and 2% verbs make up the syntagmatic relation between primes and responses.

Verbs and infinitives

There were fewer verbs maintaining their word class in the Hungarian responses (50%) but this is still the dominant category only to a lesser extent compared to nouns. The syntagmatic relation is manifested by

25% nouns, 7% adjectives, 5% pronouns, 2% modifiers, 1% cardinal numbers, and in 5% phrases were set up. Thus, the ratio of paradigmatic and syntagmatic relations is 50 : 45 with 5% no answers. In L2 answers, the maintenance of the word class is overwhelming (90%); however, less frequently than in the case of nouns. Word classes of other types in L2 responses are as follows: nouns 8%, adjectives 1% and phrases 1%.

Adjectives

Similarly to verbs, adjectives maintain their word class in 51% of the Hungarian responses, which means they tend to create paradigmatic relations only in half of the responses. Other word classes, 38% nouns, 3% verbs, 1% pronouns, modifiers, adverbs and phrases, set up the syntagmatic relations, respectively. In L2 answers, 89% of the responses are of paradigmatic character, however, 10% of responses given to nouns and 1% of those given to verbs created syntagmatic links.

Discussion

Nouns

Nouns appear to be the most consistent in preserving their word class in the word retrievals. When answers are recalled from both languages, the occurrence of noun responses is 67%; however, when we examined answers from L2 only, this proportion was much bigger (95%). This also means that nouns tend to create paradigmatic relations to a greater extent than other word classes. This tendency is most apparent in L2 responses. It should be presumed that most of the paradigmatic relations are manifested by lexical equivalency, which we could consider a kind of cross-linguistic synonymy. The large number of lexical equivalents may be due to the way the subjects store lexical items in their lexicon. As the results show, subjects who became bilingual at a later age tend to store lexemes in a co-ordinate way. However, it is not the case with all late bilinguals, and even those who had quite a lot of lexical equivalent answers also had quite a large amount of compound storage. There was no one who would have shown only co-ordinate or compound storage. It should also be mentioned that apart from the 80% lexical equivalency, there are other types of meaning relations showing up in all L2 responses. The second biggest category in the remaining 20% are words expressing co-ordination or super-ordination. One third of the answers are hyponyms or hyperonyms, for example:

- *ablak* 'window' – *door, ajtó* 'door';
- *anya* 'mother' – *papa, tata*, 'father';

- *asszony* 'woman' – *старуха* (Ru.) 'old woman';
- *asztal* 'table' – *chair*;
- *betegség* 'illness' – *stomach-ache, pneumonie* (Fr.);
- *gyümölcs* 'fruit' – *food, pomme* (Fr.) 'apple', *яблоко* (Ru.) 'apple';
- *láb* 'foot' – *ruka* 'hand' (Slo.);
- *négyzet* 'square' – *trojuholnik* (Slo.) 'triangle', *viereck* (Ger.) 'quadrangle';
- *óceán* 'ocean' – *sea, jazero* (Slo.) 'lake', *meer* (Ger.) 'sea';
- *szék* 'chair' – *stol* (Cro., Ru., Serb.);
- *szoba* 'room' – *коридор* (Ru.) 'corridor', *hala* (Slo.) 'hall';
- *szombat* 'Saturday' – *Freitag* (Ger.) 'Friday', *Sonntag* (Ger.) 'Sunday';
- *ünnep* 'holiday' – *воскресенье* (Ru.) 'Sunday', *рождество* (Ru.) 'Christmas', *Christmas*;
- *zene* 'music' – *rock, soul, house*.

Here we can observe co-ordinate (*table* – *chair*) and super-ordinate (*illness* – *stomach-ache, pneumonie* (Fr.)) terms as well.

Let us examine the links in two co-ordinate terms which could be expected to be the responses to each other (Table 2.1).

The numbers in Table 2.1 relate to all responses, that is, word retrievals from both languages. The frequencies of appearance of the relations are amazing. They are very similar, even in the commonest retrievals in the hyponym class, too, and this meets our expectations: they mutually

Table 2.1 Links in two co-ordinate terms

asztal 'table'		*szék* 'chair'	
Lexical equivalent:	10	Lexical equivalent:	13
Miscellaneous:	23	Miscellaneous:	20
Syntagmatic:	8	Syntagmatic:	3
Hyponym:	45 (total)	Hyponym:	44 (total)
chair	36	*table*	32
furniture	2	*place to sit in*	6
cupboard	1	*wooden chair*	3
round table	2	*bed*	1
dining table	2	*sofa*	1
desk	2	*bench*	1

triggered each other to the greatest extent. In both cases, there were super-ordinate terms recalled: *'furniture'* and 'place to sit in', whereas both terms became super-ordinate themselves when they triggered retrievals denoting different kinds of table and chair. The answers create linear and hierarchical orders as well, but the linear ones are stronger in both cases, perhaps because of the reflected world in our mind: a chair and a table belong together in most cases. And this tie is stronger than the one with the different kinds of objects.

In order to display super-ordination in the mental lexicon, the super-ordinate term *szín* 'colour' and its sub-ordinate terms *zöld* 'green' and *kék* 'blue', which are co-ordinates to each other, were taken and the responses of their meaning relations were analysed (Table 2.2).

The hyponyms of the super-ordinate term are just the sub-ordinate colour names; there are no linear links, in contrast with what we could see with concrete nouns. The co-ordinate terms 'green' and 'blue' have triggered in some cases the appearance of the super-ordinate term; however, the retrieval of other colour names are much more frequent. It is interesting to see that both prime words associated each other; 'green' had 11 (44%) 'blue' answers and 'blue' 20 (53%) 'green' retrievals. To what extent culture plays a role in the mental representation and in storage is shown in the associative links of 'green' and 'blue'. There are hardly any miscellaneous responses to 'blue', for example, *ice, my favourite*

Table 2.2 Super-ordination in the mental lexicon

Szín 'colour'		zöld 'green'	kék 'blue'
Lexical equivalent:	14	15	12
Miscellaneous:	15	33	5
Hyponym:	49 (total)	25 (total)	38 (total)
	21 blue	11 blue	20 green
	12 red	5 colour	8 colour
	5 yellow	4 yellow	6 red
	4 black	4 red	2 white
	3 green	1 grey	1 black
	2 lilac		1 lilac
	2 white		

colour, her beautiful eyes, but on the contrary, many more to 'green', for example, *forest, garden, vegetation, spring, grass, tree*, and so on.

Verbs and infinitives

Half of the responses given to verbs and infinitives maintain their word class and the other half is shared between other word classes, providing many more syntagmatic and miscellaneous relations compared to nouns. The largest number of collocations are nouns (e.g. *küld* 'send' – *levelet* 'letter', *mond* 'say' – *mondatot* 'sentence'), but there are quite a few of them with adjectives (e.g. *kíván* 'wish' – *jót* 'good', *vesz* 'buy' – *sokat* 'much'), and adverbs *ígér* 'promise' – *soha* 'never', *csinál* 'do' – *jól* 'well', *dolgozik* 'work' – *gyorsan* 'fast'), too. Due to the activity of the associative memory, there are responses that do not show any linguistic links to the prime word, for example, *leül* 'sit down' – *fáradt* 'tired', *tart* 'hold' – *nehéz* 'heavy', *tanul* 'study' – *okos* 'bright'.

As for the meaning relations, it can be stated that the number of hyponyms is smaller, but synonymy and antonymy show up in larger quantities, as shown in Table 2.3. Here, we must distinguish between cross-linguistic synonyms, that is, what we called lexical equivalents, and synonyms. What do we mean by synonyms? Although hyponyms express any kind of verb of movement (*walk, stroll, go, run, dash*, etc.), synonyms show a tighter link in meaning, that is, they are verbs of fast movement (*rush, hurry, jog, dash*, etc.). Obviously, cross-linguistic synonyms are the same notions in different languages, that is, the different lexical representations of the same or very similar meaning across languages.

Adjectives

Adjectives, similar to verbs, establish paradigmatic links to a much lesser extent than nouns. Only half of the answers showed a paradigmatic relation. The most frequent collocations of adjectives were nouns (e.g. *hosszú* 'long' – *út* 'road', *kék* 'blue' – *ég* 'sky'), and there were some

Table 2.3 *Fut* 'run'

Lexical equivalent:	14
Miscellaneous:	24
Hyponym:	30 (verbs of movement)
Synonym:	8
Antonym:	5

Table 2.4 Analysis of meaning relations of adjectives

	hosszú 'long'	keserű 'bitter'
Lexical equivalent	14	6
Miscellaneous	7	11
Antonym	38	0
Hyponym	0	45
Collocation	22	19

with adverbs and verbs. Intensifiers were retrieved quite often, for example, 'very', 'hardly'. Modifiers also played a small role in making up structures with adjectives.

The analysis of the meaning relations of adjectives showed that gradable adjectives set up different relations depending on whether they have binary opposition pairs (e.g. *long–short, big–small*) or not (e.g. *bitter, thirsty, Hungarian*) (Table 2.4).

It is interesting to study the categories of antonyms and hyponyms. The word *bitter* has no antonym pair, as all of the words denoting taste exclude the meaning of bitterness and none can stand opposite this notion. However, from among the other kinds of taste retrieved by the subjects, the most frequently recalled one was *sweet*, which shows a sort of oppositeness between the two terms. Thus said, it cannot be claimed that if something is not bitter, it should be sweet: it can also be salty or sour or even sweet-sour. On the other hand, *long* had no hyponyms retrieved but had a lot of antonyms, which means the category of oppositeness, the either/or relation is much stronger than that of measurement or size or spatial expansion. Miscellaneous relations are quite rare, for example, *thin, slow, distant* when recalling words to prime *long*. There are slightly more for the prime *bitter*: *sorrow, bad, lemon*. There are a few more collocations with the adjective *long* (e.g. *struggle, road* (six times), *finger, discussion*) than with the adjective *bitter* (e.g. *grapefruit, medicine, chocolate*).

Responses of early and late bilinguals categorised according to their word classes

In both groups it can be shown that the word class of the prime word does determine that of the response (Table 2.5). However, it is also true that early bilinguals recall more words with identical word classes to

Table 2.5 The proportion of word class appearance in early and late bilinguals' responses (%)

	WC of prime words					
	Noun		Verb + Infinitive		Adjective	
WC of responses	Early	Late	Early	Late	Early	Late
Noun	**75**	**68**	19	24	31	36
Adverb	0	0	2	3	1	1
Verb + infinitive	5	5	**62**	**49**	2	2
Adjective	14	17	6	7	**62**	**53**
Modifier	0	0	2	2	1	1
Pronoun	1	1	3	6	0	1
Numeral	1	1	1	2	0	0
Phrase	1	2	2	2	1	1
No answer	3	6	3	5	2	5

WC, word class.

some extent; thus they are more inclined to give paradigmatic answers. The difference is smaller in the case of noun primes (7%), with adjectives it is 9%, and the biggest difference is in the verb and infinitive group (13%).

Apart from the occurrence of identical word classes in the vast majority of cases, we must notice that late bilinguals tend to recall responses in a greater variety of word classes than early ones, thus creating more syntagmatic relations with the prime word. The relatively large number of pronouns in late bilinguals' answers in the case of verbs and infinitives is remarkable: in many cases the subjects retrieved indefinite or interrogative pronouns in response to verbs, for example, *promise – what, somebody, something, I; love – who, somebody, me*. With regard to the 'no response' category, it is also quite striking that late bilinguals had almost double the number of omitted responses as compared to early bilinguals. Although early bilinguals gave no response 289 times (3.1%), late bilinguals did so 409 times (5.7%).

Figure 2.1 summarises the links traceable in mapping the lexicon of early and late bilinguals. There are significant differences between the appearances of paradigmatic and syntagmatic links ($\chi^2 = 85,927$, $df = 2$, $p < 0.000$). Early bilinguals gave a significantly larger number of paradigmatic responses, whereas syntagmatic links were established in a

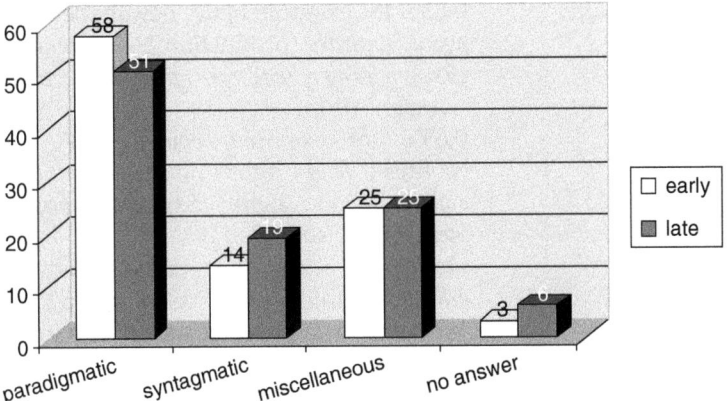

Figure 2.1 Links in the lexicon of early and late bilinguals.

significantly bigger proportion among late bilinguals. The 'no response' category was significantly larger in the data of late bilinguals as well. It is interesting to see that miscellaneous answers appear to the same extent, independently of the age of becoming bilingual.

Meaning relations in L2 responses

Nouns (9.8%)

As was mentioned above, the occurrence of lexical equivalents is quite high in the case of nouns (80%), but there is another 15% where the word class of the retrieval is noun:

- Lexical equivalent: 80%
- Miscellaneous: 10.2% for example, *pénz* 'money' – *buy*; *apa* 'daddy' – *hard*; *termelés* 'production' – *management*;
- Hyponym: 3.3% see pp. 23–24.
- Synonym: 1.2% for example, *csoport* 'group' – *team*; *fény* 'light' – *sun*; *asszony* 'woman' – *lady*;
- Antonym: 0.54% for example, *betegség* 'illness' – *health*; *barát* 'friend' – *enemy*; *baj* 'unluck' – *noroc* 'luck' (Ro.);
- Meronym: 0.65% for example *erdő* 'forest' – *bush*; *sarok* 'corner, heel' – *topánky* 'shoes' (Slo.); *négyzet* 'square' – *corner*;

- Semantic field: 0.83% for example *újság* 'newspaper' – *newsagent*; *termelés* 'production' – *урожай* 'yield' (Ru.); *leány* 'girl' – *daughter*; *женщина* 'woman' (Ru.);
- Derivation: 0.65% for example, *pont* 'point' – *exact* 'pontos'; *fény* 'light' noun – *svetlo* (Slo.), *swiatło* (Po.) 'light' adjective, *bright*; *erő* 'strength' – *strong*;
- Inflection: *utca* 'street' – *по улице* 'in the street' (Ru.);
- Compound: *erő* 'strength' – *soup* 'clear soup'; *négyzet* 'square' – *квадратный метр* 'square meter' (Ru.);
- Collocation: 1.4% for example, *lámpa* 'lamp' – *горит* 'burns' (Ru.); *nap* 'sun' – *светит* 'shines' (Ru.); *tolvaj* 'thief' – *steals*; *oldal* 'side' – *left*;
- Phrases: 0.54% for example, *név* 'name' – *my name is*; *vendég* 'guest' – *ждать гостей* 'expect guests' (Ru.).

Verbs (7.9%)
- Lexical equivalent: 83%
- Semantic field: 2.2% for example, *tanít* 'teach' – *teacher*; *jön* 'come' – *come in*;
- Antonym: 1.6% for example, *ad* 'give' – *receive*, *возьмёт* 'takes' (Ru.); *keres* 'searches' – *найдёт* 'finds' (Ru.).
- Hyponym: 1.3% for example, *felel* 'answer' – *говорит* 'speak' (Ru.), *talk*; *fut* 'run' – *walk*; *mond* 'say' – *think*; *sétál* 'walk' – *go*; *ül* 'sit' – *стоит*, *stojí* 'stand' (Ru., Slo.);
- Phrase: 1.3% for example, *lát* 'see' – *я вижу солнце* 'I see the sun' (Ru.); *tanul* 'learn' – *я хочу учиться* 'I want to study' (Ru.).
- Collocation: 1.1% for example, *tart* 'last' – *long*; *kíván* 'wish' – *zyczy* 'to live' (Po.);
- Inflection, derivation: 0.7% for example, *ad* 'gives' – *daj* 'give' (imperative) (Cro.); *elmegy* 'leaves' – *odoh* 'left' (Cro.);
- Miscellaneous: 7.9% for example, *fut* 'run' – *goal*; *vásárol* 'buy' – *money*, *Harrods*; *ül* 'sit' – *chair*; *sétál* 'walk' – *улица* 'street' (Ru.).

Infinitives (1.1%)

- Lexical equivalent: 79%
- Antonym: 3.6% for example, *aludni* 'to sleep' – *вставать* 'get up' (Ru.); *kérdezni* 'to ask' – *отвечать* 'answer' (Ru.); *répondre* 'answer' (Fr.), *answer*; *élni* 'to live' – *die*;
- Semantic field: 3.6% for example, *élni* 'to live' – *survivre* (Fr.), *survive*; *hallani* 'to hear' – *слушать* (Ru.), *to listen*;
- Derivation– collocation: 2.5% for example, *emlékezni* 'to remember' – *memory*, *memories*; *kérdezni* 'to ask' – *question*; *hallgatni* 'to listen' – *music*; *érteni* 'to understand' – *un texte* (Fr.);
- Hyponym: 2% for example, *nézni* 'to look' – *see*, *to see*; *állni* 'to stand' – *сидеть* 'to sit' (Ru.);
- Inflection: 1.5% for example, *érteni* 'to understand' – *understood*;
- Phrase: 1% for example, *kérdezni* 'to ask' – *не могу ответить* 'I can't answer', (Ru.); *állni* 'to stand' – *на ногах* 'on one's feet' (Ru.);
- Miscellaneous: 4.6% for example, *hallgatni* 'to listen' – *un squelette* 'skeleton' (Fr.); *állni* 'to stand' – *boring*; *emlékezni* 'to remember' – *story*.

Adjectives (3.9%)

- Lexical equivalent: 82%
- Antonyms: 3.2% for example, *lassú* 'slow' – *rýchly* (Slo.), *slow*; *öreg* 'old' – *mladý* (Slo.), *young*;
- Hyponym: 2.9% for example, *édes* 'sweet' – *nice, bitter*, *amar* 'bitter' (Fr.);
- Synonym: 1.5% for example, *egyszerű* 'simple' – *easy*; *kedves* 'kind' – *сладкий* 'sweet' (Ru.);
- Phrase: 1.3% for example, *drága* 'dear' – *un hotel* (Fr.); *gyors* 'quick' – *la course* (Fr.); *szomjas* 'thirsty' – *я не хочу пить* 'I don't want to drink', (Ru.);
- Semantic field, derivation: 0.8% for example, *fiatal* 'young' – *детство* 'childhood' (Ru.); *szabad* 'free' – *outside*;
- Miscellaneous: 5.4% for example, *zöld* 'green' – *vegetation*; *orosz* 'Russian' – *ушанка* 'a kind of Russian hat', *здравствуйте* 'a form of greeting in Russian'.

From the above examples, it can clearly be seen that when accessing a word, bilinguals search both their lexicons. When retrieving a word either from one language or the other, meaning and meaning relations are the most important factors. This is why there are a huge number of lexical equivalents. Thus said, besides lexical equivalents, which might be called cross-linguistic synonyms to a certain extent, other meaning or sense relations (hyponyms, antonyms, meronyms, etc.) can be observed to be very active in the same person's lexicon. Thus, we cannot claim that a bilingual individual can be categorised on how he/she stores the lexical items in their lexicons because each of them shows both co-ordinate and compound storage at the same time.

Answers given in the other language of the bilingual do not always agree with the prime word in terms of word class, and they also establish many different kinds of meaning relation. Although the number of these examples is much smaller as compared to the number of examples taken from Hungarian answers, there is still a great variety of word classes and meaning relations occurring in the answers. The relatively small number of retrievals from L2 can be explained by the test words being in Hungarian.

The comparison of early and late bilinguals according to their language choice

There is no significant correlation between the language choice in word retrieval and the word class in either group (Table 2.6). In general, it can be

Table 2.6 The proportion of appearance of L2 responses among early and late bilinguals (%)

	WC of prime words					
	Noun		Verb + infinitive		Adjective	
WC of responses	Early	Late	Early	Late	Early	Late
Noun	93	96	7	9	9	10
Adverb	0	0	0	1	1	0
Verb + infinitive	2	3	90	88	1	1
Adjective	5	1	2	1	89	89
Modifier	0	0	0	0	0	0
Pronoun	0	0	0	0	0	0
Numeral	0	0	0	0	0	0
Phrase	0	0	1	1	0	0

claimed that there are more code-switches, or rather retrievals, from L2 among the late bilinguals' responses, but there was no word class that would have promoted/triggered the code-switch better than the other. If compared, the proportions of the switches in the two age groups: 15% of the nouns, 16% of the verbs and infinitives and 14% of the adjectives were responses from the other language among early bilinguals. The same proportion, but with a greater number of occurrences of code-switches was observed among late bilinguals: 23% of nouns, 22% of verbs and infinitives and 21% of adjectives are recalled from the L2 lexicon.

Word class has an even more dominant role in word retrieval in the L2 responses, which must be due to the large number of lexical equivalents among the answers. In the case of nouns, the identical word classes in prime words and responses are greater in the late bilingual group than among early bilinguals. This must be due to the co-ordinate storage of words. In the case of verbs and infinitives, early bilinguals had more responses identical with the prime word class, whereas late bilinguals had more responses of a syntagmatic character. With adjectives, there is no difference between the two age groups' retrievals from L2 in terms of word classes. There are no examples of modifiers, pronouns or numerals appearing during the recall in any word class, only the occasional occurrence of phrases can be observed in the verbs and infinitives column.

Conclusions

It is only recently that De Groot (1995), based on an extensive review of the literature, comes to the conclusion that the bilingual memory does not exist. However, as can be seen in the tests, fluent bilinguals can sometimes use conceptual representations that are shared across their two languages. The memory of every individual is likely to contain structures of various types and these structures will occur in different proportions across bilinguals. This will depend on factors such as the level of proficiency in the languages known, the characteristics of the words, the strategy used to learn them, the context in which the languages are used, and the age at which a language was acquired.

Our data have shown that the tightest link in the lexicon is the paradigmatic one, but its appearance is significantly dependent on the age of the onset of second language acquisition. Late bilinguals gave more responses of a syntagmatic character, that could make us conclude that the declarative memory stores set phrases and expressions in late second language acquisition, especially after age 18. However, we must also remark that neglecting the role of the procedural memory would be a mistake because the responses showing syntagmatic links are not always set expressions or the expected collocations. Consequently, phrases are created, and in many cases they are mixed utterances. This might support the idea that the memory activity of fluent bilinguals is very similar (if not the same) as that of monolinguals, that is, both the declarative and procedural memories are involved in speech processing.

Based on the evidence given in this paper, we tend to argue for the common storage of languages in the bilingual lexicon. Apart from the large number of lexical equivalent responses, there are other meaning relations represented in the lexicon across the languages. Thus, next to the coordinative storage, there is a good deal of common storage of lexical items that makes us assume that the bilingual lexicon does not work as a bilingual dictionary. Rather, it works as a coherent unit which prefers arranging elements according to their notions rather than according to their forms.

References

Appel, R. and Muysken, P. (1987) *Language Contact and Bilingualism*. London/New York/Sydney/Auckland: Edward Arnold.

Balló, L. (1983) *Magyar Verbális Asszociációk 1 [Hungarian Verbal Associations* I]. Szeged: JGYTF.

Bialystok, E. (1998) *Beyond Binary Options: Effects of Two Languages on the Bilingual Mind. Studia Anglica Posnaniensia* 33, 47–60.

Chee, M.W.L., Tan, E.W.L. and Thiel, T. (1999) Mandarin and English single word processing studied with functional magnetic resonance imaging. *The Journal of Neuroscience* 19, 3050–3056.

Cook, V.J. (1996) Competence and multi-competence. In G. Brown, K. Malmkjaer and J. Williams (eds) *Performance and Competence in Second Language Acquisition* (pp. 57–69). Cambridge: Cambridge University Press.

De Bleser, R., Dupont, P., Postler, J., Bormans, G., Speelman, D., Mortelmans, L. and Debrock, M. (2003) The organization of the bilingual lexicon: A PET study. *Journal of Neurolinguistics* 16, 439–456.

De Groot, A. (1993) Word-type effects in bilingual processing tasks. In R. Schreuder and B. Weltens (eds) *The Bilingual Lexicon*. Amsterdam/Philadelphia: John Benjamins.

De Groot, A. (1995) Determinants of bilingual lexicosemantic organisation. *Computer Assisted Language Learning* 8 (2–3), 151–180.

Fabbro, F. (1999) *The Neurolinguistics of Bilingualism*. Hove: Psychology Press.

Fabbro, F. (2000) Introduction to language and cerebellum. *Journal of Neurolinguistics* 13, 83–94.

Fabbro, F. (2001) The bilingual brain: Cerebral representation of languages. *Brain and Language* 79, 211–222.

Fabbro, F. and Paradis, M. (1995) Differential impairments in four multilingual patients with subcortical lesions. In M. Paradis (ed.) *Aspects of Bilingual Aphasia* (pp. 139–176). Oxford: Pergamon Press.
Gósy, M. (2005) *Pszicholingvisztika [Psycholinguistics]*. Budapest: Osiris.
Green, D. (1993) Towards a model of L2 comprehension and production. In R. Schreuder and B. Weltens (eds) *The Bilingual Lexicon*. Amsterdam/Philadelphia: John Benjamins.
Grosjean, F. (1989) Neurolinguists, beware! The bilingual is not two monolinguals in one person. *Brain and Language* 36, 3–15.
Grosjean, F. (1998) Studying bilinguals: Methodological and conceptual issues. *Bilingualism and Cognition* 1, 131–149.
Heredia, R.R. (1996) Bilingual memory: A re-revised version of the hierarchical model of bilingual memory. *CRL Newsletter* 10(3). On WWW at http://crl.ucsd.edu/newsletter/10-3/.
Hernandez, A.E., Martinez, A. and Kohnert, K. (2000) In search of the language switch: An fMRI study of picture naming in Spanish-English bilinguals. *Brain and Language* 73, 421–431.
Illes, J., Francis, W.S., Desmond, J.E., Gabrieli, J.D.E., Glover, G.H., Poldrack, R., Lees, C.J. and Wagner, A.D. (1999) Concergent cortical representation of semantic processing in bilinguals. *Brain and Language* 70, 347–363.
Jackson, H. and Zé Amvela, E. (2000) *Words, Meaning and Vocabulary*. London and New York: Cassell.
Jagusztinné, U.K. (1985) *Magyar Verbális Asszociációk 2 [Hungarian Verbal Associations 2]*. Szeged: JGYTF.
Kim, K.H., Relkin, N.R., Lee, K.M. and Hirsch, J. (1997) Distinct cortical areas associated with native and second languages. *Nature* 388, 171–174.
Kroll, J.F. and Stewart, E. (1994) Category interference in translation and picture naming: Evidence from asymmetric connections between bilingual memory representations. *Journal of Memory and Language* 33, 149–174.
Lamb, S. (1999) *Pathways of the Brain*. Amsterdam/Philadelphia: John Benjamins.
Meisel, J.M. (1989) Early differentiation of languages in bilingual children. In K. Hyltenstam and L.K. és Obler (eds) *Bilingualism Across the Lifespan. Aspects of Acquisition, Maturity, and Loss* (pp. 13–40). Cambridge: Cambridge University Press.
Paradis, M. (1989) Bilingual and polyglot aphasia. In F. Boller and J. Grafman (eds) *Handbook of Neuropsychology* 2, 117–140. Amsterdam: Elsevier.
Paradis, M. (2001) Bilingual and polyglot aphasia. In R.S. Berndt (ed.) *Handbook of Neuropsychology* (2nd edn) (pp. 69–91). Oxford, UK: Elsevier.
Singleton, D. (1999) *Exploring the Second Language Mental Lexicon*. Cambridge: Cambridge University Press.
Ullman, M.T. (2001) The neural basis of lexicon and grammar in first and second language: The declarative/procedural model. *Bilingualism: Language and Cognition* 4 (1), 105–122.
Weber-Fox, C.M. and Neville, H.J. (1997) Maturational constraints on functional specializations for language processing: ERP and behavioral evidence in bilingual speakers. *Journal of Cognitive Neuroscience* 8, 231–256.

Part 2
L2 Lexical Perception and Production

Chapter 3
Speech Perception Processing in First and Second Language in Bilinguals and L2 Learners[1]

MÁRIA GÓSY

Introduction

Languages differ in the sounds they use to make up words and in the rules they use to construct sentences. Obviously, these differences have consequences for perceptual processing. While acquiring their mother tongue, children gradually learn the properties of the speech signals they are exposed to during their language acquisition. There are several important issues to be considered when comparing the acquisition of perceptual processing in listeners who grow up in bilingual surroundings and those who learn an L2 from the age of six under classroom conditions. The obvious differences in L1 and L2 acquisition might lead to differences in speech processing. The processes of speech perception are crucial factors in both first and second language acquisition as well as in bilinguals' dominant language (if they have one) and subdominant languages. The perceptual basis of the learner's first language exerts an influence on second language learning as well, and the L1 and L2 mental lexicons are somehow distinguished in the children's storage mechanism (from a certain age). By the age of six the bilingual mental lexicon is supposed to be well differentiated according to the languages used.

The biological background of these facts can be found in certain brain areas that are specialised to perform specific mental functions such as speech perception (Corballis, 1991; Changeux, 2004). It is assumed that there are three functional units assigned to the task of coordinating the three functional systems. The first one is responsible for arousal and attention, and is located in the limbic system. The second area is responsible for

---

[1] The research reported here was supported by OTKA (No. T049426) research grant.

sensory reception and integration, and is located in the temporal, the occipital and the parietal lobes. The third unit executes planning, evaluation and motor functions in the frontal lobe. Processing and analysing verbal information also occur within the auditory pathway. A number of nuclei in different parts of the pathway interpret the incoming information, or send fibres to improve the quality of sound input. One of these, for instance, is able to measure the time difference between the sounds reaching one or the other ear.

Speech perception is a decisive factor both in mother tongue acquisition and in foreign language learning. It is well attested that an L2 learner perceives speech through the filter of his native language (Pallier et al., 1997; Dehaene et al., 1997). Even bilinguals show implicit evidence that they categorize the non-dominant language sounds according to their dominant language representations (Navarra et al., 2005). If children hear both languages simultaneously, their brains are supposed to become wired to perceive the sounds of both languages and they will also acquire the ability to produce those sounds. However, as the flexibility of the brain decreases with ageing, the perception (and production) of the phonemes of the second language become more and more difficult. Neurophysiological evidence shows considerable experience-dependent plasticity of the brain (Kraus et al., 1995; Fabbro, 2001). The following question arises: when children have spent some time on the job of language acquisition, what specific differences do they exhibit in their speech processing, depending on whether they are bilinguals or second language learners?

Evaluation of the speech decoding mechanism is impossible by simple observation, or by single experiments focusing only on a single subprocess of perceptual processing. To learn more about the various perceptual processes, experiments using an interactive test package are needed to check children's performances in the language(s) they use and/or learn.

A fundamental problem in comparing bilingual speakers to native monolinguals is that bilinguals cannot be regarded as two monolinguals in one person. However, a growing body of cross-linguistic research has shown that different languages are characterised by different processing strategies that can be identified by comparing bilinguals' and monolinguals' performances. A number of experiments have supported the finding that L2 processing strategies differ from monolingual strategies. It is possible that different mechanisms are at work in L1 versus L2 acquisition, which seems especially obvious if we compare the strategies used by truly bilingual subjects and subjects who speak more than one language (Kilborn, 1994).

In this paper, monolingual and bilingual children's speech perception processing will be compared in their two languages with the aim of finding specific similarities and differences in their perceptual mechanisms. The actual goal of this study was to investigate the speech perception subprocesses of Hungarian-speaking children, both in their first language (Hungarian) and in their second language (English), and to compare their data to those of Hungarian-English bilingual children whose dominant language was claimed to be Hungarian. There were two factors that were common to both the bilingual and the L2-learning monolingual children: all the bilinguals were Hungarian-dominant and had been fluent in English for about three years. The monolingual Hungarian students had learnt English at school for about three years.

Our hypothesis was that monolingual children's L1 perceptual performance would be significantly superior to that of their L2. However, a very close interaction was also expected between their L1 and L2 processing mechanisms. It was assumed that the poorer the L1 speech perception, the greater the children's perceptual difficulties in L2. In other words, successful L2 acquisition requires a well-developed, age-related perceptual mechanism, and if this is the case, then an underdeveloped L1 speech perception mechanism will hinder L2 speech perception and processing. We also hypothesised that the same would apply to bilingual children's speech processing in their two languages. We assumed that our bilingual children's performance in English would be superior to the L2 English performance of monolingual children, and specific differences would depend on the type of the subprocess involved. Large individual differences were also suspected in both tested groups. Children who have acquired more than one language from birth are often seen to be at a higher risk of difficulties in academic performance at school. We assumed that our data would support this experience.

To test our hypotheses, a series of experiments were designed with two groups of children. The bilinguals were all preschool children who had started speaking close to the second year of their lives. According to their parents' information, all of them had been using both languages since the age of three. The participants of the monolingual group were selected on the basis of their L2 learning time in an ordinary elementary school in Budapest. All of them were fourth-graders who had started learning English at school at the age of six. According to their teachers, they had been doing well or acceptably in English during the previous three years. Although there was a three-year age difference between the subjects of the two groups, the length of their exposure to English was the same, although under different circumstances.

Subjects, Method and Procedure

Subjects

Thirty bilingual (Hungarian-English) preschool children and thirty monolingual Hungarian fourth-graders learning English at school were selected for participation in a speech perception experiment. The bilingual children had been exposed to both languages from birth; either the mother or the father was a monolingual speaker of English. The native Hungarian parents were all adult bilinguals. All the children were born in Hungary and had been at a monolingual Hungarian kindergarten for about two years. The families used both languages at home, depending on the English-speaking parent's presence or absence. This way, the 'one parent, one language' rule was applied with all children. They had high levels of conversational fluency in both languages and, according to their parents, they acquired both languages simultaneously. However, all the families agreed that the children's dominant language was Hungarian, and all of them were going to be sent to Hungarian (monolingual) schools. The mean age of the children was 6;8 (between 6;5 and 6;9). There were 19 girls and 11 boys in the group. There was no articulation disorder or hearing loss detected in any of the children.

Initial selection of the fourth-grader participants was based on classroom teachers' estimates of 'good' and 'weaker' learners considering their achievements in Hungarian language, reading and writing. However, all of them showed a normal language acquisition process. They had learnt English at school (and at school only) for four years, taught by the same teacher. The mean age of the fourth-graders was 9;7 (between 9;5 and 10;2). There were 19 girls and 11 boys in this group, too. No children had any speech defect, and no hearing loss was detected in any of the children.

Method

Two series of tests were conducted with both groups. One of them was the standardised GMP test package developed to test Hungarian-speaking children's speech processing abilities between the ages of 3 and 13 (cf. Gósy, 1997). The age-specific values of correct performances allow us to define the expected processing level of all tested subprocesses. On the basis of the philosophy of this test-package, the English version (GMPeng) has been developed with the same goals considering the phonetic, phonological and syntactic differences between the two languages. The primary aim of GMPeng was to obtain information about the Hungarian-speaking schoolchildren's second language proficiency (independently of the teaching method used). However, it is appropriate to test native English children's performances as well.

For this study, seven subtests were selected to evaluate the perceptual abilities of the bilingual children and the monolingual L2 learner children. Five subtests highlight acoustic, phonetic, phonological and serial perception, and two of them focus on sentence and text comprehension by the tested children. In everyday communication, the spoken message is frequently covered by noise of various types and intensities. For successful communication to take place, the speech understanding process should work correctly even under noisy circumstances. The 'cocktail-party problem' might be very disturbing, especially for children, because they do not have as much practice in understanding speech as adults do. Acoustic speech perception processing was evaluated by asking participants to identify 10 well-formed Hungarian and English sentences (GMP2) and 10 Hungarian and English words (GMP3) masked by white noise. The signal/noise ratio was 4 dB. The average intensity level used during the testing procedure was 65 dB. The following are examples of sentences used in the test:

- Hungarian:
  A sütemény nagyon finom volt ['The cake was very delicious'].
  Az őzikét kergeti az oroszlán ['The lion is chasing the deer'].

- English:
  The aeroplane landed just now.
  The dog is running after the cat.

Examples for the test words:

- Hungarian:
  csillag ['star'];
  csörgőkígyó ['rattlesnake'];

- English:
  strawberry;
  hand.

To evaluate the children's phonetic perception, filtered sentences (GMP4) were used in both languages (passband filtration with a slope of 36 dB). After filtration, all sentences were confined to the frequency range of 2200–2700 Hz. In the case of this filtration, identification can be made only on the basis of secondary acoustic cues both in Hungarian and English. Hungarian examples: *A munkások estig dolgoznak* ['The workmen work till night']; *A kulcs a zsebemben van* ['The key is in my pocket']. English examples: *My friend has broken his leg*; *In winter some birds go South*. For the evaluation of phonological speech perception, speeded-up sentences containing relatively complex morphology and syntax, and composed of uncommon words were used (GMP5). For example, *Az irígység rossz tulajdonság* ['Jealousy is a bad feature']; *Átkokat szórt mások fejére* [literally: 'He threw curses on others' heads', that is, 'he was cursing others'); *Fires are put out by firemen*; *He was angry with his neighbour*. Identification of speeded-up sentences, with the normal speech rate electrically speeded up to 130% of the original version, allowed us to detect central perceptual problems in decoding a speech signal. The actual speech rate of the 10 sentences was 15 sounds per second on average in both languages. Serial perception (GMP10) was tested with 10 nonsense words of 2, 3, and 4 syllables depending on the actual phonotactic rules of the language (for example, Hungarian: *galalajka, zseréb, námük, siszidami* and English: *stent, dag, pikshadary, shtriki, kraws, brunda*). The skill being assessed in this subtest is that of breaking words down into their components, a necessary skill for language and literacy acquisition.

A short tape-recorded story (about animals) was played to the children in order to assess their inferential comprehension (text comprehension: GMP12). Comprehension of the story in this test is checked by questions to be answered by the children. Responses to the carefully prepared questions show the comprehension processes and strategies used either successfully or unsuccessfully. The comprehension questions concern various facts in the text: location, time, object, action, instrument, characters, cause/effect, problem/solution, and so on, as well as interrelations. There is only one correct answer for each question. For the sentence comprehension test (GMP16), a special set of 10 sentences and 10 picture pairs was developed to test the first-language acquisition processes of the Hungarian-speaking and English-speaking monolingual children. The sentences were constructed so that both their real meaning and its opposite could be pictorially represented. The following are a couple of examples of test sentences:

- Hungarian: *A kislány megette volna a tortát, ha elérte volna a tálat.* ['The girl would have eaten the cake if she had been able to reach the bowl']. One of the pictures agreed with the meaning of the sentence, whereas the other showed a girl who was able to reach the bowl.

- English: *The bear and the rabbit were both climbing a tree and one of them fell.* (In one of the pictures, neither of them was shown as falling.) *The book is going to be given to the boy.* (The misleading picture showed the opposite meaning: the book was going to be given to a girl.)

Procedure

Children had to fulfill three different tasks during the sessions: repetition, answering and selection. The five subtests used to evaluate the children's speech perception processes required prompt responses. The children's task was to repeat correctly what they had heard from the tape recorder. Comprehension questions were asked after they had listened to the story. The questions were asked in English with bilinguals in the English session, but the L2-learning schoolchildren were asked questions in Hungarian in order to avoid incorrect answers due to misunderstanding the question. In the sentence comprehension subtest, the examiner read out the sentence to the child, who had to point at the picture that he thought matched the meaning of the sentence. The tests were performed individually, first in Hungarian and, after the lapse of a few days, in English to both groups (in the mornings). The procedure took about 12 minutes with both languages.

The statistical evaluation of the data was carried out using ANOVA (GLM multivariate analysis, paired sample t-tests and correlation tests by SPSS 12.0.1. for Windows software package). In all cases, the confidence level was set at the conventional 95%.

Results

Bilingual children

There are significant differences in the speech perception performances of bilingual children depending on their dominant and their subordinate language, as shown by numerous experiments and suggested by various theories (Paradis, 2004). Accepting this, our hypothesis was that the performance levels achieved by the children in their dominant language – in the present case, Hungarian – would be higher in all the tested subprocesses than the performance levels achieved in the same subprocesses in English (Table 3.1).

Although this study was not designed to compare the data for bilingual preschool children to those of Hungarian monolingual 6-years-olds, the values of the standardised GMP test do make such a comparison possible. It is safe to say that almost all the perceptual processes were poorer in the bilinguals than in the monolinguals, with individual differences range from slight to considerable. Considering the fact that the bilingual children are thrown together with monolingual Hungarian children in the kindergartens and that they will go to Hungarian schools, such comparisons could be valuable from the point of view of their future efforts in learning to read and write (Francis, 2002). The phonological and serial

Table 3.1 Bilingual children's speech perception performances

Perception subtests	Correct responses (%)			
	Hungarian		English	
	Mean	S.D.	Mean	S.D.
Noisy sentences	63.6	24.28	43.6	18.65
Noisy words	80.3	13.76	61.3	21.45
Filtered sentences	81.6	20.18	54.0	18.86
Fast sentences	50.3	20.59	17.0	16.43
Nonwords	66.6	18.63	31.0	22.18

S.D., standard deviation.

subprocesses of perception in the bilingual children, which are extremely important for the acquisition of the written language, seem to considerably lag behind the expected level (these are the subtests where fast sentences and nonwords had to be repeated). Differentiation and identification of Hungarian speech sounds caused problems for the bilingual children and their lexical access also showed deficiencies. Their errors were very similar to those made by monolingual 4- to 5-year-old Hungarian children. In sentence repetition, they often re-structured the utterance they heard, with the consequence that they committed either morphological or syntactic errors or used misperceived word(s).

The English speech perception of the bilingual participants was compared to the speech perception data from 20 eleven-year-old English monolinguals in Britain, whose subprocesses were checked using the same method (see Simon, in this volume). The data show similar tendencies, except for phonological and serial perception: these two were much worse with our preschool bilinguals than for the English monolinguals. Errors in the repetition of English sentences also concerned phoneme identification and dropping or changing some words, resulting in the production of an incorrect grammatical form. Thus, for example, the original sentence *When is he going to get married?* was repeated by the child without the particle *to*; and the sentence *It snows a lot in winter* was repeated as *It snow a lot in winter*. The sentence *Do not forget to do your homework* was repeated by one of the subjects as *Do not forget to do you work*. Poor performance in the phonological and serial subprocesses was not expected with children acquiring two languages at the same time. The explanation might be that phonological processing develops more slowly when acquiring two languages. Serial perception is of crucial importance for the acquisition of the correct articulatory movements in a language. Based on tests with various groups of bilingual and monolingual children, it was concluded that the phonological short-term memory is not a language-independent mechanism, but functions in a highly language-specific way (Thorn & Gathercole, 1999). If this is the case, it may explain our preschool children's difficulty to performing the phonological and serial perception tasks in both languages but substantially worse in their subdominant language.

In general, verbal speech comprehension does not show much difficulty with normally developed children of any age. During language acquisition, sentence comprehension seems to be easier for children than text comprehension. Young children's speech processing requires much elaboration concerning the segmentation, phonology, morphology or syntax of long utterances; this takes time and prevents easy access to higher cognitive levels. The comprehension data from the present experiment support the above mentioned facts. The preschool children's sentence comprehension was significantly better in both languages than their text comprehension (paired sample t-test: $t(29) = -8.235$, $t(29) = -6.136; p = 0.000$). However, there was no significant difference found in their text comprehension depending on the language, cf. Table 3.2.

As all the bilingual children in the experiment were fluent in both languages, we did not expect too many problems in their verbal speech comprehension. Although their sentence comprehension levels in Hungarian met the age-requirements of 6-year-old monolinguals, this was not the case with their text comprehension. Presumably, their sentence and text comprehension in English also show some backwardness. Many of the bilingual participants could not understand correctly the sentence *Although it is snowing heavily, the girl has not gone sledding*, or the sentence *The mouse has just reached the cheese*. Despite these errors and uncertainties, they did not experience any comprehension problems in English in their everyday lives. Obviously, there are several factors that can help them achieve a relatively high level of speech comprehension, such as logical reasoning, good short-term memory capacity, the communication situation, gestures that may clarify what could have remained ambiguous on the basis of linguistic elements alone, knowledge of pragmatic principles and perhaps some other special strategies, which are not yet fully understood.

Monolingual children

In general, the Hungarian speech perception processes of monolingual schoolchildren showed the expected levels (corresponding to the standard values of the test package). An analysis of the data for selected 'good' and 'weaker' children showed significant differences (multivariate $F(7, 22) = 30.669, p < 0.0005$) (Table 3.3).

The perception results of weaker but older monolingual children were slightly better than those of the bilingual preschool children. (Table 3.4.) They showed the very same deficiencies in phonological and serial perception as the younger children. The results of English speech perception performances revealed large differences between the two subgroups of schoolchildren. As a consequence, weaker students had difficulties learning English at school, particularly with spelling, storing and recalling new words – both their phonological forms and their meanings.

Statistical analysis revealed significant differences between the stronger and weaker students in their English test results, which confirmed

Table 3.2 Bilingual children's speech comprehension performances

Comprehension	Correct responses (%)			
	Hungarian		English	
	Mean	S.D.	Mean	S.D.
Sentence	78.0	16.27	62.3	19.41
Text	51.6	20.85	43.3	19.53

S.D., standard deviation.

Table 3.3 Monolingual schoolchildren's speech perception performances in Hungarian

Perception subtests	Correct responses (%)					
	Good subjects		Weaker subjects		All subjects	
	Mean	S.D.	Mean	S.D.	Mean	S.D.
Noisy sentences	96.6	4.87	74.6	12.45	85.6	14.54
Noisy words	96.6	4.57	90.6	4.57	93.6	5.56
Filtered sentences	98.66	3.51	92.0	8.61	95.3	7.30
Fast sentences	94.66	6.39	66.0	16.38	80.3	19.02
Nonwords	98.00	4.14	72.0	12.64	85.0	16.13

S.D., standard deviation.

Table 3.4 Monolingual schoolchildren's speech perception performances in English

Perception subtests	Correct responses (%)					
	Good subjects		Weaker subjects		All subjects	
	Mean	S.D.	Mean	S.D.	Mean	S.D.
Noisy sentences	86.0	13.52	36.0	18.04	61.0	29.86
Noisy words	90.6	7.98	70.6	8.83	80.6	13.11
Filtered sentences	54.66	15.05	40.6	15.33	47.66	16.54
Fast sentences	46.0	12.98	20.66	14.86	33.3	18.81
Nonwords	66.6	11.75	48.66	18.84	65.0	27.16

S.D., standard deviation.

our hypothesis that first language processing skills heavily affect L2 performances ($F(1,28) = 73.736, p < 0.0005$). The better the L1 speech perception, the better the L2 speech processing and vice versa. Weaker students were not able to correctly identify the grammatical structures of sentences under noisy conditions; however, they did much better when they had to identify noisy words. The less acoustic information is available for decoding, the worse the children's performance – as is clearly shown by the poor results achieved by both stronger and weaker students in identifying the filtered sentences. Processing time is a decisive factor in L2 operations and, in these experiments, it was this factor that was responsible for most of the difficulties of the Hungarian-speaking children. Many L2-learning students failed to finish the sentence heard and had problems identifying words. This suggests that the grammatical structure of the sentence does not help them transform the acoustic signal into speech sounds, words or structures. Correctness of serial perception needs improvement as well; however, the monolingual English 10-year-olds performed better at this task than the monolingual English 11-year-olds (Simon, this volume). Further investigations could reveal the reason for this unexpected fact.

The monolingual schoolchildren's L1 sentence comprehension was slightly better than their text comprehension, but the difference was not significant (92.0% and 85.0%, S. D.: 9.61 and 14.79 respectively). Stronger students showed good performance both in their L1 sentence and in their L1 text comprehension, while weaker students had severe difficulties in these tests, their scores showing significant differences ($F(1,28) = 110,906, p < 0.000$ for text and ($F(1,28) = 27,723, p < 0.000$ for sentence comprehension), cf. Table 3.5.

The monolingual children's L2 comprehension showed great variety depending both on the children's ability and on the actual task. Their English text comprehension was extremely poor: they were only able to answer three questions on average, and they were generally unable to follow the story heard in L2. There may be multiple reasons for these performances, such as, the inadequacy of the students' word knowledge, gaps and uncertainties in their knowledge of grammatical structure or poor text comprehension strategies (Mack, 1988). The latter was also evidenced in the present study in the Hungarian text comprehension performances of weaker students. English sentence comprehension was much better for all students, even though they understood only about half the test sentences on average. (Some of the students admitted after the testing procedure that they were unable to follow the English story and could understand only a couple of words from isolated sentences.) There were great differences between the stronger and weaker

Table 3.5 Hungarian monolingual schoolchildren's comprehension in L1 and in L2

Comprehension	Correct responses (%)							
	Hungarian				English			
	Stronger		Weaker		Stronger		Weaker	
	Mean	S.D.	Mean	S.D.	Mean	S.D.	Mean	S.D.
sentence	98.6	4.14	85.3	9.15	66.6	11.75	40.0	13.09
text	98.0	3.51	72.0	8.61	46.6	16.76	22.6	12.22

students: the latter hardly understood any of the isolated English sentences, and did not understand the gist of the story they had heard ($F(1,28) = 20.071$, $p < 0.000$ for text and $F(1,28) = 34.462$, $p < 0.000$ for sentence comprehension).

Bilinguals and monolinguals: A comparison

The effect of bilingualism versus monolingualism was significant in Hungarian (multivariate $F(7, 52) = 7.885$, $p < 0.0005$) as well as in English ($F(7, 52) = 11.103$, $p < 0.0005$). The results of the bilingual preschool children were significantly lower in all the Hungarian perceptual subtests than those of the monolingual schoolchildren, except for phonetic perception, where there was practically no difference (Figure 3.1). Detailed analyses showed that the bilingual listeners made far more errors in their repetitions than the monolingual listeners. Noisy speech perception conditions also resulted in significantly poorer performance in bilinguals compared with monolinguals in another experiment

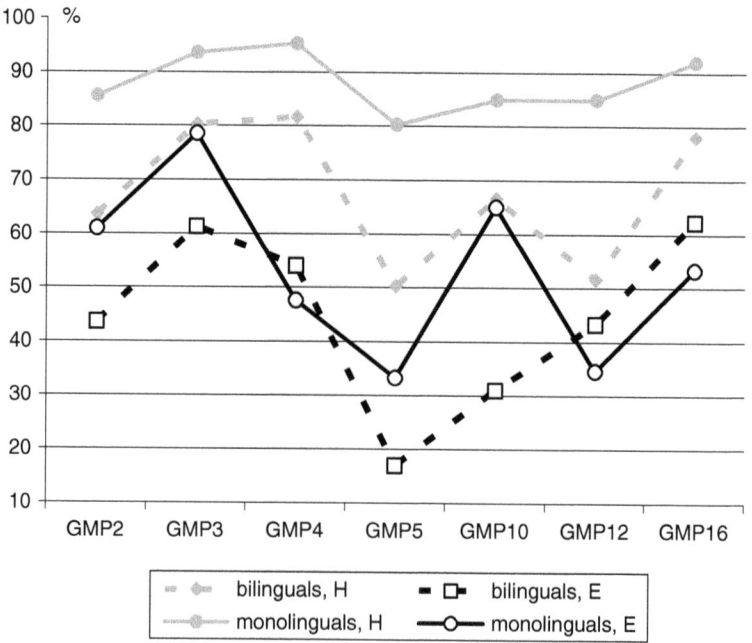

Figure 3.1 Monolinguals' and bilinguals' performances in Hungarian subtests.

(Hapsburg *et al.*, 2004), involving a group of Spanish-English bilinguals and English monolinguals.

The monolinguals' higher perceptual scores in English subtests (Figure 3.2) can be interpreted as a consequence of literacy instruction in second language learning and higher language awareness. The latter could also have been influenced by their age (Bruck & Genesee, 1995; Singleton, 2003). The fact that phonetic identification showed no significant difference between the bilinguals and the L2 learners indicates that this perception level seems to be decisive in achieving the expected level of phonological awareness needed in language acquisition.

The bilingual preschool children performed better in English speech comprehension, in both tasks, than the L2 learners (Figure 3.3). There were great individual differences in both groups and in both languages, which is clearly seen in all the figures.

Comparison of the participants' speech perception processes across the two languages revealed that, independently of their bilingual or

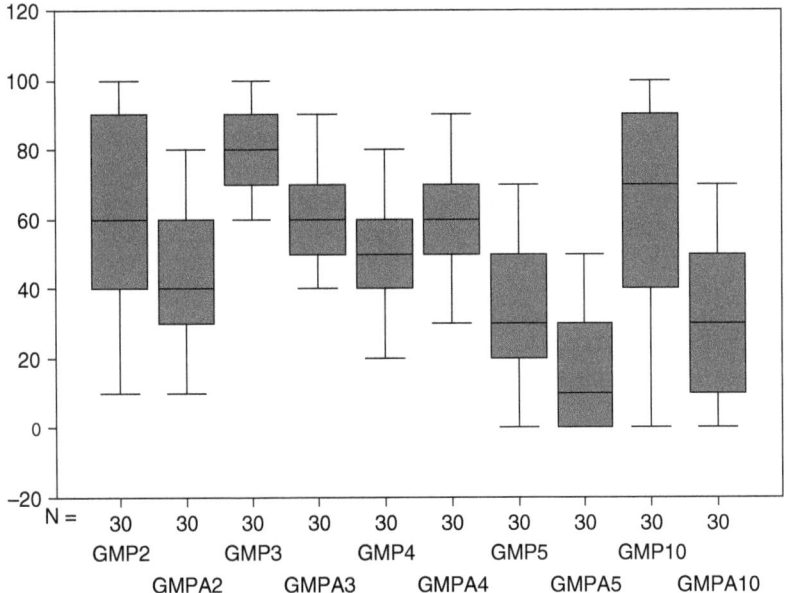

Figure 3.2 Bilinguals' and monolinguals' English speech perception processes (the letters GMP stand for monolinguals while GMPA for bilinguals)

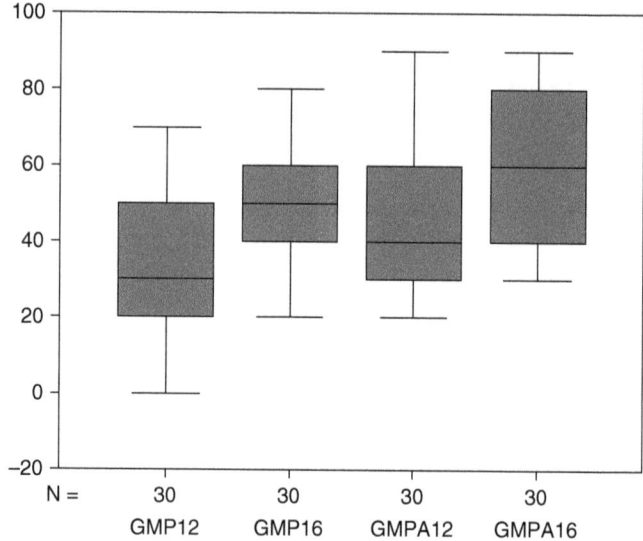

Figure 3.3 Comprehension results in English in the two tested groups (the letters GMP stand for monolinguals while GMPA for bilinguals).

monolingual second language learner status, there was a significant difference between their performance in the two languages. However, if we take a closer look at the actual differences in the subtests and the tendencies obtained, it becomes clear that perception performance was closer between the two languages in the bilingual group (Figure 3.4).

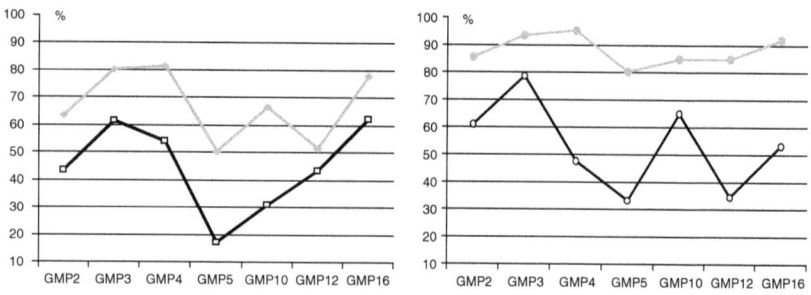

Figure 3.4 Bilinguals' (left) and L2 learners' (right) performance in the various decoding subprocesses (upper lines = Hungarian; lower lines = English).

The figures show different tendencies in the performances between the two languages in the two groups. The distance between the correct perception performances depends on the language: it is shorter with the bilinguals, and longer with the schoolchildren. There are two questions here that require further research:

(1) Do the present results mean that the bilinguals' further development will have an impact on both of their languages, and will their speech perception therefore improve, independently of the language itself? If this is the case, how deeply will this development be influenced (positively and negatively) by various internal and external factors? Or will it happen the other way round, with speech processing in the dominant language suppressing the operations of the subdominant language, depending (again) on various external factors?
(2) Will second language learners, in developing their L2 speech perception and comprehension processes, rely mainly on transferring some of their L1 strategies, or will they only use the strategies provided by the methods of language teaching?

Conclusions

Inevitably, there are many differences between acquiring a language as a bilingual speaker and learning a second language as a monolingual speaker. Of course, in later life, when someone encounters a situation where s/he has to use two languages, no one will ask them how they acquired the language or at what age they started. Indeed, nobody, not even the person concerned, will be interested any more in the strategies they used for acquisition (and they will probably have forgotten about the difficulties). However, there are more differences and more similarities between the two processes from the point of view of speech perception processing than have so far been assumed. This might be the reason behind findings that do not support the maturational factor in second language acquisition (Birdsong & Molis, 2000; Singleton, 2003). On the basis of the present results, there are two major facts to be emphasized:

(1) The data in this study support the present author's view about the need to devote more attention to perceptual processes in teaching a second language.
(2) Secondly, speech processing – even in the 'dominant' language of bilingual children – might show backwardness masked by the compensatory strategies children use in everyday communication. These

slight, but occasionally quite severe, perceptual disorders may cause further problems at school (Francis, 2002; Schelletter & Parke, 2004).

The results of the study confirmed our hypothesis about the importance of the L1 speech perception mechanism in L2 language acquisition, and it also confirmed our assumption that bilingual children are at risk due to deficiencies in processing even in their dominant language. However, we could not confirm in all cases, without exception, the hypothesis that three years of bilingual life before the age of six results in generally better English speech perception and comprehension than three years of L2 learning at school between the ages of 6 and 9. There were only two processes at which the bilingual children were better than the monolinguals or showed performances equal to those of the L2 learners: phonetic speech perception and text comprehension. All the other tested processes showed similar deficiencies in both groups.

Kilborn, (1994) assumes that L1 cues may derive from principles of optimality as opposed to learning an L2 at school, where learners are taught to communicate according to certain pedagogical principles, and losing certain strategies and cues that are typical of language acquisition under natural conditions. The present data seem to support this view, particularly in the case of speech comprehension processing. Although we are fully aware of the difficulties in comparing bilinguals with monolinguals who are not matched by age, we are convinced that these experimental data will prove extremely useful in teaching a foreign language, when study of the foreign language starts simultaneously with the study of L1 reading and writing.

References

Birdsong, D. Molis, M. (2001) On the evidence for maturational constraints in second-language aquisition. Journal of Memory and Language 44, 235–249.

Bruck, M. and Genesee, F. (1995) Phonological awareness in young second language learners. *Journal of Child Language* 22, 307–324.

Changeux, J.-P. (2004) *The Physiology of Truth. Neuroscience and Human Knowledge.* Cambridge, Massachusetts: The Belknap Press of Harvard University Press.

Corballis, M.C. (1991) *The Lopsided Ape. Evolution of the Generative Mind.* New York, Oxford: Oxford University Press.

Dehaene, S., Dupoux, E., Mehler, J., Cohen, L., Paulesu, E., Perani, D., Van De Moortele, P.F., Lehericy, S. and Le Bihan, D. (1997) Anatomical variability in the cortical representation of first and second language. *Neuroreport* 17, 3809–3815.

Fabbro, F. (2001) The bilingual brain: Cerebral representation of languages. *Brain and Language* 79, 211–222.

Francis, N. (2002) Literacy, second language learning, and the development of metalinguistic awareness A study of bilingual children's perception of focus on form. *Linguistics and Education* 13, 373–404.

Gósy, M. (1997) Developmental language impairment: Aspects of speech perception and comprehension. *ALinguH* Vol. 44. (1–2), 175–201.

Hapsburg, D., von, Champlin, C.A. and Shetty, S.R. (2004) Reception threshold for sentences in bilingual (Spanish/English) and monolingual (English) listeners. *Journal of American Academic Audiology* 15, 88–98.

Kilborn, K. (1994) Learning a language late: Second language acquisition in adults. In M.A. Gernsbacher (ed.) *Handbook of Psycholinguistics* (pp. 917–945) San Diego, New York: Academic Press.

Kraus, N., McGee, T., Carrel, T., King, C., Tremblay, K. and Nicol, T. (1995) Central auditory system plasticity associated with speech discrimination training. *Journal of Cognitive Neuroscience* 7, 25–32.

Mack, M. (1988) Sentence processing by non-native speakers of English: Evidence from the perception of natural and computer-generated anomalous L2 sentences. *Journal of Neurolinguistica* 3, 293–316.

Navarra, J., Sebastian-Gallés, N. and Soto-Paraco, S. (2005) The perception of second language sounds in early bilinguals: New evidence from an implicit measure. *Journal of Experimental Psychology* 31, 912–918.

Pallier, C., Bosch, L. and Sebastián-Gallés, N. (1997) A limit on behavioral plasticity in speech perception. *Cognition* 64, 9–17.

Paradis, M. (2004) *Neurolinguistic Theory of Bilingualism.* Amsterdam, Philadelphia: John Benjamins.

Schelletter, C. and Parke, T. (2004) Using story re-tell in bilingual assessment. *Academic Exchange Quarterly* 8/3, 25–37.

Singleton, D. (2003) Critical period or general age factor(s)? In M.P. García Mayo and M.L. García Lecumberri (eds) *Age and the Acquisition of English as a Foreign Language* (pp. 3–22) Clevedon: Multilingual Matters.

Thorn, A.S. and Gathercole, S.E. (1999) Language-specific knowledge and short-term memory in bilingual and non-bilingual children. *Quarterly Journal of Experimental Psychology* 52, 303–324.

Chapter 4
A Comparative Study of Mother-Tongue and Foreign Language Speech Perception, Lexical Access and Speech Comprehension Processes

ORSOLYA SIMON

Introduction

Crucial to the success of human verbal communication and cognitive development are several closely interrelated but nevertheless relatively autonomous and complex mental operations that psycholinguists have termed speech processing (perception and comprehension) and speech production. The ability to understand and be understood in a conversation is a seemingly effortless and spontaneous process that demands a minimum of one's cognitive resources. Psycholinguistic literature, however, underlines the active nature of these abilities (Bond & Garnes, 1980; Clark & Clark, 1977); verbal communication consists of consecutive stages of automatic, semi-automatic and conscious mental operations functioning in continuous interaction (Gósy, 2004). One of the central tasks facing researchers of verbal communication is to determine the underlying principles that ensure its successful accomplishment. One relatively established principle is the asymmetrical development of decoding and production. In both L1 and L2 acquisition, the development of speech perception and comprehension normally precedes that of speech production (Gósy, 1997a; Lengyel, 1994; White, 1989). One can conclude that the decoding mechanism plays a crucial role in communication, as without age-appropriate level decoding operations, L1 and L2 production will not develop successfully. The present study analyses the characteristic features of the speech decoding process in first language acquisition and foreign language learning.

The decoding mechanism of human speech

'Processing' or 'decoding' speech ('the decoding mechanism') can be divided into two separate components: perception and comprehension. 'Speech perception' is the term for the recognition and identification of the smallest meaningless units of the spoken language (speech sounds and their combinations). 'Speech comprehension' involves the understanding and interpretation of meaningful linguistic units, for example, words, sentences and texts (Gósy, 1999; further definitions may be found in Clark & Clark, 1977; Garman, 1990; Gósy, 2004; Pisoni & Sawusch, 1975). In the complex decoding process, these two component parts do not normally operate independently and speech is not normally separated into its meaningful and meaningless elements or into segmental and suprasegmental features (Gósy, 1999). The auditory-acoustic stimulus, which is manifested by various signals in spontaneous speech, passes through several consecutive processing stages, transforming it into increasingly larger information units and deeper layers of understanding. These stages working in systematic interaction ensure that the final aim of the decoding mechanism, that is, finding and understanding the semantic representation of the message, is accomplished (Garman, 1990; Massaro, 1994). The listener is able to perform these mental operations without any difficulty with the help of both the acquired first language system (acoustic, phonetic, phonological, lexical, syntactic, semantic, contextual and pragmatic knowledge) and numerous extralinguistic factors (encyclopaedic knowledge, situation-specific schemata, working memory capacity, and so on). The relative smoothness of processing is due to the highly selective and adaptive nature of the decoding process and its resistance to the distractions that may come up in the course of communication (for example, background noise, unusual tempo of speech, age, gender, regional differences, and so on). In addition, the listener frequently relies on and creatively employs various underlying universal principles, constraints, operations and strategies that can assist the decoding mechanism (Bárdos, 2002; Clark & Clark, 1977; Pisoni & Sawusch, 1975). Two of them, which are closely related to the findings of the present study, will be elaborated on in detail in this chapter.

Ongoing perception and comprehension are a mixture of top-down and bottom-up processing and inferencing (Bárdos, 2002; Forster, 1989; Garman, 1990; Skehan, 1989), which, in addition, reflect the modular and hierarchical character of the decoding mechanism (see Figure 4.1).

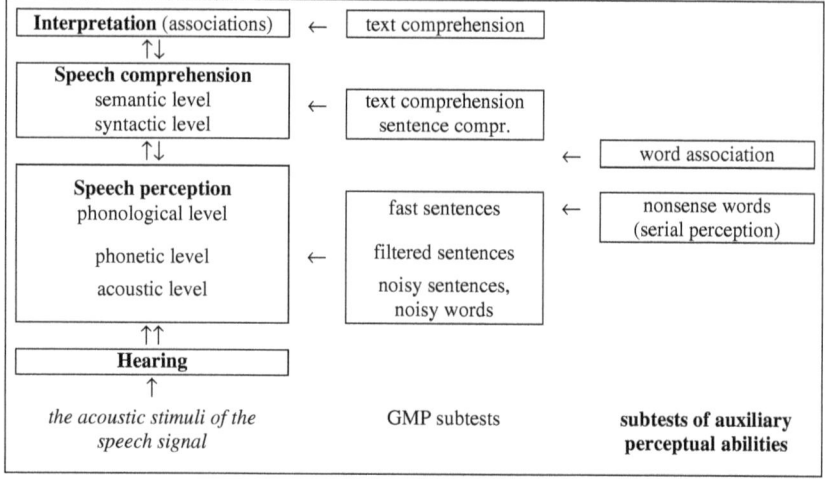

Figure 4.1 The hierarchical, interactive model of the speech decoding process and the corresponding subtests of the GMP test package.

'Bottom-up' processing begins with the sensory analysis of a stimulus and proceeds toward higher levels of analysis. As this type of processing is based on the acoustic and phonetic features of the speech signal, it is dominantly applied in speech perception. In contrast, processing is 'top-down' when analyses at higher levels (for example, the semantic and/or syntactic levels of the language) influence lower ones. Top-down effects are suggested by the sequential nature of the spoken message and by the principle of immediacy. The interpretation of the meaning of an utterance in a top-down manner therefore only involves partial analysis of the input, that is, the listener's expectations and predictions guide the decoding process, in which final perceptual decisions are made only after comprehension has taken place (Singer, 1990; Yeni-Komshian, 1998).

The 'perceptual basis' develops in childhood through the course of L1 acquisition in close relation with the child's articulation skills. It is a combination of unique neural and auditory mechanisms that monitor and determine the operation of the individual's perception system and comprise both universal and language-specific features. The perceptual basis filters the incoming speech signal contrasting it with first language speech sounds and phonemes. It is flexible to some extent in the recognition and identification of foreign sound patterns, yet it has a deep (positive or negative) impact on the learning of a foreign language (Gass & Selinker, 1994; Gósy, in this volume, 1999, 2004; Singleton, 1995; White, 1989).

The interactive and hierarchical model of speech processing

Several models have been created to describe either the perception/comprehension of human speech or the whole decoding process. (For more details on the models, see Cole & Jakimik, 1980; Garman, 1990; Gósy, 1999; Klatt, 1989; Massaro, 1994; Yeni-Komshian, 1998.) Even the most widely accepted model, however, can only serve as a general theoretical framework because of the crucial importance of language specificity in any particular model (Gósy, 1999).

The present study analyses speech perception and comprehension within the framework of the three-componential, hierarchical, interactive decoding model. The entire process is represented in terms of interconnected levels of analysis, which partly correspond to the levels of the psychological hierarchy and partly to the degrees of linguistic abstraction (Pisoni & Luce, 1987). These components work in cooperation to ensure the understanding of the spoken message. The psychological relevance of the model is strengthened by its incorporative nature; however, in the final comprehension and interpretation of the message, extralinguistic information is also taken into account. The test package (Gósy, 1995, 1997b) used in the experiment below was compiled in accordance with this theory.

The model is based on the hypothesis of gradual (bottom-up) perception (Gósy, 1990–1991, 1999; see Figure 4.1). That is, the processing of the speech signal starts with a preliminary auditory analysis, which is followed by recognition, identification and interpretation on the following consecutive and interrelated levels:

- acoustic, phonetic and phonological (perception);
- syntactic and semantic (comprehension); and
- association (interpretation).

Lexical access mediates between the stages of perception and comprehension. The decoding task (involving, for example, the size and character of the input) determines the way these levels are activated (Gósy, 1997a).

Differences in L1 and L2 acquisition and speech processing abilities

Figure 4.1 illustrates all general features of the speech decoding mechanism. One of the central issues in second and foreign language acquisition (SLA) research is whether a single language learning mechanism is flexible enough to cope with differences in external setting (the learning situation, the age and linguistic awareness of the learner, and so on). Do L2 learners use two qualitatively different processing systems for the L1 and L2 or the same perception, comprehension and production mechanisms?

Empirical evidence supports the view that although there are significant similarities between L1 and L2 learners, there remain key differences not accounted for by totally independent mechanisms (Ellis, 1990; Hatch, 1983; Odlin, 1989; Selinker, 1992; White, 1989). L2 acquisition is also a process of creative construction not dissimilar to that of L1 acquisition. The learner in both cases formulates an internalised system of abstract linguistic rules on the basis of innate principles and exposure to the language being learned, which determines the comprehension and the production of the language. However, most L2 learners are motivated by different factors from those in L1 acquisition; L2 learners are more mature in terms of cognitive development, start language learning at a later age, can exploit the prior knowledge and the availability of another language (usually the L1 system) and consciously monitor their own progress. Yet, only few of them can develop native-like language proficiency. In most cases, L2 learners' mental grammar is likely to fossilise at some point short of native-like grammar, and they may come to rely too heavily on the L1. L2 learners' approach to the target language is systematic and rule-governed, as they usually acquire the L2 through explicit language instruction, a certain teaching method and negative evidence. In addition to making use of their general (and L1) language-processing ability and experience, they must create language-specific processing skills as well, especially in cases where the L2 is not closely related to the L1.

Early contrastive and error analysis of the 1960's revealed many language-specific errors in L2 learners' performance. These errors were interpreted according to behaviourist language acquisition theory (which advocated the complete difference underlying L1 and L2 acquisition) as reflecting the learners' attempts to make use of their L1 knowledge. The nativist/mentalist view of the 1970's emphasised innate principles and the universal, developmental nature of errors, thus suggesting the fundamental identity of the L1 and L2 acquisition processes (Ellis, 1990; Gass & Selinker, 1994; Odlin, 1989).

Recent research (Gass & Selinker, 1994; Odlin, 1989; Selinker, 1992) on cross-linguistic influence (the influence resulting from similarities and differences between the target language and any other language previously acquired; see Odlin, 1989: 26), reveals that L1 transfer can occur in all linguistic subsystems of both comprehension and production among children and adults alike, and can have a negative/positive (facilitating/inhibiting/modifying) effect on L2 acquisition. The likelihood of native language influence is affected by the typological distance between the languages involved and by several interacting nonstructural, extra-linguistic factors (Ellis, 1990; Gass & Selinker, 1994; Skehan, 1989), such as different social and psychological conditions (the context of learning and the learner's background knowledge, personality, willingness to take risks, anxiety, learning style, language awareness, aptitude, motivation, learning strategies, and so on).

The concept of interlanguage (the internalised language system of the learner, most of which are native and target language elements and other ones) offers a general account of how L2 acquisition takes place, and the learner's native language is an important determinant in this process. However, there is a consensus today that the native language is not the only determinant in L2 acquisition and it may not even be the most important (Ellis, 1990; Gass & Selinker, 1994; Odlin, 1989). Importantly, universal developmental processes and transfer seem to operate in cooperation rather than in conflict.

Several models describing the relationship between L1 and L2 acquisition have been outlined in SLA research (for example, Fodor's and Bates & McWhinney's Competition Model, Krashen's Monitor Model, Bialystok & Sharwood Smith's model; see Gass & Selinker, 1994; Krashen, 1989; Skehan, 1989; White, 1989). Although most suggest that the L1 or a previously learned language can have an impact on every target language level, not one details similarities and differences in the production and decoding processes. The most salient consequences of cross-linguistic influence are production errors, but it can have important consequences for perception and comprehension, too. It is a given fact that without understanding the language, no learning can take place. L2 comprehension is fundamentally determined by prior linguistic knowledge, which includes native language knowledge, existing L2 knowledge, language universals and the knowledge of other languages (Gass & Selinker, 1994). Very little empirical evidence is available to illustrate L1 influence on L2 perception and comprehension abilities (Odlin, 1989; Gass & Selinker, 1994). For example, although major differences in phonemic inventories have been found to cause perceptual confusions, neither a different phonemic inventory nor the listener's low level phonetic sensibility totally impede the perception of L2 sounds. A large body of similar vocabulary, well-developed lexical skills and word perception strategies have been shown to accelerate the development of L2 lexical access and vocabulary size. It has likewise been demonstrated that the degree of similarity between the structural and semantic conceptual systems of the languages in question influence the learners' success in their efforts to read and understand the target language.

In other words, there is an interdependence between the first and second languages because acquiring one's first language gives one a certain 'routine' or experience, strategies and metacognitive skills, which can be generalised to subsequent languages, but there are also language-specific constraints in L2 perception and comprehension (Krashen, 1989; Lengyel, 1994).

These findings have several pedagogical implications: it is safe to claim, for instance, that delay or deficiency detected in the development of a child's mother-tongue perception and comprehension abilities will result in difficulties in the same L2 operations (Gósy, in this volume; Simon, 2001). The development of speech perception and comprehension, therefore, should start during L1 acquisition. In language teaching, it is also beneficial to measure learners' first language perception and comprehension abilities at the beginning of a course and to teach the target language based on the results (Bárdos, 2002). Teachers of a L2, who know the native language of their students, may draw helpful contrasts between the L1 and L2. Similarly, textbooks and other teaching materials that present analogies between the L1 and L2 may either promote or inhibit some kinds of transfer. In the same way that listening and reading comprehension are prerequisites for fluent speaking and writing, positive transfer may play an especially important role in the beginning stages of the acquisition of a language.

Aims and hypotheses

The aim of the present study is to gather empirical evidence about the relationship between the L1 (Hungarian) and L2 (English) decoding mechanisms of the same Hungarian school children. Results comprise a statistical analysis and comparison of the L1 and L2 processing abilities of the Hungarian test subjects, a description of differences and/or similarities between the two main components (perception and comprehension) of processing speech, and the impact of certain variables such as age and gender on these mental operations. By analysing the perception and comprehension abilities of a British control group, we also gain insight into the decoding operations and strategies applied when English is not a second but a first language. According to our hypothesis, L2 learners tend to map their first language perception and comprehension experience and strategies onto the second language rather than develop new ones adjusted to the features of the target language. The findings and conclusions of the study may have direct application to first language acquisition and development, language pedagogy and the methodology of language teaching.

Subjects and Method

In order to obtain data on the operations of each hypothetical level of the speech perception and comprehension processes (see Figure 4.1) the equivalent subtests of two corresponding test batteries, the *GMP* and *GMP Listening to English* (henceforth: GMPeng), were used. Due to space limitations, the present study will only attempt a quantitative analysis of the mean test results; no individual differences will be discussed here.

The subjects of the experiment were 11- and 12-year-old native Hungarian primary school children with normal processing, mental and hearing abilities from a Hungarian provincial capital (Veszprém). At the time of testing (2000–2002) these 200 students were attending either the fifth or sixth grades of junior school and had been learning English – mainly at school – for at least two years, for the same number of hours each year (thus meeting the requirement for GMPeng). The age difference, as well as the difference in time spent studying English as a foreign language, between the two tested subgroups was an average of one year. We aimed to test an equal number of subjects in each age group (100/100) and with the same gender distribution (50% boys and 50% girls). (The reason why this particular age group was chosen is that by this age, basic decoding errors in native language generally do not occur. We can therefore obtain a more nuanced picture from the speech decoding mechanism (L1) and implicitly of the general learning processes from children reaching the end of the critical period in language acquisition. The testing of two subgroups with only one year of difference in age offers a comparison of L1 speech decoding abilities at an age when age-specific differences are no longer expected. The choice of subjects was also guided by the fact that research carried out on the operation of the speech perception and comprehension mechanisms near puberty is scarce. In addition, a comparison of the two subgroups provides valuable information on the relationship between native language awareness and foreign language learning and the correlation between success in language learning and classroom hours invested.)

A control group of twenty 11-year-old native English speakers from Princethorpe Junior School (Birmingham, UK) took part in the experiment

Table 4.1 Basic data on the subjects of the study

Class/Age	Gender		Total
	Male	Female	
English (11-year-old)	8	12	20
Fifth grade (11-year-old)	61	47	108
Sixth grade (12-year-old)	40	52	92
Total	109	111	220

as well. These children had no foreign language experience at the time of testing. Their GMPeng (L1) results can be compared with both the fifth grade Hungarian children's GMPeng (L2) results (the same biological age) and the sixth grade Hungarian children's L2 results (the same number of years at school). Table 4.1 summarises the age and gender distribution of the subjects.

Seven subtests (containing 10 test items each) from the GMP testpackage (Gósy, 1995) and the equivalent GMPeng battery (Gósy, 1997b) were chosen to test the consecutive levels of speech perception and comprehension in L1 and L2 (see Figure 4.1). Most of the subtests require subjects to repeat an authentic speech signal recorded on tape, and the evaluation process is the same in each case: the student who repeats every single test item or answers every single test question correctly scores 100%, the one who repeats 9 scores 90%, and so on.

The three levels of speech perception (the recognition and identification of the auditory speech signal) are tested by four subtests:

(1) acoustic level: the identification of sentences masked by white noise (henceforth: noisy s.) and that of words masked by white noise (noisy w.);
(2) phonetic level: the identification of sentences after pass-band filtration confined to the frequency range of 2200–2700 Hz (filtered s.);
(3) phonological level: the identification of artificially speeded up or sped-up sentences (fast s.).

A fifth subtest, the identification of nonsense words (nonsense w.), gives empirical information on serial perception and perceptual segmentation abilities, which are indispensable for both the decoding and production of speech.

Lexical access (the speedy and efficient recognition, identification and interpretation of lexical units) mediates between speech perception and comprehension. This interface level is tested by the word association subtest, that is, by listing, in writing, within two minutes as many words as possible beginning with the stimulus syllables **ma-**, **ke-** [in Hungarian] and with the stimulus sounds /**m**/, /**k**/ [in English].

The two consecutive levels of speech comprehension (the interpretation of different syntactic structures of a language and the meaning of semantic units) are analysed with the help of the following two subtests:

(1) (dominantly) syntactic-level: a sentence comprehension subtest, in which subjects must choose from two similar drawings the one which best fits a test sentence (henceforth: sent. compr.). This test was only administered in English to obtain a more sophisticated picture of the nature of L2 speech comprehension.
(2) (dominantly) semantic-level: a text comprehension subtest, with a listening exercise followed by answering comprehension questions in writing. This subtest (text compr.) also tests the interpretation level (the association of the message understood with our encyclopaedic knowledge and experience) at the top of the decoding hierarchy.

The GMP test results can be evaluated against standardised age-specific assessment scores. For GMPeng, however, only informatory mean test scores are available, which are based on the duration of foreign language study. (See the following references for greater detail on the test batteries: Gósy, this volume and Gósy, 1995, 1997a,b). For statistical analysis the SPSS 9.0 software package was used (confidence level = 95%).

Results

Some very basic features of the interrelation between the two main components of the speech decoding mechanism (perception and comprehension) and of the efficiency of the lexical access supporting these operations can be easily discerned by comparing the mean results of the test group in both the L1 and L2 and with those of the control group (see Figures 4.2 and 4.3). As age and gender were not found to significantly affect the Hungarian subgroups' L1 and L2 decoding abilities (exceptions to this finding are mentioned later), the study only discusses the performance of the whole Hungarian test group of 200 children.

Mother-tongue decoding abilities of the Hungarian test group

The findings reveal that the lower levels of the L1 decoding hierarchy – that is, the levels of speech perception – operate routinely, automatically and

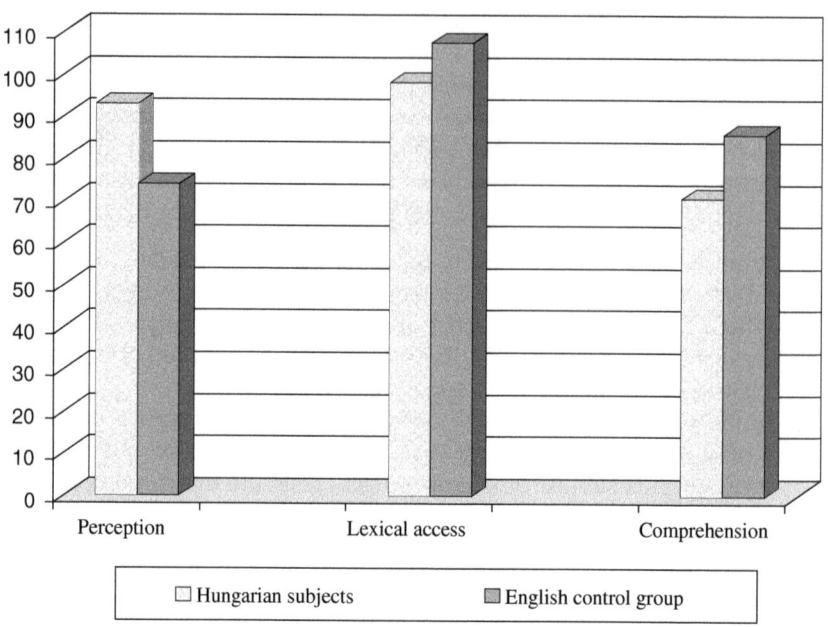

Figure 4.2 Speech perception and comprehension GMP results in L1 (%). (lexical access: number of words ×10).

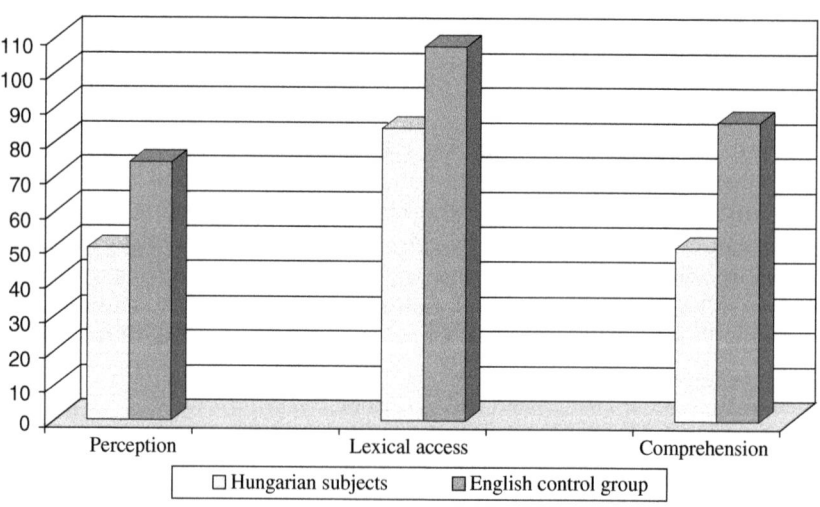

Figure 4.3 Speech perception and comprehension GMPeng results in L2 (%). (lexical access: number of words ×10).

spontaneously, and hence significantly faster and better than the more conscious and slower comprehension component (Wilcoxon test: $Z = -10.047$, $p < 0.000$), which depends heavily on contextual and factual knowledge. Lexical access proves to be fast and accurate: the children associate far more words, on average, than the expected standard of six to seven items. The Hungarian children's L1 lexical access abilities are significantly more developed than their L2 lexical access (Wilcoxon test: $Z = -5.688$, $p < 0.000$). In addition, lexical access proves to be heavily dependent on age in the L1 and/or language learning experience in the L2 (see Figures 4.2 and 4.3), as in both cases the sixth graders outperform the fifth graders.

A more detailed analysis of each particular level of the decoding process (see Table 4.2) shows that the children were not all able to reach the expected 100% standardised age-score at the levels of perception that were tested, but achieved a mean result in text comprehension over the standard (60–70%). In text comprehension, however, individual differences were marked resulting in the most extremely low and high scores.

The order of difficulty of the mental operations to be performed in the L1 appears to be the same for the whole test group irrespective of age and gender. In all cases, this order (see Table 4.5) precisely reflects the consecutive stages of the hierarchical speech decoding model introduced earlier (see Figure 4.1). That is, the acoustic, phonetic and serial perception levels work more automatically and effortlessly than the phonological level and the higher levels of speech comprehension, which require

Table 4.2 The L1 (GMP) results of the Hungarian test group

	N	*Minimum*	*Maximum*	*Mean*	*S.D.*
Noisy sentences	190	60.0	100.0	91.158	9.1851
Noisy words	190	70.0	100.0	96.789	5.7004
Filtered sentences	190	80.0	100.0	97.895	4.5762
Fast sentences	190	50.0	100.0	86.895	11.2847
Nonsense words	190	50.0	100.0	91.8421	8.80574
Mean perception results	190	78.0	100.0	92.9158	4.04515
Word association	199	3.5	45.5	9.809	3.7924
Text comprehension	199	10.0	100.0	70.653	24.1539
Valid N (listwise)	190				

S.D., standard deviation.

more complex and conscious operations and rely heavily on the cooperation of several levels. Similar findings were presented by Simon (2001) and by Vančóné Kremmer (2002) in her study of 110 dominantly Hungarian-speaking 11- and 12-year-old Hungarian-Slovak bilingual students and 34 Hungarian children, based on the same GMP subtests.

No correlations have been detected in our study between L1 perception, comprehension and lexical access in any case. The close interdependence of the particular levels of perception, however, is significant. Successful perception in the mother tongue is primarily determined by the operation of its highest, phonological level (Spearman's rho = 0.644, $p < 0.001$). (And the more effortlessly this level functions, the faster the speech comprehension is.)

Foreign language (English) decoding abilities of the Hungarian test group

The L2 speech perception and comprehension results and individual deviations from the mean are more balanced and levelled up (see Figure 4.3 and Table 4.3). The reason for the finding that individual L2 listening abilities do not show as many variations as in the L1 probably derives from the homogeneity of the language learning environment (the teaching method, the teaching material, the pace of instruction, and so on, as well as the uniformity of input and of memory requirements). Foreign language

Table 4.3 L2 (GMPeng) results of the Hungarian test group

	N	Minimum	Maximum	Mean	S.D.
Noisy sentences	196	0.0	100.0	39.388	25.2502
Noisy words	196	40.0	100.0	76.684	14.3838
Filtered sentences	196	0.0	100.0	34.337	21.4612
Fast sentences	196	0.0	90.0	14.643	19.1184
Nonsense words	196	40.0	100.0	82.194	13.1181
Mean perception results	196	22.0	92.0	49.4490	14.36172
Word association	198	1.5	32.5	8.409	3.8135
Sentence comprehension	196	20.0	100.0	61.378	18.8826
Text comprehension	198	0.0	100.0	38.409	23.9048
Mean comprehension results	196	15.0	100.0	49.8852	19.05507
Valid N (listwise)	196				

decoding processes are also noticeably less automatic and the students' L2 performances are significantly lower than their corresponding native language results (Wilcoxon test – $p < 0.000$: perception $Z = -11.926$; comprehension: $Z = -9.171$). (This latter finding also proves that it is not enough to depend solely on mother-tongue decoding abilities, techniques and strategies to understand an L2 utterance.) If we compare the Hungarian test group's GMPeng results with the expected norm set by Gósy (1997b), our test results correspond to a period of three to four years of language study (only 35.5% of the tested children had been learning English for that long). The average time spent on language learning is four and a half years. Neither language exposure duration is considered a very long time, several students were still able to score 100% in various GMPeng subtests. A detailed analysis reflects low mean results (see Table 4.3) and the frequent occurrence of extreme scores (standard deviation results reaching twice as much as for native speakers of English – see Table 4.4). Interestingly, and in keeping with L1 results, L2 lexical access proves to be unexpectedly fast and accurate. Most tested children associated more words than the set norm, that is, they could effectively navigate their L2 mental lexicon.

With regard to age and time spent in language learning, a significant improvement in L2 perception abilities, but only a slight increase in L2

Table 4.4 L1 (GMPeng) results of the native English control group

	N	*Minimum*	*Maximum*	*Mean*	S.D.
Noisy sentences	20	50.0	100.0	77.000	13.8031
Noisy words	20	70.0	100.0	89.000	10.2084
Filtered sentences	20	40.0	90.0	76.500	13.0888
Fast sentences	20	60.0	100.0	80.500	10.9904
Nonsense words	20	20.0	70.0	47.500	15.5174
Mean perception results	20	62.0	88.0	74.1000	7.38348
Word association	20	4.0	17.5	10.750	3.7187
Sentence comprehension	20	30.0	100.0	88.000	16.7332
Text comprehension	20	10.0	100.0	84.000	21.9209
Mean comprehension results	20	35.0	100.0	86.0000	17.00232
Valid N (listwise)	20				

comprehension, is found when comparing the fifth and sixth graders (noisy sentences and words, fast sentences, word association). There are also more differences found in the language processing abilities of boys and girls in the L2 than in the L1. Although the boys' scores are heterogeneous and frequently lie at the extremes, they still outperform girls (noisy words, filtered sentences and text comprehension).

However, the above differences are mainly of a quantitative nature, and all tested Hungarian subjects seem to face the same difficulties in L2 perception and comprehension (see Table 4.5). The order of difficulty of the GMPeng subtests found in our study is identical with that presented in Gósy's research (1997a,b) on subjects of the same age. The hierarchy of the decoding mechanism (see Figure 4.1) is not reflected fully in the findings above as the Hungarian test group's perception and comprehension of English are very similar.

The levels of speech comprehension can operate effectively even with the higher (phonetic and phonological) levels of perception working only partially. L2 perception achieves its fullest potential with word-level input, as children tend to focus on meaning rather than form when the task is to process entire sentences. The dominance of top-down processing in the L2 can be explained by several factors: for example, the structural properties of the English language, the temporal limitations on processing ongoing speech, the qualitative and quantitative influence of previous

Table 4.5 The order of task difficulty in L1 and L2 decoding processes (1 = very easy, 7 = very difficult)

Decoding task difficulty ranks	GMP (L1) Hungarian test group	GMPeng (L2) Hungarian test group	GMPeng (L1) English control group
1	Filtered sentences	Nonsense words	Noisy words
2	Noisy words	Noisy words	Sentence comprehension
3	Nonsense words	Sentence comprehension	Text comprehension
4	Noisy sentences	Text comprehension	Fast sentences
5	Fast sentences	Noisy sentences	Noisy sentences
6	Text comprehension	Filtered sentences	Filtered sentences
7		Fast sentences	Nonsense words

language learning experience, the underdeveloped L2 verbal short-term memory capacity, and so on.

Similarly, strong correlations have been detected between L2 perception, comprehension and lexical access in all combinations (Spearman's rho – $p < 0.000$: perception and lexical access $r = 0.501$, comprehension and lexical access $r = 0.569$, perception and comprehension $r = 0.691$). Therefore, it is safe to assume that there is a close interdependence and mutual development of foreign language perception and comprehension. In addition, both the ability to access the acquired vocabulary and the size of this vocabulary are likely to determine the operation of these two components and the outcome of the whole L2 decoding process. First language acquisition and the development of metalinguistic awareness take place in much more heterogeneous circumstances, which more often result in individual differences in the levels of the decoding mechanism. These particular levels are likewise able to operate more independently and autonomously in the L1 decoding process. One can conclude from the above that such an intricate network of connections between all levels of perception and comprehension does not exist in the L1 (including the control group, see GMPeng results of the native English control group below).

Another remarkable finding is the significant correlation between L1 and L2 abilities in perception, comprehension and lexical access (Spearman's rho – $p < 0.01$: $r = 0.303$, $r = 0.375$, $r = 0.407$), respectively, that is, a person with developed speech perception, comprehension and word association in his mother-tongue processes foreign language utterances equally well. From this, we conclude that mother-tongue speech perception and comprehension experience and abilities (interacting with a host of other factors) are indispensable for efficient and accurate L2 decoding. Therefore, the development (or 'cultivation') of L1 perception and comprehension is clearly necessary even through the fifth and sixth grades. In addition, the significant role of lexical access (the highest correlation rates detected) in both the L1 and L2 suggests that lexical access abilities considerably influence speech perception and comprehension in any language, but to a greater extent in the L2.

Mother-tongue (GMPeng) decoding abilities of the native English control group

The control group's speech processing results show significant differences from those of the Hungarian test group. Operations at the levels of perception are impeded to a greater extent than those at the comprehension levels. Moreover, although their perception abilities in the L1 are weaker and more heterogeneous than those of the Hungarian subjects, their comprehension abilities are much stronger and more consistent (see Figure 4.2, Table 4.4). These findings reveal the relative independence of perception and comprehension processes (as was also seen in the test group's L1 results), but also the significant impact of lexical access abilities on comprehension (Wilcoxon test: $Z = -2.763$, $p < 0.006$. Spearman's rho $= 0.666$, $p < 0.001$). The native English control group's GMPeng scores not surprisingly exceed the Hungarian test group's L2 results in each test (see Figure 4.3, Kruskal-Wallis test – $p < 0.000$: perception – df $= 2$, $\chi^2 = 41.598$; comprehension – df $= 2$, $\chi^2 = 39.926$). Their lexical access abilities do not differ from either the L1 or L2 lexical access abilities of the 12-year-old Hungarian subjects – who have learned English for a maximum of five-and-a-half years (control group: 10.75 words; sixth graders: 10.7, and 9.368 words), but the lexical abilities of the control group are significantly better (two more words on average) than those of the Hungarian subgroup of the same age (Kruskal-Wallis test: df $= 2$, $\chi^2 = 17.655$, $p < 0.000$).

If we rank the subtest performances in order of difficulty (see Tables 4.4 and 4.5), it turns out that text comprehension (an easy task) precedes some lower-level perception tasks restricted to identifying isolated words and sentences, although the former is considered the most complex level of the decoding process and depends greatly on the interaction and the output of the lower ones. The control group's relatively low perception scores derive from weakness at the phonetic and phonological levels and in serial perception (Spearman's rho – $p < 0.01$: filtered sentences $r = 0.678$, fast sentences $r = 0.799$, nonsense words $r = 0.803$). The latter has a strong impact on the development of an individual's vocabulary and thus implicitly on the general learning process; it is indispensable for learning to read and write, for learning a new language and also for the development of L1 metalinguistic awareness. The difficulty detected at this perception level is probably due to structural features of the English language and to the control group's lack of foreign language learning experience. The hierarchy of the decoding mechanism (see Figure 4.1) is not reflected fully in the findings above, either. The control group compensates for its perceptual shortcomings by using global, top-down strategies and relying greatly on contextual, semantic cues. (Table 4.5 sets out the list of tasks ranked by difficulty for the control group and the test group in each language.)

Comparative Study 77

Discussion

In accordance with the aim of this study, this chapter sets out to:

(1) compare the Hungarian test group's L1 and L2 processing abilities to find basic differences and similarities between them.

An analysis of the English control group's results enables us to examine two more aspects of the decoding mechanism:

(2) whether speech perception and comprehension abilities and strategies depend on the type of acquisition (as a L1 or L2) of the same language; and
(3) which characteristics of L1 speech perception and comprehension are universal and which are language-specific.

General speech perception and comprehension patterns revealed by the experiment

Figure 4.4 summarises both the Hungarian test group's and the English control group's L1 and L2 scores at each level of the speech decoding process. The three main data groups in the figure are quantitatively fully independent of one another; yet an obvious similarity between the Hungarian test group's mother-tongue and foreign language processing

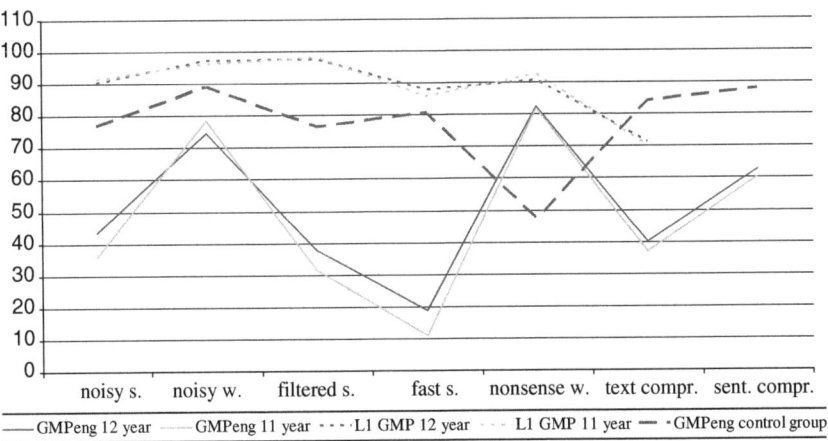

Figure 4.4 L1 and L2 speech perception and comprehension characteristics of the Hungarian test group and the English control group (%).

abilities and a partial similarity between these and the English L1 data can still be seen.

L1 and L2 perception and comprehension abilities of the Hungarian subjects

Figure 4.4 reflects a relationship between the L1 and L2 perception and comprehension abilities of the Hungarian subjects. The graphs follow the same pattern with the exception of one subtest (filtered sentences). Mother-tongue speech perception operates automatically at every single level at the tested age, whereas speech perception in the foreign language (at the phonetic level) is not solely determined by L1 experience, because the L2 graph declines at this point. As the English control group's graph also declines at this stage, one may conclude that the phenomenon can be explained by specific structural and phonemic features of the English language.

L1 processing abilities of the English control group

Tendencies in the L1 processing abilities of the English control group differ from those in the perception and comprehension of English as a foreign language by the Hungarian subjects at three levels. They are the most complex levels of perception and comprehension: phonological perception (fast sentences), serial perception (nonsense words) and text comprehension.

The accuracy of the Hungarian test group's perception of L2 (and even L1) utterances is deeply influenced by the tempo of the speech. This factor becomes especially significant in situations when the listener cannot compensate for the distortion of the acoustic stimulus with the help of semantic and contextual cues, because the utterance appears to be syntactically and semantically too complex. This condition is aggravated in a foreign language by the lack of authentic L2 perception experience.

In the case of serial perception (the identification of the sound pattern of new and foreign words and phrases) the situation is reversed. That is, identifying nonsense words was the easiest task for the Hungarian children irrespective of the language used. Gósy (1997a) presents the same findings after testing 160 primary school children. However, this ability is not universal, as the identification of nonsense words proved the most difficult task for the control group. An explanation should take into consideration the impact of the first language perceptual basis and positive transfer, the previous language learning experience and general perceptual awareness in the Hungarian test group.

The Hungarian test group ran into difficulties in both L1 and L2 text comprehension while the English subjects did not. This finding suggests that the control group, most likely influenced by language-specific factors, relies more often on top-down processing. The Hungarian subjects also depended heavily on this meaning-based processing strategy in completing the GMPeng tasks, although they frequently blended it with its counterpart, bottom-up processing, which they dominantly apply for first language perception and comprehension.

First Language decoding mechanisms

When comparing the first language decoding mechanisms, the English L1 pattern appears to be different from the Hungarian L1 pattern at four levels: filtered sentences (phonetic), fast sentences (phonological), nonsense words (serial perception) and text comprehension.

The above tendencies and graph patterns (illustrated by Figure 4.4 and in accordance with their statistical analysis) suggest that the decoding methods of the English control subjects do not resemble either the Hungarian test group's L2 or L1 perception and comprehension strategies. Nevertheless, the L1 and L2 results of the Hungarian test group are remarkably similar. The findings of this study indicate that, with respect to speech perception and comprehension, people tend to learn a foreign language under the influence of the mother-tongue. This may facilitate, or sometimes hinder, the acquisition of native-like proficiency in the target language.

Conclusion

Our original hypothesis has been proved as the patterns of decoding speech clearly reveal interdependence between the Hungarian subjects' L1 and L2 perception and comprehension development (with a nearly identical order of task difficulty, although the mother-tongue results are, of course, at a higher level than the foreign language results).

One can also conclude from this that Hungarian speakers mainly map their first language decoding strategies onto the processing of speech in the L2 (Vančóné Kremmer, 2002), although there are examples (similarities with the control group's GMPeng results) that illustrate that L2-specific features may also influence the outcome.

Our test results only partly (in the L1) correspond to the hierarchy of gradual perception and comprehension given in the theoretical framework of this study. Mother-tongue perception appears to be so automatic, effortless, rapid and accurate that it cannot cause comprehension difficulties. But the two components of the decoding process in the L2 are related to such an extent that if perception becomes slower or impeded, and easy access to the higher levels is prevented, the listeners compensate for their difficulties by resorting to top-down processing and inferencing strategies in comprehension. (The selection of meaning-based cues is considered universal in comprehension. See Gass & Selinker, 1994.)

Accurate and rapid lexical access abilities both precondition and ensure the precise recognition and identification of the meaningful and meaningless units of the lexicon regardless of the language (L1/L2) used. The development of lexical access strengthens the decoding operations, which themselves become faster and more accurate. Hence, the role of this mediator level in the decoding process should not be neglected in either L1 or L2 development and teaching even at the later ages of schooling.

There is indeed an important relationship between L1 and L2 perception and comprehension, implying that the development of mother-tongue processing abilities should be emphasised in second language acquisition (Gósy, this volume). This has implications for SLA theory, language pedagogy and for language teaching (for example, in selecting the appropriate teaching method and material). Specific features of the first language and cross-linguistic influence should be highlighted not only in the development of L2 speech production and communication strategies but also during the development of perception and comprehension. Although L1 positive transfer should be exploited in language teaching whenever possible, L1 negative transfer should be prevented or avoided. This goal can be accomplished by publishing textbooks and developing teaching methods based on the cross-linguistic comparison of the first and target languages concerned in the teaching process.

Still, one should not forget that successful L2 perception and comprehension operations are not determined solely by mother-tongue decoding abilities at a given age, but that transfer also interacts with a host of other factors in acquisition.

References

Bárdos, J. (2002) *Az idegen nyelvi mérés és értékelés elmélete és gyakorlata*. [*The Theory and Practice of Foreign Language Testing and Assessment*]. Budapest: Nemzeti Tankönyvkiadó.

Bond, Z.S. and Garnes, S. (1980) Misperceptions of fluent speech. In R.A. Cole (ed.) *The Perception and Production of Human Speech* (pp. 115–132). Hillsdale, NJ: Lawrence Erlbaum.

Clark, H.H. and Clark, E.V. (1977) *Psychology and Language. An Introduction to Psycholinguistics*. New York: Harcourt Brace Jovanovich.

Cole, R.A. and Jakimik, J. (1980) A model of speech perception. In R.A. Cole (ed.) *The Perception and Production of Human Speech* (pp. 133–164). Hillsdale, NJ: Lawrence Erlbaum.

Ellis, R. (1990) *Instructed Second Language Acquisition: Learning in the Classroom.* Oxford: Blackwell.
Forster, K.I. (1989) Basic issues in lexical processing. In W. Marslen-Wilson (ed.) *Lexical Representation and Process* (pp. 75–107). Cambridge, MA: The MIT Press.
Garman, M. (1990) *Psycholinguistics.* Cambridge: Cambridge University Press.
Gass, S.M. and Selinker, L. (1994) *Second Language Acquisition. An Introductory Course.* Hillsdale, NJ: Lawrence Erlbaum.
Gósy, M. (1990–91) Lower Levels of the Speech Perception Process. *Acta Linguistica Hungarica* 40 (3–4), 315–327.
Gósy, M. (1995) *GMP Diagnosztika.* [The GMP Diagnostic Test Battery] Budapest: Nikol.
Gósy, M. (1997a) Assessment of L2 speech perception and comprehension. In Z. Lengyel, J. Navracsics and O. Simon (eds) *Applied Linguistic Studies in Central Europe* I (pp. 170–182). Veszprém: Veszprémi Egyetem.
Gósy, M. (1997b) *Listening to English. Tesztcsomag az angol nyelvi beszédészlelés és beszédmegértés vizsgálatára* [*Listening to English. A Test Battery for Measuring the Perception and Comprehension of English Speech*] Budapest: Nikol.
Gósy, M. (1999) *Pszicholingvisztika* [*Psycholinguistics*]. Budapest: Corvina.
Gósy, M. (2004) *Fonetika, a beszéd tudománya.* [*Phonetics. The Study of Speech*]. Budapest: Osiris Kiadó.
Hatch, E.M. (1983) *Psycholinguistics. A Second Language Perspective.* Rowley, MA: Newbury House.
Klatt, D.H. (1989) Review of selected models of speech perception. In W. Marslen-Wilson (ed.) *Lexical Representation and Process* (pp. 169–226). Cambridge, MA: The MIT Press.
Krashen, S. (1989) *Language Acquisition and Language Education. Extensions and Applications.* New York: Prentice Hall International.
Lengyel, Z. (1994) *Nyelvelsajátítási és nyelvtanulási formák.* [*Language Acquisition and Language Learning*] Veszprém: Egyetemi Kiadó.
Massaro, D.W. (1994) Psychological aspects of speech perception: Implications for research and theory. In M.A. Gernsbacher (ed.) *Handbook of Psycholinguistics* (pp. 219–264). New York, London: Academic Press.
Odlin, T. (1989) *Language Transfer. Cross-Linguistic Influence in Language Learning.* Cambridge: Cambridge University Press.
Pisoni, D.B. and Luce, P.A. (1987) Acoustic-phonetic representations in word recognition. In L.K. Tyler and U.H. Frauenfelder (eds) *Spoken Word Recognition* (pp. 21–52). Cambridge, MA, London: The MIT Press.
Pisoni, D.B. and Sawusch, J.R. (1975) Some stages of processing in speech perception. In A. Cohen and S.G. Nooteboom (eds) *Structure and Process in Speech Perception* (pp. 16–35). Berlin, Heidelberg, New York: Springer Verlag.
Selinker, L. (1992) *Rediscovering Interlanguage.* London: Longman.
Simon, O. (2001) A magyar és az angol beszédészlelési és beszédmegértési teljesítmény összefüggései 11-12 évesek körében. [The relationship between Hungarian and English speech perception and comprehension abilities of 11- and 12-year-old Hungarian children] *Alkalmazott Nyelvtudomány* 1(2), 45–61.
Singer, M. (1990) *Psychology of Language. An Introduction to Sentence and Discourse Processes.* Hillsdale, New Jersey, London: Lawrence Erlbaum.
Singleton, D. (1995) Introduction: A critical look at the critical period hypothesis in second language acquisition research. In D. Singleton and Z. Lengyel (eds) *The*

Age Factor in Second Language Acquisition (pp. 1–29). Clevedon: Multilingual Matters.

Skehan, P. (1989) *Individual Differences in Second-Language Learning*. London, NY: Edward Arnold.

Vančóné Kremmer, I. (2002) A beszédészlelés és a beszédmegértés vizsgálata magyar-szlovák kétnyelvű gyermekeknél. [The study of Hungarian-Slovak bilingual children's speech perception and comprehension] In I. Lanstyák és Sz. Simon (eds) *Tanulmányok a Kétnyelvűségről* (pp. 71–94). Pozsony: Kalligram.

White, L. (1989) *Universal Grammar and Second Language Acquisition*. Amsterdam: John Benjamins.

Yeni-Komshian, G.H. (1998) Speech perception. In B.J. Gleason and B.N. Ratner (eds) *Psycholinguistics* (pp. 107–156). NY, London: Harcourt Brace College Publishers.

Chapter 5
Slip of the Doctor's Eye: Recognising English Contact Induced Features in Hungarian Medical Texts

CSILLA KERESZTES

Introduction

In some speech communities, the prestige and the socio-economic dominance (Thomason, 2001) of English as a foreign language (EFL) can create a language contact situation that affects the native language (Peterson, 2004). This paper observes how physicians and medical students are influenced by the knowledge of English language in proofreading medical texts, and what new insights it can give to the research field of psycholinguistics.

In the 20th century, a much closer contact of English (E) with other European languages developed due to new means of communication (Odlin, 1989). The result was a very free and versatile linguistic borrowing of English words by European languages, including the Hungarian (H) language. This phenomenon can be found in various fields of culture, but can be best detected in the field of sciences (Navracsics, 2004; Singleton, 2003), and especially in the field of medicine (Keresztes, 2003; Kontra, 1981). Although this influence is mostly reflected in the appearance of English loan words in H, it can be detected at all levels of the language (Farkas & Kniezsa, 2002).

After the Second World War, the influx of English words in H increased dramatically, but there was a strong tendency for the purging of E elements for obvious political reasons (Farkas & Kniezsa, 2002). Medicine was one of the fields which was most affected by this phenomenon (Kontra, 1981). During the 1980's, there was a clear opening toward the west, that led to an unprecedented boom in the adoption of E words in almost all areas of life, including the field of medicine. The result of the English influence is that H borrows E loans, adapts them as Anglicisms and subsequently integrates them into the H (medical) vocabulary (Keresztes, 2003). But at what phase are they really integrated into H? When can we declare that they are part of the mental lexicon of the individual or that of the community? Are these words/phrases represented in the active part of the mental lexicon or in the passive part?

We can try to identify this integration by analysing the interference categories:

(1) the orthographic interference;
(2) the use of loan words and abbreviations;
(3) the grammatical interferences; and
(4) the semantic interferences (Bánréti, 1999; Besner & Johnston, 1989).

Foreign elements in the native lexicon have been studied for almost two centuries. The impact of some major European languages (mainly Latin, German and French) on the Hungarian language and its lexicon has been investigated, however, English has hardly been studied as one of the sources of foreign elements (Farkas & Kniezsa, 2002). Consequently, studies, surveys and lists of English contact induced features in the H language of medicine are extremely rare compared to those of other European languages (Kontra, 1981).

Any analysis of E borrowings into the medical lexicon of H shows that unsurprisingly, nouns (for example, *stroke, bypass, biofeedback*) are in the majority: they represent 80% of the English words. Recently, hybrid compounds (for example, *trigger-pontok* H – *trigger-points* E, *véna-stripping* H – *vein-stripping* E) have become very popular. In all these cases, the foreignness of the English element is very apparent. Calques (loan translations) are also frequent since the morphological structure of English and Hungarian composition is similar, translation is easy for example, *cost-effective* E – *költséghatékony* H, *islet cell* E – *szigetsejt* H, *target organ damage* E – *célszervkárosodás* H (Farkas & Kniezsa, 2002; Keresztes, 2003; Kontra, 1981).

In our study, we try to trace the influence of E on H from another aspect, namely by investigating the mental lexicon of medics, as it comprises all our knowledge related to words (Marslen-Wilson, 1989). According to Fillmore (1971), our mental lexicon contains information about the phonological form of a given unit of speech, the meaning of it, its syntactic surroundings, the grammatical rules that can be applied with it, its possible argumentations, the conditions of its use, and its semantic and morphological relations to other given units of the lexicon. The identification of a word/expression or structure is performed, on one hand, in the mental lexicon and, on the other hand, in its peripheries (Lengyel, 1998). This identification or recognition is accelerated by associations of words, and by the adjoining semantic and grammatical information. In word recognition, we first make use of perceptual information, and we are later helped in the process by the complex contextual information (Gósy, 1998). Generally, word recognition is influenced by the language of the text, the type of the text, the age of the reader, and the reading experience of the reader (Wheeler, 1970).

Most linguists agree that lexical entries contain information regarding a word's semantic, syntactic and phonological properties (e.g. Gósy, 1999b; Levelt, 1989; Schreuder & d'Arcais, 1989). However, some cognitionists propose that words do not have meaning as much as they provide clues to meaning (Elman, 2004). Thus, the importance of context is highly emphasised in the recognition of words (see Figure 5.1): information flows from input to hidden to output layers. In addition, at every time step t, the hidden-unit layer receives input from the context layer, which stores the hidden unit activations from time t-1 (Elman, 2004).

Perfetti (1986) states that context has a very essential role in reading texts and understanding them. Reading is a decoding skill, it is the transformation of written words into uttered ones. Information is processed by a certain code-switching and visual transformation. This decoding is the segmentation of words, recognising their equivalence with sequences of phonemes. Readers then understand this sequence, that is, recognise the morphological structure of the segmented word, and finally, identify meaning. It is the visual stimulus that activates the proper unit in the mental lexicon of the reader. Thus, we can say that written word recognition is identifying a printed item as being familiar. Visual stimuli – the written text – are processed at high speed during normal reading. The purpose of the reading, as well as other textual factors, can influence

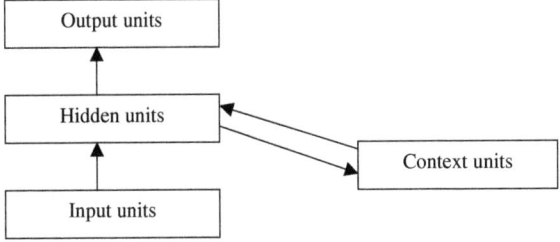

Figure 5.1. Simple recurrent network.

this speed (Smith, 1969). If the pace of the reading is determined externally, and not chosen by the reader, word recognition can be hindered and reading errors might occur (Besner & Johnston, 1989).

In visual word recognition, context has a huge impact on our reading process. Similarly to that of spoken word recognition, it can also have a positive effect on our global understanding (Gósy, 1998). But the contextual effect might also hinder us in recognition, namely in the recognition of errors or foreign language influences (Fromkin, 1980).

Identifying these errors or 'language contact induced features' and their interpretation in the light of contrastive linguistics can help us understand English-Hungarian cross-linguistic influences.

Subjects and Methods

In this study, data were gained during an experiment in which participants had to proofread two medical texts in H, and had to spot E induced contact features or errors. Recognising a printed word involves automatic processing of perceptual input and may also involve controlled (or attentional) processing (Baker, 2001), as in our case, in a certain experimental task. The task had to be performed within a given period of time. The two texts mimicking research articles had several English contact induced features in addition to three Hungarian spelling mistakes hidden in them.

In the experiment, medics had limited time to concentrate on various types of contact induced features or 'errors'. The proofreading task demands close and careful reading as it is the final stage of the editing process, focusing on surface errors such as misspellings and mistakes in grammar and punctuation. This task involved not only visual word recognition but lexical access as well, that is, eliciting all information pertaining to a word (Editing and proofreading, 1998).

The study was carried out in the spring of 2005 at the Medical University of Szeged, Hungary. The research was based on two reading texts (see Appendix) on Cardiology (one on Kawasaki disease and the other on anti-hypertensive treatment). I used two Hungarian articles (with the kind permission of the authors) as sources for my texts, and rewrote them in a way to be appropriate for my linguistic purposes. First, I selected certain parts of the articles, then I changed some words/expressions of the original piece, rearranged the word order and made some further grammatical changes. I also inserted some Hungarian spelling mistakes into the text as distractors. The 'new' texts were of two-page length ($n = 5650$) altogether containing 23 changed items, which were phonological, morphological, syntactic and semantic borrowings from the English language, calques, English abbreviations without explanation, grammatical patterns of direct and indirect E interferences (Klaudy, 1999).

At the end of the proofreading task, participants had to fill in some data concerning their sex, age, knowledge of the English language (self-evaluation between 0 and 5; 5 being the highest level), exposure to English language, and whether they took or had taken part in the English-Hungarian Medical Translator course. There was also a *Notes* section where they could write comments in connection with the task.

Sixty questionnaires were dispensed during the survey, and 32 fully filled ones were returned. Subjects ($n = 32$) were categorized into three groups (see Table 5.1) according to their age (17 to 21 year-old: students in the preparatory or pre-clinical course, 30 to 40-year-old: residents and junior doctors, and over 50 years old: senior doctors). Residents, junior and senior doctors were selected from various fields of medicine. They were also selected for the task on the basis of whether they had taken part in the translator course or not, as in this course the students' awareness of direct and indirect interferences of E on H is raised.

There were six translator students in the first age group, and eight translators in the second age group (being in the course or having finished it), and there was nobody in the third group who had completed this course as the programme was launched in 1987.

Medics had limited time (15 minutes) to proofread the texts. They were asked to underline anything in the text they would change should these texts be submitted for publication.

My hypotheses were that those medical professionals who had high-level knowledge of English (4 or 5; Self-evaluation on a 5-grade scale where 5 is the highest level) and who were extensively exposed to E, would not recognise E contact induced features in H written texts, or at least would not mark them as errors/items to be changed. I also hypothesised that age could be another factor in the spotting results. On the other

Table 5.1 Distribution of the subjects involved in the experiment

Age groups	17–21 years	30–40 years	Over 50 years	Total
No. of subjects	11	15	6	32
No. of translators	6	8	0	14

hand, I was strongly convinced that participation in the translator course would have an effect on the results of proofreading, that is, they would identify more E contact induced features than their colleagues.

Results

In evaluating the results, I kept two aims in mind: how many E contact induced features and other 'errors' subjects could identify, and what type of features and 'errors' had not been spotted.
Influences could be grouped according to linguistic categories:

- **Orthographical interferences**. For example: *non-purulent, ágent, beta-blockolók* (in Hungarian *non-purulens, ágens* and *beta-blokkolók* are the standard expressions);
- English **loan words** and **abbreviations** instead of the existing Hungarian expressions. For example: *Kawasaki-disease, Nyerges et al., strawberry tongue, concordance, UK-ban* (whereas there are Hungarian words for these: *Kawasaki-betegség, Nyerges és mtsai, málnanyelv, együttműködés, Egyesült Királyságban (EK-ban?)*);
- **Grammatical interferences**. For example: *egy ismeretlen etiológiájú betegség* (in Hungarian, in this case, the indefinite article is not generally used – indirect interference), *Rövid eliminációs idejű szer hatástartama* (in Hungarian, the definite article is always used in this case – direct interference), *6.5%* (in Hungarian, commas are used and not a dot to separate decimals), *vérnyomáscsökkenés eredményeződhet*, and *a készítmény nem bizonyul naponta egyszer adagolhatónak* (these are passive structures which are very rarely used in Hungarian);
- **Semantic interferences**: calques/loan translations. For example: *coronaria érintett* (coming from the literally translated form of the English *affected/non-affected coronary artery*), or *célszervkárosodás* H (*target organ damage* E).

There were also two English abbreviations used in the text without giving the original meaning (for example, *FDA* = *Food and Drug Administration*, and *ABPM* = *ambulatory blood pressure measurement*). I also inserted two words, now considered to be part of the (mental) lexicon of the H medical discourse community (for example, *ACE-inhibitorok* H (*ACE-inhibitors* E) = *ACE-gátlók* H, or *stroke* H (*stroke* E) = *agyérkatasztrófa* H). They used to be E loanwords some 20 years ago (Kontra, 1981). Finally, I changed the correct spelling of three Hungarian words (I used *kiegyensulyozott, iletve*, and *külömbségei* instead of the correct *kiegyensúlyozott, illetve*, and *különbségei*) to see if subjects were able to identify H errors.

Keeping the so called 'bath tub' effect in mind, all three spelling mistakes were difficult to spot as they were in the middle of the words (Aitchison, 1987). Nevertheless, I was surprised to find that *iletve* was spotted only by three readers, and *kiegyensulyozott* by nine ($n = 32$).

The distribution of E interference items was varied, they were inserted both in the middle of lines and to the left and right sides of the pages (Gósy, 1999a). The number of E contact induced features was approximately the same on both pages, and according to my expectations, more features were identified on the first page than on the second one. As proofreaders grew tired, they did not seem to identify the same type of interferences toward the end of the second text. For example, *strawberry tongue* (málnanyelv H), which is in the first third of the first text, was underlined by 20 subjects, whereas *smoothness index* (*simasági mutató* H) in the one before last paragraph was spotted only by nine people.

Subjects who spotted the most features were in their early twenties, participating in the translator course. All 14 translators found 18 interferences or more. Altogether, nine people identified more than 20 features ($n = 26$). Generally, women were better at identifying the English influences in all age groups. The fewest features (12 or less) were identified by people between 30 and 40, especially males who did not take part in the translator course, had extensive exposure to the English language and evaluated their English knowledge as level three or above.

Considering the type of errors, the most frequently identified items were loan words from E and orthographical interferences (see Table 5.2): 26 subjects ($n = 32$) marked *risk-faktor* (*risk factor* E) as problematic (*rizikó tényezö* or *rizikó faktor* are the generally accepted Hungarian versions of it), and 24 subjects identified *half-life* (*félélet/felezési idö* H) and *ágent* (*ágens/tényezö* H). The least frequently spotted features were syntactic interferences: the use of definite and indefinite articles – nobody identified them, spelling mistakes – *iletve* was found by only three subjects, and the abbreviations that were taken over directly from English – *FDA* ($n = 9$), and *UK*-ban ($n = 9$).

Three people mentioned at the end of the task in the *Notes* that we should not use foreign (Greek, Latin and English) words in medical writing at all when there is a Hungarian equivalent for them.

Conclusions

Word specific visual pattern information (WSVP) can be used successfully when the context permits the reader to generate expectations for upcoming words. This fact might compensate the reader for unknown

Table 5.2 The distribution of recognition of English induced features and Hungarian spelling mistakes in the experimental texts

English contact induced features/errors and H spelling mistakes	No. of spottings (n = 32)
risk-*faktor*	26
agent	24
half-life	24
concordance	23
Nyerges et al.	21
cost-*effektivitás*	21
strawberry tongue	20
non-purulent	19
Kawasaki-**disease**	19
külömbségei	17
coronaria érintett	13
vérnyomáscsökkenés **eredményeződhet (passive)**	13
beta-blockoló	12
Trough-to-peak ratio (T/R)	11
Smoothness index	9
A készítmény nem bizonyul naponta egyszer **adagolhatónak** (passive)	9
FDA (no explanation)	9
kiegyensulyozott	9
UK-ban	9
6.5 %	6
célszervkárosodás	6
stroke	5
iletve	3
ABPM (no explanation)	3
(A Kawasaki-disease) **egy** ismeretlen etiológiájú betegség	0
(0 article) Rövid eliminációs idötartamú szer hatástartama ...	0

words and context could help follow the train of thoughts even without realising that some foreign words are hidden in the text (Elman, 2004). Such context-generated expectations are presumably the basis for whatever effects sentence context has on word processing. As Besner and Johnston (1989) state when sufficient context is available, WSVPs facilitate word identification. The mental lexicon is the store of all our knowledge related to words, but it is not something fundamentally separate from other knowledge systems, that is, not a separate submodule within the language module. This view of the mental lexicon is an important relay station connecting certain specific sensory events or output patterns with mentally represented knowledge structures (Schreuder & d'Arcais, 1989). The lexicon is an essential mediator between conceptualisation and grammatical and phonological encoding (Levelt, 1989).

Subjects, in our case health professionals, who regularly use EFL and who participate in multicultural networks (that is, take part in international meetings regularly, or work/study/research in English speaking countries, or simply read extensively in English in their field of speciality) exhibit E features in writing/reading (printed word recognition or word specific visual pattern information) that distinguish them from other members of the medical and the general Hungarian community. Linguistic features being distinctive for this type of speaker/reader are evident in domains in which speakers/readers exhibit a high level of metalinguistic awareness (Ellis, 1986).

People in the field of medicine are highly under the influence of the English language, both when communicating orally and in writing. Medics tend to use various types of Anglicisms in writing their research articles (Keresztes, 2003). It can be attributed to several factors: English has become the lingua franca of medicine, recently doctors have travelled to English speaking countries more extensively than before, they regularly take part in international conferences where English is the working language, they read scientific articles mostly in English (according to a World Health Organization report, 75% of all medical articles are published in this language), and doctors working at university clinics mostly publish in English (or at least write abstracts/summaries in that language).

Medics whose English is poor or who do not speak this language (they mostly speak German over the age of 50), or whose attention was called to the phenomenon of the English influence (medical translators) seem to be more aware of the presence of Anglicisms in written texts. (It is one aim of our translator programme to present the students with the 'standard' or most widely accepted use of the Hungarian language.) Translators, on average, were able to spot a higher number of E contact induced features as their attention was called to this phenomenon several times during their studies and their eyes were focused onto them.

Non-translator professionals with high level (above three) knowledge of English did not tend to identify E interferences, not even E loan words with H equivalents, and which have kept the original English orthography. The lowest spotting results were found among these people. Age was also of relevance (Singleton, 2001) in the distribution of the results as subjects between 30 and 40 spotted the least number of items. Members in this age group (non-translators) have achieved a high level of E knowledge, have learned the English language at school and use it quite extensively in their everyday practice. Thus, detectable changes may have appeared in their mental lexicon due to EFL exposure. On the other hand, members of the first age group seem to be too young for these changes in the mental lexicon as not only general H (and E) knowledge is required in understanding (reading) a medical text, but considerable amount of professional knowledge as well. So we suspect that in the case of this group, members devoted more attention in the experiment to the text to grab the message, and have read the texts more carefully than members of the second age group. In the case of the latter group, contextual assumptions might also have helped them with visual word recognition and lexical access. Whereas in the case of the younger age group, their mental lexicon does not seem to contain certain elements, and they do not seem to have the right context in mind for making presumptions while reading medical texts.

While these findings are drawn from a group of speakers in just one speech community, the results offer insight into a largely unexplored type of language contact, the one resulting from English as a global lingua franca. The findings presented in this paper might shed light on the need for further research to prove that EFL exposure does lead to changes in the mental lexicon of the individual.

Acknowledgements

Thanks are due to all the 32 subjects who were willing to devote their precious time to my project. Special thanks are to Mária Gósy and Erzsébet Barát for their valuable discussions concerning methodological issues, and also to Eszter Szabó-Gilinger for suggestions concerning the realisation of the project.

References

Aitchison, J. (1987) *Words in the Mind: An Introduction to the Mental Lexicon*. Oxford and New York: Basil Blackwell.
Baker, L.A. (2001) Critical concepts – 'Microscopic revision': Spotting and revising idiom glitches. On www at www.ksu.edu/english/baker/english320/cc-revision.htm (date of reading: 8th April 2005).
Bánréti, Z. (ed.) (1999) *Nyelvi struktúrák és az agy. Neurolingvisztikai tanulmányok. [Linguistic Structures and the Brain. Studies in Neurolinguistics.]* Budapest: Corvina.
Besner, D. and Johnston, J.C. (1989) Reading and the mental lexicon: On the uptake of visual information. In W. Marslen-Wilson (ed.) *Lexical Representation and Process* (pp. 291–316). Cambridge: Cambridge University Press.
Editing and proofreading (1998) at http://www.unc.edu/depts/wcweb (date of reading 6th April 2005).
Ellis, R. (1986) *Understanding Second Language Acquisition*. Oxford: Oxford University Press.
Elman, J.L. (2004) An alternative view of the mental lexicon. On WWW at http://www.sciencedirect.com TICS 216 (date of reading: 3rd April 2005).
Farkas, J. and Kniezsa, V. (2002) Hungarian. In: M. Görlach (ed.) *English in Europe* (pp. 277–291). Oxford: Oxford University Press.
Fillmore, C.J. (1971) Types of lexical information. In: D. Steinberg and L. Jakabovits (eds) *Semantics: An Interdisciplinary Reader in Phylosophy, Linguistics, and Psychology* (pp. 74–124). Cambridge: Cambridge University Press.
Fromkin, V.A. (ed.) (1980) *Errors in Linguistic Performance. Slips of the Tongue, Ear, Pen and Hand*. New York: Academic Press.
Gósy, M. (1998) Szókeresés a mentális lexikonban [Word retrieval in the mental lexicon]. *Magyar Nyelvör* 122, 189–201.
Gósy, M. (1999a) Hibaüzenet kezelése olvasáskor [Handling error messages when reading]. *Magyar Nyelvör* 123, 27–35.
Gósy, M. (1999b) *Pszicholingvisztika* [Psycholinguistics]. Budapest: Corvina.
Keresztes, Cs. (2003) Az angol nyelv hatása a magyar szakmai nyelvre [The influence of English on Hungarian jargon]. In: Sz. Tóth (ed.) *Nyelvek és kultúrák találkozása* (pp. 168–172) Szeged: Szegedi Tudományegyetem Juhász Gyula Tanárképzö Föiskolai Kara.
Klaudy, K. (1999) *Bevezetés a fordítás elméletébe [An Introduction into Translation Theory]*. Budapest: Scholastica.
Kontra, M. (1981) A nyelvek közötti kölcsönzés néhány kérdéséröl, különös tekintettel 'elangolosodó'orvosi nyelvünkre. [On some questions of borrowing with a special emphasis on our anglicized medical language]. *Nyelvtudományi Értekezések* 109, 5–64.
Lengyel, Zs. (1998) *Az írás. Kezdet-Folyamat-végpont. [Writing.Start-process-endpoint.]* Budapest: Corvina.
Levelt, W.J.M. (1989) *Speaking: From Intention to Articulation*. Cambridge: Massachusetts Institute of Technology.
Marslen-Wilson, W. (ed.) (1989) *Lexical Representation and Process*. Cambridge: Cambridge University Press.
Navracsics, J. (2004) Kapcsolatok a kétnyelvü mentális lexikonban [Links in the bilingual mental lexicon]. *Modern Filológiai Közlemények* 6 (1), 21–32.

Odlin, T. (1989) *Language Transfer: Cross-Linguistic Influence in Language Learning*. Cambridge: Cambridge University Press.
Perfetti, C. (1986) Continuities in reading acquisition, reading skill, and reading disability. *Remedial and Special Education* 8 (1), 11–21.
Peterson, E. (2004) EFL as a contact language: Evidence from variation in an L1. On www at http://www.ling.upenn.edu/NWAVE/abs-pdf/peterson.pdf (date of reading: 6th April 2005).
Schreuder, R. and d'Arcais, G.B.F. (1989) Psycholinguistic issues in the lexical representation of meaning. In W. Marslen-Wilson (ed.) *Lexical Representation and Process* (pp. 409–436). Cambridge: Cambridge University Press.
Singleton, D. (2001) Age and second language acquisition. *Annual Review of Applied Linguistics* 21, 77–89.
Singleton, D. (2003) Perspectives on the multilingual lexicon: A critical synthesis. In J. Cenoz, B. Hufeisen, and U. Jessner (eds) *The Multilingual Lexicon* (pp. 167–176). Dordrecht: Kluwer Academic.
Smith, F. (1969) Familiarity of configuration vs. Discriminability of features in the visual quality in a word–non-word classification task. *Journal of Verbal Learning and Verbal Behaviour* 14, 261–262.
Thomason, S. (2001) *Language Contact*. Edinburgh: Edinburgh University Press.
Wheeler, D. (1970) Processes in word recognition. *Cognitive Psychology* 1, 59–85.

Appendix

In the texts we have indicated the changes concerned in italics.

Text 1

A *Kawasaki-disease* (KD) cardiovascularis és epidemiológiai vonatkozásai

Bevezetés

A Kawasaki betegség (mucocutan nyirokcsomó szindróma) *egy ismeretlen etiológiájú, akut lázas megbetegedés,* mely döntően az öt év alatti gyermekeket érinti. A betegséget 1967-ben T. Kawasaki írta le. Az első hazai esetről *Nyerges et al.* 1976-ban számolt be. Az eleinte jóindulatúnak tartott betegségről kiderült, hogy a coronariák vasculitisével járhat, ami coronaria aneurysmák kialakulásához vezethet. Az elsö *coronaria érintett betegről* 1991-ben számolt be a hazai irodalom. A betegség diagnosisa alapvetően klinikai. A klasszikus Kawasaki betegség diagnosisa kimondható, ha a 4–5 napnál tovább tartó (antibiotikumra, gyulladás csökkentőre nem szűnő) magas láz mellett, a következő major tünetek közül négy jelen van: (1) kétoldali *non-purulent* conjunctivitis, (2) oropharyngeális nyálkahártya elváltozások (gyulladt hyperaemiás torok és ajak vagy száraz berepedezett ajak, *strawberry tongue*), (3) distalis végtagtünetek (kéz- vagy lábháti ödéma és/vagy erythema, periungualis hámlás), (4) döntően a törzsön jelentkező, polymorph, nem vacuolás kiütések, (5) nyaki lymphadenopathia (15 mm>, fájdalmatlan, egyoldali, non-purulens duzzanat). A major tüneteken kívül valamennyi szervrendszer megbetegedése megfigyelhető. Jellegzetes minor tünet: irritabilitás, lethargia, asepticus meningitis, myocarditis, szívelégtelenség, steril pyuria, epehólyag hydrops, arthritis, arthralgia, hasi fájdalom, hasmenés, hányás. A betegség abortív, atipusos formája, amikor a major tünetek közül csak egy vagy kettő van jelen egyre gyakoribb, viszont echocardiographiás vizsgálattal coronaria megbetegedés kimutatható. Irodalmi adatok alapján az esetek 10-45%-a atípusos megjelenésű; a betegség ezen formája döntően az egy év alattiakat érinti és nagyobb a coronaria megbetegedés (64%) incidenciája is.

Epidemiológia

A KD világszerte előfordul, és növekvő tendenciát mutat. A 90-es évek előtt epidémiák formájában jelentkezett, manapság a sporadikus megjelenés a gyakoribb. A betegség incidenciája (100 000 öt év alatti gyermekre vonatkoztatva) országonként változik, a legmagasabb Japánban 90; míg az USA-ban 6.5-15,2, UK-ban 3,4, Svédországban pedig 6,2. Döntően a fiatalkor betegsége, hisz az érintettek 70-80%-a öt évnél fiatalabb. Jellegzetes a fiúk dominanciája, a fiú-lány arány 1,5:1 körüli, bár Svédországban (2,3:1) és Ausztráliában (2,1:1) nagyobb arány mutatkozott. A betegség szezonalitása változó, Japánban és USA-ban téli-tavaszi, az Egyesült Királyságban tavaszi-nyári, Chilében téli halmozódást írtak le, míg Kanadában és Svédországban nem volt jellegzetes eltérés. Az ismétlődés ritka, USA-ban 1,9%, Japánban 3,0%. A betegség mortalitása 2% alatti, Japánban 0,04-0,08%.

Etiológia

A betegség etiológiája a kiterjedt kutatások ellenére mindeddig ismeretlen. A klinikai sajátságok és epidemiológiai adatok alapján a betegséget jelenleg egy ismeretlen *ágent* okozta fertőző betegségnek, vagy egy fertőző ágens indukálta immunbetegségnek tartják. Az infectiós elméletet a betegség szezonális és járványszerű megjelenésére alapozzák, bár baktérium tenyésztési és vírus izolálási kísérletekkel, valamint szerológiai vizsgálatokkal eddig III. típusú kollagén ellenes, anti-cardiolipin, anti-neutrophil cytoplasmaticus (ANCA) és anti-endothel antitesteket izoláltak. Cunningham és mtsai (1999) vizsgálata alapján az akut myocarditist Kawasaki betegségben a myosin ellenes antitestek okozhatják. Állatkísérletekben ezen antitestek cardiotoxicusok voltak. Az ellentmondó vizsgálati eredmények további kutatásokat tesznek szükségessé, azonban az akut szakban adott IVIG hatékonysága alátámasztja az immunológiai faktorok szerepét a vasculitis kialakulásában.

Text 2

A 24 órás hatástartam jelentősége az antihipertenzív kezelésben

Az alkalmazott gyógyszerek *kiegyensúlyozott*, tartós 24 órás hatása kiemelt jelentőségű az antihipertenzív kezelés során. Az egyenletes vérnyomáscsökkentő hatás mérsékli a *célszervkárosodás* kialakulását, növeli a *concordance*-t és jelentősen, emeli az antihipertenzív terápia *cost-effektivitását*. A 24 órás hatást a hatóanyag farmakokinetikája, vagy a tartós receptorkötődése biztosíthatja. *Rövid eliminációs idejű szer* hatástartama felszívódást elnyújtó formulációval növelhető. A 24 órás hatástartam vizsgálatára szolgáló módszerek sokrétűek és megítélésük/ értékelésük sem mindig azonos.

A hipertónia fontos kardiovaszkuláris *risk-faktor* és epidemiológiai jelentősége sem kisebb. Kezelésének egyik elsödleges célja a *stroke* és myocardiális infarktus megelőzése.

A terápiás együttmüködés azt mutatja meg, hogy a betegek mennyi ideig tartják be az orvos terápiás utasításait, *illetve* milyen rendszerességgel veszik be az előírt időben a gyógyszerüket. A hipertóniások terápiás együttműködését rontó két alapvető faktor a magasvérnyomás-betegség tünetszegénysége és a betegség egész életen át tartó volta.

A 24 órás vérnyomáscsökkentő hatás vizsgálata

Trough-to-peak ratio (T/P) A 24 óra alatti vérnyomáscsökkenés egyenletességét mutatja a T/P. *ABPM*-vizsgálattal határozható meg. Számítási módja: a következő dózis bevételekor még észlelhető vérnyomáscsökkenés értékét elosztjuk a maximális vérnyomáscsökkenés mértékével. Ennek az értéke az *FDA* ajánlása szerint a naponta egyszer adagolható készítmények esetén 50% feletti kell, hogy legyen. Nagyobb dózisok alkalmazásakor a szerek hatása megnyúlik, tehát a dózisnöveléssel önmagában is elérhető tartósabb hatás. Ebben az esetben azonban nemkívánatos mértékű *vérnyomáscsökkenés eredményeződhet* a csúcshatás növekedése által, a T/P arány csökken és *a készítmény nem bizonyul naponta egyszer adagolhatónak*. Megjegyzendő, hogy azoknál a szereknél, amelyeknél a dózis, plazmakoncentráció és hatás közötti összefüggés nem lineáris (pl. *ACE-inhibitorok, béta-blockolók*), a dózis növelésével elérhető a kívánatos, 50%-nál nagyobb T/P arány.

Smoothness index

A teljes vérnyomáscsökkentés homogenitását az előbbinél jobban jellemző, reprodukálható és a célszervkárosodások regressziójával jól korreláló paraméter. Kiszámítási módja: a placebo és aktív kezelés alatti óránkénti vérnyomásátlagok *különbségei* átlagértékének és az átlag standard deviációjának hányadosa.

A 24 órán át tartó hatás alapja A gyógyszerek tartós hatását biztosíthatja a kedvező farmakokinetika: hosszú plazma *half-life*, vagy tartós receptorkötődés, de rövid hatású hatóanyagok 24 órás effektivitását lehet biztosítani a felszívódást elnyújtó formuláció alkalmazásával.

Part 3
The Lexicon in L2 Writing

Chapter 6
Vocabulary Assessment in Writing: Lexical Statistics

EWA WITALISZ

Introduction

This paper discusses vocabulary assessment in writing, both qualitative and quantitative, with the focus on Laufer and Nation's (1995) Lexical Frequency Profile. The measures are analysed in reference to the study of the written English produced by Polish EFL learners applying to the English Department of the Jagiellonian University in Kraków, Poland (Witalisz, 2004). Although this paper concentrates on the tool rather than the results of the study, a brief description of the study is needed to understand the subsequent references. The study was inspired by the striking quality of the output produced by the least successful candidates, namely the discrepancies between various features in their texts. In the same text, several indicators of advanced language skills, such as length of production, syntactic complexity or lexical sophistication, contrasted with serious deficits, that is, both the number and gravity of errors. The data for the study consisted of specific samples of written English collected cross-sectionally, that is, 60 texts constituting a corpus of about 14,800 words. The texts were part of the entrance examination, namely the writing task that involved producing a 250-word English summary of a Polish article of about 500 words. Since writing assessment requires a point of reference, the poorest texts were compared with the most successful ones in order to examine the differences and to highlight the similarities. While the differences between the two groups helped identify and evaluate the linguistic and composing deficits of the poor writers, the similarities indicated the features of advanced language and writing skills. So the texts selected for the study came from two ends of the scale: 30 most successful texts and 30 texts that received the lowest scores.

This paper shows how my attempt to use Laufer and Nation's Lexical Frequency Profile for the lexical analysis of the texts revealed its shortcomings, and how I tried to overcome them by adjusting their tool for the purpose of my analysis.

Qualitative Versus Quantitative Assessment

The role of vocabulary in language assessment can be seen from two contrasting perspectives outlined by Read (2000: 7) in the following way: learners' knowledge of vocabulary (meaning and usage) can be tested separately (words are taken as independent semantic units) or vocabulary must always be assessed in the context of a task, where it interacts with other components of language knowledge. Since this distinction, as any dichotomy, is seen by Read as an oversimplification, he proposes three dimensions of vocabulary assessment as set out in Table 6.1.

Table 6.1 Read's dimensions of vocabulary assessment (2000: 9)

Discrete A measure of vocabulary knowledge used as an independent construct	⟵⟶	**Embedded** A measure of vocabulary that forms part of the assessment of some other, larger construct
Selective A measure in which specific vocabulary items are the focus of the assessment	⟵⟶	**Comprehensive** A measure that takes account of the whole vocabulary content of the input material (reading/listening tasks) or the test-taker's response (writing/speaking tasks)
Context-independent A vocabulary measure in which the test-taker can produce the expected response without referring to any context	⟵⟶	**Context-dependent** A vocabulary measure which assesses the test-taker's ability to take account of contextual information in order to produce the expected response

These three dimensions shed light on the type of vocabulary assessment made in assessing writing. The vocabulary measure in writing is embedded because it contributes to the assessment of a larger construct, and it is context-dependent because the learner's vocabulary is assessed in relation to the task. Generally, it is comprehensive because it takes account of the whole vocabulary in the learner's written output. However, one may claim that in certain types of writing tasks using specific prompts (for example, pictures or a text in L1), particular lexical items have to become the focus of the assessment (otherwise the task cannot be fulfilled), so in that case, the vocabulary measure can also be seen as selective to some extent.

The role of vocabulary assessment depends on the type of writing assessment used. The qualitative assessment of writing relies basically on two main approaches:

(1) Global or holistic rating, which employs a single rating scale providing descriptions of several levels of performance; and
(2) Analytic rating, which uses several scales, each focusing on a different aspect of writing.

As Read (2000: 214) observes, the analytic approach has more to offer for vocabulary assessment: the results can be reported as a profile consisting of separate ratings for the various components of the scale, thus providing the diagnostic information of the learner's strengths and weaknesses. He also quotes other scholars who strongly advocate the use of analytic rating (Bachman & Palmer, 1996; Hamp-Lyons, 1991) as more reliable, because it is based on multiple measures and reflects raters' behaviour.

The analytic scales give a much more elaborate description of each component, and it is an advantage if the results are presented as a profile with a separate mark for each component. However, considering the raters' behaviour and the challenge involved in assessing writing, one may argue that both global and analytic ratings present similar problems, and their choice might be dependent on the rater's personal preference, particularly if, in the case of the analytic rating, the marks are simply added up and given as a single result. It is interesting to notice that in mark schemes based on the global approach, vocabulary is frequently listed as the first feature in the descriptor of a particular band. The example of the description of vocabulary in the general mark scheme for the Certificate of Proficiency in English, Paper 2 Writing (UCLES, 2000) is presented in Table 6.2.

In the analytic rating, different aspects of the text are evaluated separately. For example, the assessment scale for written work presented by

Table 6.2 Description of vocabulary in the CPE general mark scheme (2000: 22)

5	**Outstanding** realisation of the task: Sophisticated use of an extensive range of vocabulary, collocation and expression, entirely appropriate to the task
4	**Good** realisation of the task: Fluent and natural use of a wide range of vocabulary, collocation and expression, successfully meeting the requirements of the task
3	**Satisfactory** realisation of the task: Reasonably fluent and natural use of a range of vocabulary and expression, adequate to the task
2	**Inadequate** attempt at the task: Limited and/or inaccurate range of vocabulary and expression
1	**Poor** attempt at the task: Severely limited and inaccurate range of vocabulary and expression
0	**Negligible** or **no attempt** at the task: Totally incomprehensible, irrelevant, insufficient language to assess, illegible

Tribble (1996) consists of five scales: task fulfilment/content, organisation, vocabulary, language, and mechanics (Table 6.3).

It is interesting how the role of vocabulary assessment in writing is underlined by the fact that it is extracted from 'language', which, as the descriptor shows, is understood as grammar: structures and errors. The same distinction is also used in ESL Composition Profile (Jacobs *et al.*, 1981; in Read, 2000: 217). The descriptors of vocabulary in these two analytic scales are presented in Table 6.4.

Table 6.3 Components of Tribble's scale (1996: 35)

Area	*Score*
Task fulfilment/Content	0–20
Organisation	0–20
Vocabulary	0–20
Language	0–30
Mechanics	0–10

Table 6.4 Comparison of descriptors of vocabulary in two analytic scales: Tribble (1996: 35) and Jacobs et al. (1981: 30)

Tribble		Jacobs et al.	
20–17	**Excellent to very good:** Wide range of vocabulary; accurate word/idiom choice and usage; appropriate selection to match register	20–18	**Excellent to very good:** Sophisticated range; effective word/idiom usage; word form mastery; appropriate register
16–12	**Good to average:** Adequate range of vocabulary; occasional mistakes in word/idiom choice and usage; resister not always appropriate	17–14	**Good to average:** Adequate range; occasional errors of word/idiom form, choice, usage *but meaning not obscured*
10–8	**Fair to poor:** Limited range of vocabulary; a noticeable number of mistakes in word/idiom choice and usage; register not always appropriate	13–10	**Fair to poor:** Limited range; frequent errors of word/idiom form, choice, usage; *meaning confused or obscured*
7–5	**Very poor:** No range of vocabulary; uncomfortably frequent mistakes in word/idiom choice and usage; no apparent sense of register	9–7	**Very poor:** Essentially translation; little knowledge of English vocabulary, idioms, word form; or not enough to evaluate
4–0	**Inadequate:** Fails to address this aspect of the task with any effectiveness		

If the two types of scales (global and analytic) are compared, one can see that they have a lot in common. Whether the description of the vocabulary is only one feature of a band descriptor or has its own scale with its own descriptors, it operates within the same criteria, and although the descriptions in the analytic scales are longer, they do not cover more criteria.

(In the CPE scale, errors are a separate feature.) So from the raters' perspective, such two scales may be very similar but the elaboration of the descriptor in the analytic scale, promising as it looks, is not necessarily helpful.

As can be seen, the basic concepts in the qualitative assessment of vocabulary are range and accuracy. Whereas the latter might be judged in terms of errors, the first seems to refer vaguely to size. Raters are to determine if the learners' range of vocabulary is wide, extensive, adequate, limited, severely limited, inaccurate or none (Tribble's scale), the last one being particularly unclear (what exactly is 'no range of vocabulary'?). Nevertheless, all these characteristics involve the raters' judgement, which means that a rigorous process of coordination has to take place during assessment to ensure comparable and valid marks.

Having experienced the problems of qualitative assessment of vocabulary in writing, for example, deciding whether the learner's range of vocabulary is wide or just adequate, one should be relieved to discover that there are several quantitative measures of learner production or, to be more precise, of lexical richness. Before they are discussed, it should be understood, as Read (2000: 200) observes, what assumptions are made about effective vocabulary use in writing. Read enumerates these assumptions that hold that good writing has the following features:

- A variety of different words rather than repetition, the characteristic that is called 'range of expression' in writing assessment. More proficient writers are expected to have a larger vocabulary which allows them to avoid repetition. This characteristic is measured by the type-token ratio or lexical variation.
- A selection of low-frequency words (appropriate to the topic and style) rather than general, everyday vocabulary, which is another aspect of range of expression. This is measured by lexical sophistication: the ratio of sophisticated (unusual, advanced) word families to all word families in the text. (Words are classified as sophisticated according to various word lists.)
- A relatively high percentage of lexical (or content) words, as compared to grammatical (or function) words that is measured by lexical density. Ure (1971), who originated this measure, generally found the percentage of lexical words to be over 40 in written texts and below 40 in spoken texts, which shows that ideas are presented in a more concentrated way in written language.
- Few if any errors in the use of words. This can be measured by counting the number of errors found in the text.

Although these assumptions may seem easily acceptable, some of them can actually be slightly problematic if task fulfilment is the priority in writing assessment. As my study of poor writing has shown (Witalisz, 2004), repetition may be required by a particular task, and the learner's attempt to use synonyms to avoid it can be very much against the task requirements. The use of 'general, everyday vocabulary' may also be most appropriate in certain tasks, where the learner's attempt to use sophisticated vocabulary would be inappropriate. Generally, this problem could be seen as a conflict of interest to some extent. The learner's urge (frequently stimulated by language teachers) to display rare, sophisticated and varied vocabulary perceived as lexical richness and advancement in writing skills may clash with the requirements of the task, especially within the communicative approach.

Once the assumptions about lexical richness are understood, what remains to be done is to calculate the statistics, which is by no means a simple matter. Although the statistical measures are frequently referred to as 'objective', (after all, counting should provide unquestionable results), there are a number of decisions about what to count that require human judgement. Even deciding what is a single word depends on the researcher and the purpose of the study. Apart from technical differences between computer programs such as counting, for example, contracted forms as one or two words, the word count may change once the focus of the analysis changes. The texts analysed in my study (Witalisz, 2004) had numerous serious errors (for example, *a nader* for *another*, *them selves* for *themselves*), so for some texts the word count changed substantially once the spelling was corrected for the sake of the lexical analysis. In calculating the lexical frequency profile, two or three words may be counted as one if they are placed in a particular frequency band as a phrase, for example, *mobile phones*, which is justified especially when the frequencies for each individual word and the whole phrase are different. In the *Collins COBUILD English Dictionary* (2001) the word *mobile* belongs to band 3, *phone* to band 2, whereas the phrase *mobile phone*, being much less frequent, belongs to band 5. Thus what seems to be the simplest quantitative measure, that is, the number of words in a text, is not unequivocal and also depends on the purpose of the analysis.

Classifying words into frequency bands poses other problems as well. Although the information about the frequency is available (for example, in the *Collins COBUILD English Dictionary*), it is given for the headwords only, so the researcher has to decide whether particular word forms from the learner's text should be classified as the same frequency, especially if some forms are listed as separate entries with their own frequency (for example, *being, worse*) different from the frequency of the base word (*be, bad*), while in the case of other words their forms (for example, *eating, bigger*) belong to the entry describing the base word as the headword (*eat, big*). One more difficulty here is that the frequency information concerns the headword as such, without any differences in its particular meanings (sometimes very different) and, as some researchers claim (Sinclair & Renouf, 1988), this is an important distinction.

The next complicating factor is that some of the statistical measures are very sensitive to text length. For example, the type-token ratio is typically higher in shorter texts. In other words, it is much easier to avoid repetition in a shorter text; as writers write more, they have to use more words that have already been used, thus naturally achieving a lower figure for lexical variation. Any measure calculating the proportions of words in a text naturally depends on the text length. If a higher figure indicates a higher level of lexical richness (higher density, sophistication, variation), it is always easier to achieve it in a shorter text, so if they are used for any kind of comparison of texts, the texts have to be of comparable (preferably the same) length. To account for that, various adjustments can be made: for example, Laufer (1991) simply took the first 250 words from each essay and Arnaud (1984) used a random selection of 180 words from each essay. However, none of these methods seems perfect. After all, if one is interested in the comprehensive measure of vocabulary in the learner's output, any adjustment of text length eliminates some vocabulary, and the assessment is no longer comprehensive. Depriving the text of its concluding sentences may seem particularly disadvantageous for the lexical analysis: conclusions typically contain 'important' words that may substantially affect the lexical measures (density, variation, sophistication).

Considering the problems discussed above, it should be interesting to find out what results have been obtained by means of various lexical statistics. Here are some of those discussed by Read (2000: 206–7):

- Two studies compared the performance of L2 learners and native-speakers (Arnaud, 1984, and Linnarud, 1986) and found that, on average, L2 learners' vocabulary was substantially less varied and sophisticated. Waller's study (1993) showed that texts with a lexical density above 50% were either written by native speakers or were perceived that way by native-speaker readers.
- The correlation of quantitative statistics and holistic ratings produced inconsistent results. In Nihalani's study (1981), better essays tended to have more varied vocabulary and a higher percentage of

lexical words, but the differences were not statistically significant. Linnarud (1986) found that, out of the four lexical statistics she used (individuality, sophistication, variation, density), only one – lexical individuality (the ratio of lexical words unique to the writer to all lexical words in the text) – was significantly correlated with the holistic ratings of the Swedish students' compositions.

As Read (2000: 209) points out, the findings of those studies are difficult to interpret. Researchers frequently use different statistics and calculate them differently, which makes meaningful comparisons impossible. The issue of the role of vocabulary in the overall quality of learner writing has been addressed by some researchers (Laufer & Nation, 1995; Linnarud, 1986), who correlated lexical statistics with holistic ratings of the writing and with the scores of vocabulary tests. However, the correlations between 0.40 and 0.80 obtained are, as Read (2000: 209) puts it, 'notoriously difficult to interpret'.

Lexical Frequency Profile

The new measure devised by Laufer and Nation (1995) called Lexical Frequency Profile was supposed to overcome the shortcomings of other lexical statistics. They claim that the LFP shows the percentage of words a writer uses at different vocabulary frequency levels; the assumption being that the more proficient writers would use more words of lower frequency. Words are counted as word families, and the number of word families at each frequency level is converted into percentages out of the total number of word families in the text. So the LFP for a particular text may look like this: 86.5% – 7.1% – 3.2% – 3.3%, which means that 86.5% of the word families in the text come from the first frequency level (the first 1000 most frequent words), 7.1% from the second level (the second 1000 most frequent words), 3.2% from the University Word List, that is, 'a list of 836 word families containing vocabulary that is not in the first 2000 words of English, but which is frequent and wide range across a variety of written academic texts from a variety of disciplines' (Laufer & Nation, 1995: 312) and the remaining 3.3% are the less frequent words that are not in any lists. More advanced learners would be expected to have a higher percentage of the less frequent vocabulary, for example, 74% – 5.6% – 10.1% – 8.7%. (Both examples of the LFP are taken from the study conducted by Laufer and Nation.)

As the methodological advantages of this measure were discussed in detail (Laufer & Nation, 1995: 312), they were supported by the study establishing the reliability and validity of this measure (1995: 313–318), and the tool itself, that is, the computer program (Range) with the three accompanying word lists was available on Paul Nation's website, it seemed to be a perfect measure for the lexical analysis of learners' texts in my study (Witalisz, 2004). However, after processing a number of texts, I was puzzled by the results, namely the way in which the words were classified into particular frequency levels. At first glance, the classification simply did not coincide with the experienced teacher's intuition as to which vocabulary is more advanced. To confirm this impression, I checked in which frequency band the same words were placed by the *Collins COBUILD English Dictionary* (2001) and the two classifications seemed incompatible. For example, the words 'not in the lists' are supposed to be less frequent: they are not in the first and second 1000 most frequent words and not in University Word List (Laufer & Nation, 1995: 311). However, some of the words not found in the three lists were common, easy and placed in high frequency bands by the *Collins COBUILD English Dictionary*. The frequency bands used by the *Collins COBUILD English Dictionary* are presented in Table 6.5. For further discussion, I replaced the diamonds used in the dictionary by numbered bands.

Table 6.5 Collins COBUILD frequency bands (3rd edition)

♦ ♦ ♦ ♦ ♦ Band 1	circa 680 most frequent words	75% of the language	95% of the language
♦ ♦ ♦ ♦ Band 2	Next 1040 most frequent words		
♦ ♦ ♦ Band 3	Next 1580 words		
♦ ♦ Band 4	Next 3200 words		
♦ Band 5	Next 8100 words.		
Remaining			5%

Here are some examples of the words not in the lists provided by the LFP program with the *Collins COBUILD* frequency bands:

- drugs–band 1
- TV, movie, kids, abuse–band 2
- cinema, impressed, well-known, romantic, charity, pubs, alcohol, cope–band 3.

Such results may perhaps be explained by the source of the lists for the first 2000 words, namely Michael West's *General Service List of English Words* (London: Longman) published in 1953.

Another problem is that words are classified into a particular frequency band as word families, that is, the headword (for example AID) and its derived forms (AIDED, AIDING, AIDS, UNAIDED). Laufer and Nation claim that counting word families (rather than types or tokens) is

> more revealing as an indication of lexical richness, because it uses a definition of what should be counted as a word, which most closely matches how learners view words, that is ... they have no difficulty in seeing that *happy, happiness, happyish, happily* and *unhappy* are closely related. (1995: 312)

I would strongly disagree with this claim. Although learners may perceive such groups of words as related, this does not mean that they can use each member of the word family equally well, which is understandable, particularly when the words belong to very different frequency bands. This can be very well illustrated with the examples of the key vocabulary in my corpus. Table 6.6 shows three word families from Laufer and Nation's frequency word lists with the *Collins COBUILD* frequency bands.

This comparison shows marked differences between the frequencies of various words in one family, which may correspond to the level of difficulty associated with particular words. For example, in the case of *unemployment* and *unemployed*, it clearly showed in the corpus that the less frequent word *unemployed* was used only by 2 successful writers and 1 poor writer, whereas the more frequent word *unemployment* was used by many more writers – 19 successful writers and 10 poor writers – some making the lexical error of using it instead of *unemployed*, a more difficult and less frequent word.

As I found the LFP word lists inadequate, I decided to use Laufer and Nation's idea of the lexical frequency profile but coupled with the *Collins COBUILD* frequency bands, which meant that the work could not be done by the computer since the word lists were not available. The texts, with the spelling errors corrected, were then analysed in the following

Table 6.6 Classifications of the same words into frequency bands: differences between Laufer and Nation and Collins COBUILD

Laufer & Nation	Word families	Collins COBUILD
Words list 1	EMPLOY	Band 3
	UNEMPLOYMENT	Band 3
	UNEMPLOYED	Band 4
Words list 2	EDUCATE	Band 4
	EDUCATED	Band 4
	EDUCATION	Band 2
	EDUCATIONAL	Band 3
	UNEDUCATED	–
Words list 3	ECONOMY	Band 1
	ECONOMIC	Band 1
	ECONOMICAL	Band 5

way: each word was placed in a *Collins COBUILD* frequency band (1 to 5 and the remaining) or rejected if it was a non-existent word or a proper noun (names). Lexical errors were accepted as words for the profile and counted, although they were marked as errors. This was done because, in the case of poor writers, I was interested in their apparent (not only real) productive lexicon, as this was one of the factors that made the false impression of advanced language skills in their texts. The words (tokens) classified into each band were counted and converted into percentages out of the total number of words (tokens) minus those that were rejected. Lexical errors were listed separately, next to the profile, to show the difference between the writer's apparent productive lexicon and the number and nature of errors. Finally, one more figure (advanced lexis) was calculated, namely the sum of percentages in bands 3, 4, 5 and remaining, and to make the comparison of 60 texts possible, this single figure was used as an indicator of advanced lexis.

On the whole, the number of advanced words (types) turned out to be very high for both successful and poor writers, although obviously the figure for the better group was higher. Moreover, the range of vocabulary used by all writers was surprisingly wide. This was calculated by another statistical measure that I used, namely lexical distribution in the group, which shows how much of the same vocabulary is used by all writers in the group and how much their vocabulary differs. Considering the nature of the task (summarising the same text) and the fact that the groups were very homogenous in terms of their background (the same nationality and L1, the same system of education, similar coursebooks and materials used in the past), it was reasonable to expect a high vocabulary overlap. This assumption was made in the pilot study of a small sample of texts (Witalisz & Leśniewska, 2004), in which a set of key words was determined and the lexical measure used consisted in counting the correct uses of the key words in the texts. However, the subsequent analysis (Witalisz, 2004) of a large corpus by means of lexical statistics produced surprising results, and the assumption concerning key words, reasonable as it seemed at the time, was seriously challenged. In conclusion, the fact that the writers used so much advanced and varied vocabulary to present the same content is remarkable.

However, since the focus in this paper is not on the results of the study but on the tool used for the analysis, let me discuss the latter. It has to be emphasized that any quantitative analysis requires simplifications. In this case, the only criterion used for identifying advanced lexis was word frequency according to the *Collins COBUILD*. Once the actual lists of words were analysed, some shortcomings of this measure could be seen immediately. The lists show that certain low-frequency words are not necessarily perceived as advanced vocabulary. In this particular writing task, the writers used several low-frequency words that are at the same time cognate words for Polish speakers: *aggressive* (band 3), *aggression* (band 4), *alcohol* (band 3), *alcoholic* (band 4), *alcoholism* (band 5), *discrimination* (band 4), *pathology, pathological* (band 5), *tragedy* (band 3), *transformation* (band 3). Besides, the spelling errors were corrected for the lexical analysis; so if someone wrote *alkoholizm*, although it is a Polish word, its spelling had to be corrected, the word was classified into its frequency band and the writer was unduly appreciated for advanced lexis. Another problem would be the low-frequency words that are perceived as easy, because they are introduced very early in the syllabus, such as *dirty* (band 3), *hungry* (band 4) and *exam* (band 4). And one more difficulty was caused by the word *worse*, the key word for the summary in the task. It happens to be a very low-frequency word (band 5), but at the same time it is simply an irregular comparative form of a very high frequency word, the adjective *bad* (band 1). Furthermore, this adjective, as well as the grammatical rules concerning grading adjectives, is typically introduced very early in the syllabus, for example, in Unit 13 of the first level of *The New Cambridge English Course* (Swan & Walter, 1990), and therefore the word *worse* might not be perceived as an advanced lexical item. But as the corpus analysed in my study shows (as well as my teaching experience), learners have serious difficulties with it, which can be explained by its low frequency. By contrast, the words *better* and *best*, the irregular comparative and superlative forms of the adjective *good*, which are typically introduced together with *bad*, *worse* and *worst*, cause much less difficulty, and this is also well explained by their frequency: all three of them belong to the highest frequency band (band 1). So despite the fact that *worse* may be perceived as an easy item, it was classified according to its frequency as an advanced one.

These aspects, however, do not undermine the reliability of this measure for two main reasons. Firstly, all writers were selecting vocabulary from their productive lexicons in order to express the same content, so they all had the opportunity to resort to similar strategies (for example, relying on Polish cognates). Secondly, even if there are some words that do not deserve to be classified as advanced lexis, they are a marginal group considering the size of the corpus (circa 14,800 words).

It can be concluded, then, that although the lexical frequency profile I devised for my study has its shortcomings, it does indicate lexical sophistication of the writers, particularly when the uniformity of the content and the size of the corpus are taken into account. Moreover, it was used in the same way in order to compare the texts within the corpus only. Obviously, it cannot be used for any comparisons outside this study.

Conclusion

It has to be mentioned that Laufer and Nation's Lexical Frequency Profile has been recently criticised by Paul Meara (2005). It is interesting, though, that while he lists some obvious problems with LFP such as

> the way errors are handled (do we ignore errors or correct them?), the way proper nouns are counted (do we count proper names as low-frequency items simply because they are not in the word lists?), the treatment of formulaic sequences (do we treat 'Victoria Park' as two separate words, or as a single proper noun?) (2005: 34)

he questions neither the word lists used nor the concept of word families. He used a set of Monte Carlo simulations to evaluate Laufer and Nation's major claims about LFP. They showed that:

> it is not possible to distinguish between two vocabularies differing by only 500 words: for smaller vocabularies there is more tolerance, but for larger vocabularies it is increasingly difficult to find reliably

different results. Profiles generated by an 8000-word vocabulary are reliably different from profiles generated by a 5000-word vocabulary, but not reliably different from the profiles generated by a 6000- or a 7000-word vocabulary (2005: 40).

So, LFP is probably not sensitive enough to pick up modest changes in vocabulary size (2000: 32).

This objection emphasises a particular perspective taken by lexical research, where the assumption is that a written text is the learner's display of his/her productive lexicon, which directly reflects the size of his/her passive lexicon. This perspective may well be called 'vocabulary assessment in writing', where written output is elicited from learners in order to evaluate their vocabulary. From the perspective of writing research, the focus may be different, that is, the role of vocabulary in evaluating the text as a whole, so it is vocabulary in writing assessment rather than vocabulary assessment in writing. If the priority is task fulfilment and lexical accuracy, low-frequency (advanced, sophisticated) vocabulary does not necessarily contribute to a higher holistic rating. As my study showed (Witalisz, 2004), poor writers' misguided attempts to use more advanced vocabulary frequently resulted in semantic errors and, as a result, lower rather than higher scores.

As has been shown, vocabulary assessment, whether qualitative or quantitative, presents a number of problems. While the descriptors in holistic or analytic bands may seem imprecise and open to interpretation, the statistical measures also involve several decisions based on human judgement and have a number of shortcomings, which make them difficult to use or interpret. It might be claimed, though, that despite their weaknesses, the statistical measures are a powerful research tool, especially in the case of a large corpus, that can provide tangible evidence for various assumptions or hypotheses about quality in writing. Although, as has been underlined, the statistical results are difficult to compare across studies, the quantitative measures can be very useful for comparisons within the same study as long as they are consistently applied to all subjects.

References

Arnaud, P.J.L. (1984) The lexical richness of L2 written productions and the validity of vocabulary tests. In T. Culhane, C. Klein-Braley and D.K. Stevenson (eds) *Practice and Problems in Language Testing*. Department of Language and Linguistics, Colchester University of Essex.

Bachman, L.F. and Palmer, A.S. (1996) *Language Testing in Practice*. Oxford: Oxford University Press.

Certificate of Proficiency in English. Revised CPE Specifications and Sample Papers. (2000) Cambridge: UCLES.
Collins COBUILD English Dictionary for Advanced Learners. (2001) New Edition. London: HarperCollins.
Hamp-Lyons, L. (1991) Scoring procedures for ESL contexts. In L. Hamp-Lyons (ed.) Assessing *Second Language Writing in Academic Contexts*. Norwood, NJ: Ablex.
Jacobs, H.R., Zingraf, S.A., Wormuth, D.R., Hartfiel, V.F. and Hughey, J.B. (1981) *Testing ESL Composition: A Practical Approach*. Rowley, MA: Newbury House.
Laufer, B. (1991) The development of L2 lexis in the expression of the advanced language learner. *Modern Language Journal* 75, 440–48.
Laufer, B. and Nation, P. (1995) Vocabulary size and use: Lexical richness in L2 written production. *Applied Linguistics* 16, 307–322.
Linnarud, M. (1986) *Lexis in Composition. A Performance Analysis of Swedish Learners' Written English*. Malmö: CWK Gleerup.
Meara, P. (2005) Lexical frequency profiles: A Monte Carlo analysis. *Applied Linguistics* 6 (1), 32–47.
Nihalani, N.K. (1981) The quest for the L2 index of development. *RELC Journal* 12, 50–56.
Read, J. (2000) *Assessing Vocabulary*. Cambridge: Cambridge University Press.
Sinclair, J. McH. and Renouf, A. (1988) A lexical syllabus for language learning. In R. Carter and M. McCarthy (eds) *Vocabulary and Language Teaching*. London: Longman.
Swan, M. and Walter, C. (1990) *The New Cambridge English Course*. Cambridge: Cambridge University Press.
Tribble, C. (1996) *Writing*. Oxford: Oxford University Press.
Ure, J.N. (1971) Lexical density and register differentiation. In G.E. Perren and J.L.M. Trim (eds) *Applications of Linguistics: Selected Papers of the Second International Congress of Applied Linguistics*. Cambridge: Cambridge University Press.
Waller, T. (1993) Characteristics of near-native proficiency in writing. In H. Ringbom (ed.) *Near-Native Proficiency in English*. Åbo, Finland: English Department, Åbo Akademi University.
Witalisz, E. (2004) An analysis of the written English produced by Polish EFL learners applying to the English Department of the Jagiellonian University. Ph.D. thesis, Jagiellonian University, Kraków.
Witalisz, E. and Leśniewska, J. (2004) Reckless writers: An analysis of the poorest texts produced by the candidates for the English Department. In J. Leśniewska and E. Witalisz (eds) *The Legacy of History. English and American Studies and the Significance of the Past*, Vol. 2. Kraków: Jagiellonian University Press.

Chapter 7
The Use of High- and Low-Frequency Verbs in English Native and Non-Native Student Writing

KATALIN DORÓ

Introduction

Writing is a complex task that requires the author to balance and attend to a number of factors such as context, audience, purpose, vocabulary, grammar, organisation, spelling and punctuation. Language learners are often so worried about 'correct target language use' and the length of the paper they are writing, that they dedicate little attention to sophisticated vocabulary use, and tend to use basic words, even when they have a large receptive vocabulary.

When reading and evaluating a text, vocabulary greatly influences our judgement in deciding whether the given text is well-written or not. One of the key factors of the vocabulary used in written production is the vocabulary size of the writers, especially if they are second or foreign language learners with a limited vocabulary compared to that of a native speaker. Singleton (2001) points out that lexical development is a process without end, both in case of L1 and L2, and that the lexicon constantly develops in a variety of contexts where any situation may offer opportunity for vocabulary growth. Although both L1 and L2 vocabularies show some parallel features, they also have some basic differences. L1 vocabulary develops from a very early age and literary skills are also learned on the L1, leading to a boost in lexical development through reading and writing. L2 vocabulary, on the contrary, is built, in most cases, on an already existing L1 lexicon and literary skills.

Foreign language learning usually takes place in a formal institutional setting; therefore, a vast amount of the vocabulary (and language input in general) comes through the following channels:

(1) teacher talk, characterised by more frequent occurrences of high-frequency words, simple grammar, repetition, standard-like pronunciation, and limited range of topics;
(2) textbooks, which have standard, graded language in a written form; and
(3) peer interlanguage.

Of course, nowadays students also receive a vast amount of visual, oral and written input outside the classroom while traveling, listening to music, watching television or using the internet. This double input allows students to experience the target language in many different circumstances and to learn vocabulary on vast areas of topics, belonging to different varieties of the L2. However, the mastery of the meaning and the form of new words does not automatically lead to the production of the words in context and does not guarantee that the learner will produce texts that are lexically rich. When writing an essay, the semantic, syntactic, morphological and orthographical properties of the lexical items need to be activated.

Vocabulary size has been of interest to researchers for a long time, both in case of L1 and L2 (Nation & Waring, 1997). Many have also tried to estimate the rate of vocabulary growth. Some researchers have tested passive/receptive vocabulary, others have focused on what they call active/productive vocabulary. In the L2 literature, researchers use various terminology to indicate the different aspects of knowing a word. In this study, we will accept the use of the terms passive/receptive and active/productive as synonyms (for more details on the topic see Henriksen, 1999; Laufer, 1998; Melka, 1997). Whatever the terminology used, it is agreed that our passive vocabulary is larger than our active one, and what gets activated in speech or writing depends on many linguistic and extralinguistic factors.

L2 vocabulary is generally measured through tests: gap-fillings, C-tests, matching of words and meanings, check lists, word-association or translation. They all make language learners concentrate consciously on their vocabulary. But having a better score on these receptive or even productive vocabulary tests does not lead directly to a richer vocabulary in a more complex written production task. Vocabulary frequency measures, on the contrary, look not only at the size of vocabulary, but the amount of words one knows at various frequency levels.

They break down the native speakers' and L2 learners' lexicon into frequency bands and give information on how the vocabulary of given texts are distributed. This type of measure is an indicator for both learners and teachers on the amount of very frequent and less frequent words used in texts.

One of the most frequently used vocabulary frequency measures in the L2 literature is the Lexical Frequency Profile, originally designed by Laufer and Nation (1995). It describes texts in terms of frequency bands by breaking them into four lists. These four lists are:

- the first 1000 most frequently used word families;
- the second 1000 most frequently used word families;
- the University Word List; and
- the remaining words (or off-list words)

The sources of these lists are the *General Service List of English Words* by West (1953) for the first 2000 words, the *University Words List* by Praninskas (1972) and *The New Academic Word List* by Coxhead (2000) containing 570 word families. One of the major shortcomings of this vocabulary profile is that it is based on a word list as mentioned in Chapter 6 dating back to 1953; therefore, some words (especially nouns) commonly used nowadays will not appear in the first 2000 words.

The present paper concentrates on a particular aspect of the frequency band, namely the use of high-frequency verbs in written stories. In any language, some verbs are used more often both in speech and writing, and therefore, occur early in frequency lists. In English, not including *be* and auxiliaries, the following 15 verbs top any corpus-based list: *come, do, find, get, give, go, have, know, look, make, say, see, take, think* and *use* (Aarts & Meyer, 1995). Altenberg and Granger (2001) cite Viberg's study (1996) in which the author points out the following characteristics of high-frequency verbs:

- they have basic meanings, yet are characterised by a high degree of polysemy;
- they have high-frequency equivalents in most languages;
- they show various language-specific tendencies that result in specialised meanings, collocations and idiomatic uses; and
- language learners often have problems with them.

The EFL literature reports both the over- and the underuse of high-frequency verbs. Altenberg and Granger (2001), while listing some related studies, conclude that a number of these verbs are overused because students learn them early in their studies, they are often heard or seen in texts, and therefore, learners use them comfortably. On the contrary, verbs like *give, make, take* and *put* are often used with nouns as delexical verbs or idiomatic expressions. Their usage may be difficult for learners of English, so they prefer using less frequent, more sophisticated verbs. This underuse, however, often leads to awkward passages in learners' texts.

My hypothesis was that the use of these high-frequency verbs is task specific and depends on the learner's proficiency level. What can be considered as high- or low-frequency word may be strongly influenced by the text in which it is present. The vocabulary used in narratives written on an everyday topic can be expected to be different from that in an academic text or a newspaper article. Therefore, I did not attempt to compare learner data to large native corpus data that usually include different genres, topics and language proficiency levels. Instead, I preferred to look at intermediate level learner data in terms of data obtained from native children performing the same writing task under similar conditions. The main question addressed in this small-scale study is whether Hungarian learners of English tend to over- or underuse verbs that occur early in frequency lists.

Method and Subjects

Two main groups of subjects participated in this study: one group of native speakers of English and two groups of native speakers of Hungarian. Group 1 consisted of 29 native speakers of English, sixth graders enrolled in public schools in the United States, with a middle-class family background. Group 2 consisted of 26 speakers of Hungarian, made up of a subgroup of tenth graders and another subgroup of eleventh graders. Subjects in the non-native group, at the time of data collection, had been studying English for an average of seven years, and therefore, were at an intermediate or close to intermediate level of English. They had four classes per week of formal instruction at school and reported occasional use of English outside the classroom, mainly when using the internet, watching television or listening to music.

Data Collection

Students were asked to write a story using picture prompts. Studies have shown that picture elicitation is a successful data collection methodology as it provides a common background to the texts produced and eliminates the variables of free topic choice. A set of pictures also makes writing smoother as the subjects do not spend much time searching for ideas. Moreover, it helps them organise the flow of events they are writing about. Compared to written vocabulary tests, a free writing production – writing an essay or a story on a given topic – balances the learner's attention among the different factors that are needed during writing: the general organisation of ideas, grammar, vocabulary, spelling, punctuation, and text organisation. Vocabulary in a written story gives a more accurate picture of the actively used vocabulary than tests.

The four pictures used in this study depict a child who discovers smoke coming out of a window, tries to put it out with a bucket of water and, when the smoke clears, it turns out that there was no real fire. As a consequence, the child gets in conflict with a man inside the house who got the water poured at by accident. The prompt allows students to describe the events in the third person or to write it in the first person singular being the hero of the story, and also to conclude with a moral. While providing a shared basis for writing, the pictures also give freedom of vocabulary use, idea and text organisation, sophistication of grammar, and so on. Therefore, this task proves to be ideal both for native speaking children and foreign language learners. These pictures have been used in previous studies to elicit data from students of different native languages (for the first study using these pictures see B. Fejes, 1981).

Data was elicited from Hungarian high school students in the Spring of 2005 and data collection was done among American students as part of a previous research project (see Doró, 2001). The writing task was done as part of normal class work, and the time limit for the writing was 45 minutes, which was not fully used by most of the non-native subjects. No special guidance was provided about the content of the story.

For this study, sixth graders were chosen as control group, because my previous research showed that this is the age group when native students are able to organise their ideas into longer texts using rich vocabulary and a great variety of story types. Their texts are closest to the intermediate level learner texts in terms of length (with an average 215 words per text for the native group and 210 words for the non-native group), compoundness of the stories, variety of word choice and coherence.

Methodology of Data Analysis

The native and the non-native texts were combined into two text files. The two small corpora were analysed using the on line version of test tools, known as the *Complete Lexical Tutor*, designed by Tom Cobb. Out of the research tools available on Cobb's webpage, the following were used for the data analysis: VocabProfile, which is the improved version of the original frequency profile computer text tool of Paul Nation (called RANGE), the concordance, the frequency measures and the text comparison tool. The on line version of the vocabulary profile was used as, unlike the original version, it also gives data for the first 500 words and breaks down the first 1000 words band into function and content words.

Results and Discussion

Before closely analysing the verbs occurring in the texts, the frequency distribution of all words are discussed in this part of the study. In order to have a general picture of the words used in the stories the students wrote, the text files were analysed by the VocabProfile program. Results for the native students' stories are given in Table 7.1. Figures show the number of word families, word types (number of different words) and tokens (total number of words) for all four major frequency bands. The reason for some cells being empty in Tables 7.1 and 7.2 is that, in the case of the first 500 words and of the function and content words of the first 1000 words, the VocabProfile program is able to calculate only the

Table 7.1 Vocabulary profile of native students

	Families	Types	Tokens	Percentage
First 500 words			4725	75.50
First 1000 words	373	583	5269	84.20
Function words			3139	50.16
Content words			2130	34.04
First 2000 words	136	168	402	6.42
AWL words	16	17	33	0.53
Off-list words		238	554	8.85
All	525	1006	6258	100

Table 7.2 Vocabulary profile of non-native students

	Families	Types	Tokens	Percentage
First 500 words			4327	79.35
First 1000 words	347	539	4795	87.93
Function words			3007	55.14
Content words			1788	32.79
First 2000 words	114	140	436	8.00
AWL words	7	7	9	0.17
Off-list words		110	213	3.91
All	468	796	5453	100

tokens and the percent figures. Similarly, the program cannot group the off-list words into word families.

Results indicate that over 75% of the words in the native texts are made up of the first 500 words of English, and over 84% of the first 1000 words. Function words (*the, and, a,* and so on) are very frequent: half of the texts are, indeed, function words. We see much fewer words from the first 2000 words band, and very few of the Academic Word List. This may be explained by the fact that children were writing about an everyday topic and the subject of analysis is not academic texts. Almost 9% of the words were off-list words not represented in the first three lists, many of which are proper names.

The results of the VocabProfile analysis for the non-native texts are shown in Table 7.2. The figures in percentages allow for a quick comparison between the two corpora. Hungarian students used more words from the first 1000 words band, with a higher rate of function words. They also used a little higher rate of the first 2000 words band – 8% – compared to the 6.42% of the native group. These rates, however, are calculated on the basis of word tokens. If we take a closer look at the figures in the table, they show that the number of word types and families is lower in the

Hungarian group than in the American one, which means that the non-native students had a smaller variety of different words in this second band. The two other bands percentages in Table 7.2 are smaller than in Table 7.1, and the use of academic and off-list words make up just slightly over 4% of the learner corpus. The lack of use of more words from higher frequency bands fails to be accounted for by the proficiency level of the learners. They, on average, had been studying English for seven years, having come across texts with rich vocabulary. A possible explanation for the underuse of low-frequency words could be that the task did not explicitly require the writers to use sophisticated vocabulary. Furthermore, language learners may experiment little with less frequent words or expressions, and they may be happy to quickly do the writing task using the words learned early in their studies.

Figures in the vocabulary profile of the two groups show that the Hungarian students incorporated a higher number of high-frequency words from the first two frequency bands in their texts, but only a few academic words and less than half the number of off-list words used by the native children. As, on average, every fifth word in a story is a verb, it can be expected to find a great number of high-frequency verbs in data elicited for this study.

Figures for the 15 most frequently used verbs in English are given in Table 7.3. The results indicate the number of times each of these generally

Table 7.3 The use of the 15 most frequently used English verbs in the data elicited for this study

Verbs	NS	NNS	Verbs	NS	NNS
come	49	23	look	13	13
do	55	69	make	12	2
find	8	4	say	49	27
get	56	14	see	40	38
give	2	7	take	8	5
go	37	51	think	32	33
have	57	40	use	2	0
know	20	24			

NS, native student; NNS, non-native student.

high-frequency verbs occurr in the data of the present study. By looking at the figures, it can be immediately noted that some verbs, such as *give, take* and *use* are rarely used by both native and non-native students. This result supports the hypothesis that what counts as high- or low-frequency word greatly depends on the text in which it is present. The picture prompt used for data collection generated a story that did not necessarily include the interaction of giving or taking something. The verb *use* was not present at all in the non-native texts, which, of course, does not mean that students do not know this verb.

Other verbs show a close similarity in the number of times they were used. *Look, think, see* and *know* relate to the main character's state of mind, which is important in the story. The remaining verbs listed in Table 7.3 show an unbalalance in their use between the two groups. The polysemic verbs *have* and *get*, which have a general meaning, are underused by the Hungarian students. The verb *say* is missing from a number of non-native texts, since the learners wrote more descriptive, factual stories, with little communication between the characters. The verbs *go* and *come* refer to the movements mainly done by the child in the story. The American students described the movements as bidirectional using both verbs frequently. In contrast, the Hungarian students described the actions as a sequence, following the main character on his way. This fact led to the overuse of the verb *go* and the underuse of the verb *come*. The verb *do* is also more frequently used in the non-native texts. A possible explanation could be that it is often used in negation as an auxiliary verb in the form of *didn't*. There is also a great difference in the use of the verb *make* between the two groups: the native students used it six times more than the non-native students. One explanation to this unbalance is that the native speaking children used *make* not only to refer to the creation of something, but to express other meanings, and it was also used as causative. The following sentences provide some examples:

(1) ...*he was a baker and **made** some bread.* (non-native student)
(2) ***Make** sure it's fire before you put it out!* (native student)
(3) *If I became a hero it would **make** my day.* (native student)
(4) *Mr. Henrick would **make** him clean the floor with a toothbrush.* (native student)

As the results show, some generally high-frequency verbs are rarely used in the data elicited for this study. This raises the question whether the data presents other verbs not among the top 15 English verbs that can be considered high-frequency in the texts written on the basis of the picture prompts. Table 7.4 lists, in a frequency order, ten verbs that are used several times by at least one of the two groups. The verbs *run* and

Table 7.4 The top 10 most frequently used verbs in our data, not on the list of generally high-frequency verbs

Verbs	NS	NNS	Verbs	NS	NNS
run	55	38	put	17	8
walk	38	24	tell	16	9
want	3	31	ask	14	9
help	17	29	bring	1	12
throw	19	3	burn	11	9

walk are close to the frequency level of the verbs *come* and *go*. Again, they are less frequently present in the Hungarian texts, where the main character's movement is most often described by the verb *go*. The verbs *want* and *help* are used more often in the non-native corpus, which suggests that for the Hungarian students helping was a key concept of the story. Instead of using the verb *want*, the American children preferred the verb *need*. The following sentences provide further examples:

(5) But he **wanted** to **help**, he didn't **want** anything wrong. (non-native student)
(6) He **wanted** to solve the case alone. (non-native student)
(7) I was the only one on the street when I looked so I felt that I **needed** to **help**. (native student)
(8) A bucket, yes, just what I **need**. (native student)

The words *throw* and *put* relate to the action of putting the fire out in expressions such as *throwing water into the fire* or *putting the fire out* which are often missing explicitly from the Hungarian texts. The difference between the two groups in the use of the verbs *tell* and *ask* shows similarity with the verb *say* which indicates that the communication between the characters of the story is less frequently included by the non-native students. In contrast, the action of *bringing* something is very common in the Hungarian texts. This can be explained by the fact that the non-native subjects described the action of putting the fire out by making the main character first bring the water back to the house and then pouring it onto the smoke. American children, however, explain in more detail the chain of actions that lead to the water being used to put the fire out. The verb *bring* was only used by one of the native speaking children in the expression *bringing someone down*:

Table 7.5 The 10 most frequent verbs that occur in only one of the data sets

Native student corpus	Non-native student corpus
yell (21), mean (7), dump (6), need (5), pass (4), splash (4), reply (3), ruin (3), rush (3), bark (3)	arrive (8), shout (7), understand (7), laugh (3), split (3), show (3), pipe (3), invite (3), sing (3), cause (3)

(9) He found a bucket and **brought** some water. (non-native student)
(10) He had gotten a few bad grades on some tests and quizzes. And that always **brings** someone down! (native student)

When comparing the two small corpora, we see that certain verbs are more frequently used by one or the other groups. There are some verbs, however, that are only used by one of the two groups and are completely missing from the other. These verbs are listed in Table 7.5, indicating the number of times they are used.

The pair of verbs *yell* and *shout* are synonyms, and they very frequently occur in the corpora, yet, they show very different usage by the two groups: *yell* is used 21 times in the native texts and *shout* is used 7 times in the non-native texts. They both express the meaning of talking loudly, *yell* is frequently used by the native children, for them it is a high-frequency verb, but its pair *shout*, is not present at all. Similarly, none of the learners made use of the verb *yell*. For example:

(11) But there wasn't any fire!!! – **shouted** the man. (non-native student)
(12) As he poured it fast in the window, a man **started** to **shout**. (non-native student)
(13) He **yelled** "Fire, Fire!" and went to get a pail of water. (native student)
(14) He quit **yelling** for a second but started again. (native student)

Other than incorporating high-frequency verbs in their stories, the data show that native children use a greater variety of low-frequency verbs than non-native students to indicate the same or similar meaning. As quick movement from one place to another is a key element of the story, a few examples from native texts are listed below. These sentences include alternative, more expressive verbs to indicate the action described by the Hungarian students with the verb *go*:

(15) Billy fills the bucket up with water, and **dashes off** to the house.
(16) Sam **darted out** and went to the side of his house ...
(17) Mr. Crab didn't even answer! He just **stormed off** dripping wet and do you know what?
(18) He thought that is was a fire. He **rushed** to find a bucket.

(19) *So he got a bucket of water, and* **ran back** *to the smoke and heaved the water on the smoke.*

A similar variety of low-frequency verbs is found in the native student texts in the description of the other key element of the story, namely the action of putting the fire out. This variety is missing from the Hungarian texts. For example:

(20) *He* **dumped** *all the water in the window.*
(21) *Bob* **tossed** *the water on the smoke.*
(22) *. . .* **heaved** *the water on the smoke.*
(23) *. . . he* **poured** *the bucket of water over the fire.*

Conclusions

In this paper, I have looked at the verbs used in stories written by native and non-native students. The results of this study suggest that the first 1000 words in English make up over three fourth of a non-academic, narrative text. These words are usually learned early in foreign language studies and are the basis of communication even at an advanced level. A pedagogical implication is that L2 learners will hopefully benefit from instructions that focus on the correct use of the basic verbs of the target language, including the use of expressions and phrasal verbs that make language much more expressive. Along with the attention dedicated to high-frequency verbs, alternatives for basic verbs (and other parts of speech) should be taught in order to show language learners how they can make their language richer, and less repetitive in terms of vocabulary. Moreover, the results suggest that what counts as over- or underuse is task specific and thus depends on the task our students are asked to do. Therefore, including carefully selected native texts in second/foreign language syllabi could benefit both teachers' and students' work. Texts produced by native speakers could be used as sample texts or as teaching materials to show the difference between simple and sophisticated texts in terms of vocabulary use. The stories written by the American children show a great variety of verbs that express meanings for which only a restricted number of verbs and expressions are used by the Hungarian learners.

When learners were asked, after data elicitation, about their experience in writing in the target language, they reported that they seldom wrote longer texts. This corresponds with the findings published in Csapó (2002) that rank writing as the least frequently used language task in the Hungarian classrooms. However, language learners should gain experience in creating texts in the target language in order to develop skills necessary for writing rich texts. A final pedagogical implication is that language learners should be given as much opportunity as possible to experiment with their growing vocabulary in writing, not only in speech.

References

Aarts, B. and Meyer, C. (eds) (1995) *The Verb in Contemporary English. Theory and Description.* Cambridge: Cambridge University Press.
Altenberg, B. and Granger, S. (2001) The grammatical and lexical patterning of MAKE in native and non-native student writing. *Applied Linguistics* 22(2), 173-195.
B. Fejes, K. (1981) *Egy Korosztály Írásbeli Nyelvhasználatának Fejlődése* [*The Development of Written Language Use of an Age Group*]. Budapest: Tankönyvkiadó.
Csapó, B. (ed.) (2002) *Az Iskolai Műveltség* [*School Education*]. Budapest: Osiris.
Cobb, T. *The Complete Lexical Tutor.* On WWW at http://132.208.224.131.
Coxhead, A. (2000) A New Academic Word List. *TESOL Quarterly* 34(2), 213-238.
Doró, K. (2001) *'The Mistery of the Black Cloud': The Development of American Children's Written Narratives.* Unpublished MA thesis, University of Szeged.
Henriksen, B. (1999) Three dimensions of vocabulary development. *Studies in Second Language Acquisition* 21(2), 303-317.
Laufer, B. (1998) The development of passive and active vocabulary in second language: Similar of different? *Applied Linguistics* 19(2), 255-271.
Laufer, B. and Nation, P. (1995) Lexical richness in L2 written production: Can it be measured? *Applied Linguistics* 16(3), 307-312.
Melka, F. (1997) Receptive vs. productive aspects of vocabulary. In N. Schmitt and M. McCarthy (eds) *Vocabulary: Description, Acquisition and Pedagogy* (pp. 84-102) Cambridge: Cambridge University Press.
Nation, I.S.P. *RANGE.* On WWW at: http://www.vuw.ac.nz/lals/staff/Paul_Nation.
Nation, I.S.P. and Waring, R. (1997) Vocabulary size, text coverage and word lists. In N. Schmitt and M. McCarthy (eds) *Vocabulary: Description, Acquisition and Pedagogy* (pp. 6-19). Cambridge: Cambridge University Press.
Praninskas, J. (1972) *Academic University Word List.* London: Longman.
Singleton, D. (2001) *Exploring the Second Language Mental Lexicon.* Cambridge: Cambridge University Press.
Viberg, Å. (1996) Cross-linguistic lexicology. The case of English *go* and Swedish *gå*. In K. Aimer, B. Altenberg and M. Johansson (eds) *Language in Contrast* (pp. 151-182). Lund: Lund University Press.
West, M. (1953) *A General Service List of English Words.* London: Longman, Green & Co.

Part 4
The Lexicon in Second Language Acquisition

Chapter 8
Selection of Grammatical Morphemes in Early Bilingual Development

ZSUZSANNA GERGELY

Introduction

In my empirical investigations, I focus on the grammatically mixed utterances of a Hungarian-English bilingual child that come from over a short period between his 2;6–3;0 years. The paper aims to contribute additional evidence to refute the idea of an initial single system of grammar and, by analysing what linguistic expression reveals about competence, intends to encourage discussion about how this phenomenon could be accounted for by the several language acquisition theories which have, so far, conspicuously neglected bilingual data.

One System or Two – or Neither?

The proposition that early bilingual development is characterised by an initial unitary system and that lexical and grammatical differentiation of the two languages happens gradually (Volterra & Taeschner, 1978) has received heavy criticism (review by Lanza, 2004) and has now been refuted.

De Houwer (1990), in her profound reanalysis of the original claims and data, suggests that the initial question is a mistaken one. Language separation may not be a useful concept. Moreover, mixes are sporadic and idiosyncratic; they have been reported (Deuchar & Quay, 2000: 87) to constitute a minority only in the overall production of the bilingual children studied. De Houwer (1990: 38) reckons:

> After all, when the occurrence of 'mixed utterances' is seen as evidence for a 'one unit' system, by the same token the simultaneous appearance

of 'non-mixed' utterances can be seen as evidence against such an interpretation.

Research evidence has accumulated to favour the dual-system hypothesis (Meisel, 2001, 2004).

Ways to Approach Bilingual Children's Mixing

A recent question in research is whether children's mixed utterances are merely a reflection of language used in their complex sociolinguistic environment or an attribute of their underlying linguistic competence. In analysing examples, these options have to be considered.

Language mixing is a feature of bilingual speech. One approach to studying mixing is to observe the complex sociolinguistic situation in which the bilingual child perceives, comprehends and produces speech – and to account for such linguistic behaviour. Lanza (2004) regards mixing as one aspect of language socialisation, which provides a theoretical framework for her to study bilingual language acquisition.

It has been suggested that mixing results from code-switching. The ability to switch codes – as believed by Meisel (2004) – emerges at the beginning of the third year and assumes knowledge of two distinct grammatical systems and a certain level of social skill. Children's early mixing in a variety of sociolinguistic situations might be indicative of the fact that 'the child has yet to acquire a particular type of sociolinguistic knowledge' (De Houwer, 1990: 39) and not necessarily the sign of the existence of a hybrid system, one medium of communication. Lanza's view is similar in that she contends (2004: 61) that:

> (...) the question of one system or two may not be the right question to ask in regard to language mixing in infant bilingualism. We may rather ask, what are the factors that promote language mixing? (...) at the representational level, although the child may have two separate linguistic systems, she still may have to learn to differentiate them in language use according to such sociolinguistic parameters as participant and topic.

Thus, mixes are signs of insufficient sociolinguistic/pragmatic knowledge rather than undifferentiated linguistic representation. Advocates of the separate systems hypothesis believe that the reason for children mixing is that there is mixing in their linguistic environment.

This was not the case in our observed situation. A pure mismatch of languages, that is, the 'wrong' choice of language has not been recorded. Jamie is an only child in a mixed Hungarian and English family who follow the 'one parent-one language' method. This principle disallows mixed speech on the parent's behalf and also discourages, though does not punish, the child's mixing. Still, there was a short period of five months in Jamie's third year when he did not always formally differentiate his two languages. Until his third birthday, his life's primary ground was the home, where there were two languages constantly present and long grandparental stays were of about equal length. Our son's mixed utterances were noted down in the closest family – in the presence of either parent, or both. Other (monolingual) members of the family almost never got such mixes.

All the mixes in Jamie's case seem to be motivated by the 'rely-on-all-available-resources' routine or strategy and never proved to be a sheer mistake of not being able to identify the participant. Rather, his mixing of the two languages only occurred in the company of the parents, the only persons in his immediate environment who are competent in both languages. The child's linguistic behaviour presupposes some sensitivity to the sociolinguistic situation.

It is worth noting that it is the same determinant of language choice – here, the interlocutor and his/her language competence – that encourages the child to select the right language and, at the same time, allows him to mix in the presence of those he knows would understand even his mixed messages.

This rather subtle knowledge is what Lanza (2004: 67) describes as bilingual awareness: more than an ability to separate languages formally; it is also social and cultural awareness: knowing what possibilities are yielded by bilingualism (when it is appropriate to separate and when to mix languages).

'Language mixing per se is not a valid measure for determining that the child lacks awareness of the two languages' Romaine observes (1995: 207). When a child draws on his/her total bilingual repertoire as an additional communicative tool in order to be understood, it is probably a sign of a yet incomplete language acquisition rather than a deficiency of language use or of grammatical knowledge (Meisel 2001: 14).

The other approach tries to account for early morphosyntactic development. The starting point is of De Houwer's (1990: 47):

> Whether on the psycholinguistic level the child in using 'mixed utterances' operates with two different sets of knowledge or only one is an unresolved question.
>
> Language-specific utterances, that is, syntactic differentiation, can only be identified when language-specific vocabulary and language-specific

morphology have emerged, claim Deuchar and Quay (2000: 88). Production data in bilinguals' languages may reflect a differential order of acquisition of formal elements that refer to a particular meaning distinction.

Frequency in the input may be regarded as a viable explanation: certain forms are acquired earlier than others because they are more productive or more frequent in the input that the child receives. The more productive forms are those that appear on the largest number of stem-types. Clark (2003: 196) states that children

> ...tend to use more productive forms more often than less productive ones early on, and only later master less productive forms. Overall, children are more attentive to type-frequency than token-frequency: they are more likely to use the inflections that appear on many stems than those that appear on only a few, even when tokens of the latter are much more frequent overall.

Slobin attributes the difference in formal complexity of certain semantic domains or single semantic distinctions to how early children start using a form (1973 quoted in Clark 2003: 194). Brown (1973) explains emergence of grammatical morphemes on the grounds of semantic complexity. But 'complexity' defies easy definition. De Houwer found, in the case of her Kate, that the degree of complexity may not be a determining factor and not necessarily instructive, although the appearance of a particular semantic notion depends on the child's cognitive maturity (1990: 234).

MacWhinney (1985: 1086) interprets Hungarian acquisitional data of emerging inflections as their order being less dependent on semantic complexity as semantic reliability and applicability. The formal complexity of major Hungarian grammatical markers is constant, as they are all suffixes and subject to the same morphophonological rules. In contrast, in English '(...) some grammatical markers are articles, some suffixes, some auxiliaries, and some discontinuous morphemes.'

In the following, I present some examples of the dual acquisition of these typologically different languages.

Hungarian is a highly inflecting language expressing grammatical relations with invariant suffixes. Beöthy & John-Steiner (1995) believe that the one form – one function quality of such languages allows a relatively speedy first language acquisition compared to other, non-agglutinative languages.

Jamie's Examples and Discussion

All these mixed utterances were observed during Jamie's third year: 2;6 – 3;0.

Those categories that were missing during the telegraphic stage have appeared by now. Lengyel (1981) regards these function words as forming a more heterogeneous group than MacWhinney will do (1985), including in it lexical morphemes, for example, articles and postpositions, together with a rich system of suffixes. As function words do not represent a homogeneous group as far as the level of difficulty in the process of language acquisition is concerned, Lengyel (1981: 218) identifies determining factors that influence the accessibility of these words for children. These are: saliency, syllabicity, semantic transparency, allophonic variation, relative frequency, independence of the environment. Verbal prefixes – for example – are perceptually salient, stressed and syllabic, thus the use of a verbal prefix may precede that of several nominal derivational and, less frequently, inflectional morphemes (suffixes).

Verbal prefixes MEG- ('completive') and LE- ('down')

Example 1   *Daddy, én meg-rub it.*
            DADDY, I'LL RUB IT.
Example 2   *Hey, mummy meg-pinch-el me bottom.*
            HEY, MUMMY HAS PINCHED ME BOTTOM.
Example 3   *Ott is meg-clean it up. Meg-clean it properly.*
            (WE)'LL CLEAN IT UP THERE TOO. (WE)'LL CLEAN IT PROPERLY.
Example 4   *Mit megyünk meg-look?*
            WHAT ARE WE GOING TO LOOK AT?
Example 5   *Meg-stroke.*
            I'LL STROKE IT.
Example 6   *Mummy, le-push it.*
            MUMMY, PUSH IT DOWN.

These examples demonstrate that the verbal prefix is so forcefully salient that it imposes itself on English verbs. Example 3 marks the completive meaning in both languages: '*meg*-clean' and 'clean it up', revealing the child's proper understanding of this semantic content. To decide whether the synthetic or the analytic formal design is the more complex – for the child this is irrelevant: he uses both.

Past tense

Example 7   *Daddy, én come-tam vissza.*
DADDY, I'VE COME BACK. (literally, 'I come-verbal suffix 1st p.sg. for past, back')

Example 8   *Én push-tam.*
I PUSHED. (literally, 'I push-verbal suffix 1st p.sg. for past')

Example 9   *Én nem broke-ott.*
I DIDN'T BREAK IT. (literally, 'I not broke-verbal suffix 3rd p.sg. for past')

Example 10 *Jerry gone-t.*
JERRY'S GONE. (literally, 'Jerry gone-verbal suffix 3rd p.sg. for past')

The above examples reveal formal variance for a notion cognitively present. The Hungarian past tense marking is attached to English verbs. In Examples 7 and 8 a Hungarian phonological rule is applied: the allomorph *-tam* (as opposed to its pair *-tem*) is chosen to conform to the phonological process of vowel harmony.

Note the English verb forms 'come' and 'broke'. Both are irregular verbs and to both are attached the appropriate (showing agreement in person, number, definiteness) Hungarian past suffix. Both Examples 7 and 8 suspiciously conform to English word order: the subject is explicit, albeit given in Hungarian. The null-subject is the default parameter in Hungarian, though the information structure of the sentence allows its overt presence. In these examples, however, the context did not require such an arrangement. Besides, in Example 7, the vocative tells us that the addressee was the English father, so we might conclude that the language was intended to be English. Why is the verb stem 'come' used, but the past form 'broke' with Hungarian tense marking? If the child knows 'broke', why not 'came'? (Example 10 is different: generalised by the all-purpose 'gone' meaning 'past', 'no more'.) Formal complexity cannot be a variable here. And why isn't the English regular past suffix attached, if anything?

Pinker's answer is the modified word/rule theory (Pinker, 1999). Irregular verbs are few (about 180), but the most frequently used ones belong to this closed class. Regular verbs number thousands. The access to irregular forms is through a mental mechanism: memory. If retrieval fails – allegedly due to insufficient experience to encounter the word frequently enough to build strong memory traces –, the child leaves the verb stem intact. This observation is reverberated in the Full Competence Hypothesis (Borer & Rohrbacher, 2002) that claims that all functional structures, including IP, are present in early grammar, head features, such as agreement and tense, together with the lexical heads. Without IP (Inflection Phrase: functional node dominating agreement and tense) children would randomly use inflections and make tense and agreement errors. Instead, the authors claim (2002: 135):

(...) insofar as the child is not certain of the phonological realization of either head features or grammatical formatives that assign range to functional heads, the child will avoid using them altogether and opt instead for a representation that utilizes none, (...)

At a later stage of cognitive development, another psychological mechanism – symbolic computation – enables the child to form the past tense by adding the suffix -ed. Temporary memory failure at this stage might result in this rule being generalised. Memorised words, rule products – different mental operations but the same meaning. English children are in their third year when they demonstrate having acquired the regular past tense rule by overgeneralising it. Jamie resorts to the same routine – but using Hungarian past suffixes – well. It is apparently the clear and transparent nature of the Hungarian inflectional system that allows formal expression of the same content prior to that in English. Lack of confidence as to reliable use is shown by other attempted English verb forms that occurred once:

'breaked'
'breakened'
'brokened'

Here, the overgeneralised English regular past tense rule is coupled with the vacillated irregular pattern generalisation. In any case, the rule is 'there' in both languages, at approximately the same time, within the same utterance.

I take it as evidence for separate grammatical development in multiple first language acquisition. As the stems and suffixes are freely combined, it can be assumed that they reside in separate 'corners' of the mental lexicon.

Article, object, possessive

Example 11   *Daddy húzta a curtain-t.*
              DADDY WAS DRAWING THE CURTAIN.
Example 12   *Bear fújik a candles-t.*
              BEAR IS BLOWING THE CANDLES.

Example 13   *Akarok* kick the *boszorkány away.*
             I WANT TO KICK THE WITCH AWAY.
Example 14   *Odatettem a* big finger here.
             I PUT THE BIG FINGER HERE.
Example 15   *Megette a* crocodile *a Grandma* toes.
             THE CROCODILE ATE GRANDMA'S TOES. (literally,
             Eat the crocodile the Grandma toes.)
Example 16   *Tiger fog eat-ni a Bambis.*
             TIGER WILL EAT THE BAMBIS.
Example 17   *Levettem a* paper *now.*
             I'VE TAKEN DOWN THE PAPER NOW.
Example 18   Missing *a Simbá-nak a fej-é-t.*
             SIMBA'S HEAD IS MISSING. (literally, Missing Simba's
             head + objective case suffix, which is unnecessary)
Example 19   *Én* smacked *a Daddy's seggé-t.*
             I SMACKED DADDY'S BUM.
Example 20   *Ha feltöröd, meglátod a fehér-jé-t* and its *sárgá-já-t.*
             IF YOU BREAK IT YOU'LL SEE ITS WHITE AND ITS
             YOLK.
Example 21   *Eszem a rice-om.*
             I'M EATING MY RICE.
Example 22   *Az én supper-m.*
             MY SUPPER. (literally, my supper – sign of possession)

The examples illustrate the striking absence of English articles (exceptions are Examples 13 and 24); as well as demonstrating the presence of the Hungarian definite article, which consistently and correctly stands in for its English counterpart, proving that the DP (Determiner Phrase: functional node associated with reference) is fully available (Borer & Rohrbacher, 2002).

In Example 20, a Hungarian (the definite article '*a*') and an English (the possessive pronoun 'its') determiner precede their respective nominative heads within the same sentence, thus providing clear evidence of language-specific grammar.

The direct object in Hungarian is realised by the attachment of the accusative case marker *-t* on the noun; in English it is the postverbal position that gives the argument this syntactic function. Examples 11, 12, 18, 19 and 20 are instances of the former; Examples 13 to 17 are instances of the latter. Mixing happens in both directions, the syntactic solutions are definitely differentiated.

The Saxon genitive 's' (Example 19) and the English possessive pronoun 'its' (Example 20) co-exist with the Hungarian allomorphic realisations of the possessive sign -*je* (Examples 18 and 20) -*ja* (Example 20), -*om*, -*m* (Examples 21 and 22). These possessive markers can combine in the noun phrase with the possessor noun (Example 19) or pronoun (Example 22) or with the optional dative marker -*nak* on the possessor (Example 18).

The conclusion is the same as above.

Preposition: Locative

Example 23   *Én le-estem a big bed.*
             I FELL OFF THE BIG BED. (literally, I off-fell the big bed.)
Example 24   *Bele-esett in the víz-be.*
             IT FELL INTO THE WATER. (literally, into-fell in the water-into)

In Example 23, to express the locative 'off' Hungarian normally employs double marking: here the verbal prefix *le-* and the semantically related nominal suffix allomorph -*ról*, which happens to be absent from, or rather substituted by a zero suffix on the English noun phrase (functionally a prepositional object) in this mixed sentence. Example 24 opts for the 'proper' double marking in Hungarian (*bele*-V + N-*be*) coupled with the English into-NP (thus making it threefold sure that the meaning is put through). Both ways of expression are available to the bilingual child.

Auxiliaries, infinitive

Example 25   *Én nem like it.*
             I DON'T LIKE IT.
Example 26   *Nem szabad lick-ni.*
             YOU MUSTN'T LICK.
Example 27   *Nem kell put it on.*
             YOU DON'T HAVE TO PUT IT ON.
Example 28   *Én nem tudok exercise.*
             I CAN'T EXERCISE.
Example 29   *Most nem hurt.*
             IT DOESN'T HURT NOW.
Example 30   *Nem fog falling down.*
             IT WON'T BE FALLING DOWN.
Example 31   *Én voltam clever, yes?*

	I WAS CLEVER, WASN'T I?
Example 32	*Daddy beard. Jamie-nek nincs beard.*
	DADDY'S GOT A BEARD. JAMIE HASN'T GOT A BEARD.
Example 33	*Én nincs vagyok closer.*
	I'M NOT CLOSER. (lit., I not am closer.)
Example 34	*Nem vagyok hideg, nem hideg vagyok.*
	I'M NOT COLD. (literally, Not I am cold, not cold I am.)
Example 35	*I can't hallom.*
	I CAN'T HEAR IT. (literally, I can't hear-verbal suffix 1st p.sg. definite)
Example 36	*I can't see the sea because vannak trees.*
	I CAN'T SEE THE SEA BECAUSE THERE ARE TREES.
Example 37	*Elmegyünk walk-ni?*
	ARE WE GOING FOR A WALK? (literally, Are we going to walk?)
Example 38	*Elmentem wee-ni.*
	I WENT FOR A WEE. (literally, I went 'to wee'.)
Example 39	*Én már voltam wee.*
	I HAVE BEEN FOR A WEE. (literally, I have been 'to wee'.)

Examples 26, 37 and 38 show the English bare infinitive with the explicit Hungarian infinitival marker used context-appropriately; the mixed utterances are grammatically correct in both Hungarian and, if replaced by the intended construction, in English. Examples 25, 27, 28, 29 and 39 prove the same grammaticality: here the base language is obviously English where the required infinitival form finds its expression in English. It has been proven that the same grammatical principle exists in two different forms.

In Examples 25 to 30 the English 'auxiliary + not' constructions, are conspicuously substituted by the Hungarian clause-external negator *nem*. It is the normal initial pattern for English children as well, and 'as soon as they have acquired finiteness, clause-internal negation appears, and the target structures are usually acquired rapidly and without apparent effort' (Meisel, 2001: 20). Examples 35 and 36 present the use of a modal with a cliticised negator, revealing the tight bond between the negative particle and the auxiliary. It is not impossible that in the child's brain 'can't' is represented as a single unit at this phase of development.

Present progressive

Example 40   Bear *fúj-ing* a candles-*t*.
              BEAR IS BLOWING THE CANDLES.
Examples 41   *Mit csinál-ing a Bear?*
              WHAT'S BEAR DOING?
Example 42   *Fürd-ing, fürd-ing, fürd-ing.*
              BATHING, BATHING, BATHING.
Example 43   *A doggy esz-ing a butter.*
              THE DOGGY IS EATING THE BUTTER.

In the above mixes, the easily available, perceptually salient and semantically straightforward '-ing' suffix is imposed on Hungarian word stems. (Hungarian has no separate verb conjugation for aspect.) This example of bilingual speech illustrates the separate mental representation of lexical and grammatical knowledge.

Tentative Conclusions

All these mixed utterances share one particular feature. They are grammatical: examples of natural language. Even though there is mixing, the components are systematically arranged to form phrase and clause structure (DP and IP for example), always conforming to the rules of either Hungarian or English.

This situation could be likened to Grosjean's description of the bicultural (1996: 29): Jamie is bistructural from living in the linguistic environment of two grammars, adapting to and blending aspects of them.

With regard to article use, Hungarian children mark the definite-indefinite distinction in the noun phrase by the time they are two years old (Varma in Romaine 1995: 213), which is consistent with MacWhinney's findings (1985: 1147). Schaeffer and Matthewson (2005: 54) assert that English children also set the parameter correctly between the age of 2 to 3, but tend to omit them as they lack a pragmatic concept that would allow them to produce adult-like article choice. They propose that cross-linguistic semantic variation may be described in parametric difference. It is perhaps not untenable to assume that in bilingual first language acquisition such variation is levelled out and the two languages, although autonomous, reciprocally support their respective development.

Meisel's convincing arguments (2001, 2004) make claims about the availability of the principles and parameters of Universal Grammar for more than one language. Schaeffer and Matthewson (2005) consider that their research findings support the hypothesis that the intermediate stages of child grammar is a coherent system and child structures never violate either the general principles of Universal Grammar or the particular grammar of the target language.

It is to be hoped that Jamie's examples lend support to this claim and that the arguments for natural rule-governed mixed bilingual speech will contribute to the extension of the First Language Acquisition theory in order to account for Bilingual First Language Acquisition.

References

Beöthy, E. and John Steiner, V. (1995) Magyar-angol kétnyelvű gyermekek hibázási mintázatának elemzése. In Z. Telegdi, C. Pléh and G. Szépe (eds) *Általános Nyelvészeti Tanulmányok 18*, (pp. 5–12). Budapest: Akadémiai Kiadó.

Borer, H. and Rohrbacher, B. (2002) Minding the Absent: Arguments for the Full Competence Hypothesis. *Language Acquisition* 10 (2), 123–175.

Brown, R. (1973) *A First Language: The Early Stages*. Cambridge, MA: Harvard University Press.

Clark, E. (2003) *First Language Acquisition*. Cambridge: Cambridge University Press.

Deuchar, M. and Quay, S. (2000) *Bilingual Acquisition: Theoretical Implications of a Case Study*. Oxford: Oxford University Press.

De Houwer, A. (1990) *The Acquisition of Two Languages from Birth: A Case Study*. Cambridge: Cambridge University Press.

De Houwer, A. (1995) Bilingual language acquisition. In P. Fletcher and B. MacWhinney (eds) *The Handbook of Child Language* (pp. 219–250). Oxford: Blackwell.

Grosjean, F. (1996) Living with two languages and two cultures. In I. Parasnis (ed.) *Cultural and Language Diversity and the Deaf Experience* (pp. 20–37). Cambridge/New York: Cambridge University Press.

Lanza, E. (2004) *Language Mixing in Infant Bilingualism: A Sociolinguistic Perspective*. Oxford: Oxford University Press.

Lengyel, Zs. (1981) *A gyermeknyelv*. [Child Language]. Budapest: Gondolat.

MacWhinney, B. (1985) Hungarian language acquisition as an exemplification of a general model of grammatical development. In D.J. Slobin (ed.) *The Crosslinguistic Study of Language Acquisition, Volume 2: Theoretical Issues* (pp. 1069–1155). Hillsdale, NJ: Erlbaum.

Meisel, J.M. (2001) The simultaneous acquisition of two first languages: Early differentiation and subsequent development of grammars. In J. Cenoz and F. Genesee (eds) *Trends in Bilingual Acquisition* (pp. 11–41). Amsterdam/Philadelphia: John Benjamins Publishing Company.

Meisel, J.M. (2004) The bilingual child. In T.K. Bhatia and W.C. Ritchie (eds) *The Handbook of Bilingualism* (pp. 91–113). Blackwell Publishing Ltd.

Pinker, S. (1999) Words and rules. In A. Sorace, C. Heycock and R. Shillcock (eds) *Language Acquisition: Knowledge Representation and Processing* (pp. 219–242). North-Holland.

Romaine, S. (1995) *Bilingualism*. 2nd edition. Oxford UK and Cambridge USA: Blackwell.

Schaeffer, J. and Matthewson, L. (2005) Grammar and pragmatics in the acquisition of article systems. *Natural Language & Linguistic Theory* 23, 53–101.

Volterra, V. and Taeschner, T. (1978) The acquisition and development of language by bilingual children. *Journal of Child Language* 5, 311–326.

Chapter 9
The Importance of Language Specific Features For Vocabulary Acquisition: An Example of Croatian

LIDIJA CVIKIĆ

Introduction

Several hundreds of papers and dozens of books about vocabulary acquisition in a second language have been published since the 1980's, when vocabulary came within the scope of second language research (Meara & Hilton, 2005). There have been numerous topics investigated, that is second language vocabulary structure (McCarthy & Carter, 1997; Nation & Waring, 1997), mental lexicon (Singleton, 1999, 2000), vocabulary acquisition and its strategies (Schmitt, 1997), vocabulary assessment (Laufer & Nation, 1999; Meara, 1997; Melka, 1997; Mondria & Wiersma, 2004; Read, 2000), and so on. However, there is still no unique, complete and detailed model of second language vocabulary acquisition (Haastrup & Henriksen, 2001; Meara, 1997).

Meara (1997) claims that two things are needed for proposing such a model: efficient research instruments and a solid theoretical base. Both are necessary in order to explain the complex process of vocabulary acquisition in a second language.

The lexical component of second language acquisition (SLA) consists of much more than isolated words (Nation, 2001; Schmitt & McCarthy, 1997); phonology, morphology, syntax and semantics all play a role in vocabulary acquisition. Therefore, research on languages that are structurally different from those most commonly investigated and described in the field of SLA, might provide critical insight into the processes and phenomena of vocabulary acquisition in a second language. Research on one such language, Croatian, can help us raise new questions and make greater strides in improving our knowledge about vocabulary in a second language.

Croatian as a Second Language

The Croatian language is the national and official language used in the Republic of Croatia. It is estimated that Croatian is spoken by 5.5 million people (Institut za hrvatski jezik i jezikoslovlje, 2005) – 4.4 million Croatian inhabitants and 1.1 million Croatian speakers who live abroad. According to the numbers, Croatian is considered a 'small language', as well as a 'less widely taught language'. Thus, its psycholinguistic and sociolinguistic status and its relation to other languages provide a very complex picture (Jelaska, 2003, 2005; Jelaska & Kusin, 2005). Jelaska (2005: 280) differentiates various groups of monolingual and bilingual speakers within the borders of Croatia and claims that

> the situation with the Croatian language in foreign countries and with persons who have partially acquired Croatian in their families (Croatian immigrants) and have partially learned it through an educational system in their countries and/or in Croatia, is even more complicated.

Research on Croatian as a second language

Although there was some interest in Croatian as a second language earlier, more systematic research began in the first part of the 1990's (Cvikić & Jelaska, 2005). Interest in researching Croatian as L2 came about due to an increase in the number of its learners and the need for more modern and successful teaching methods and materials. The structure of Croatian significantly differs from the structure of the first languages of its learners (mostly Germanic and Romance languages) and therefore, influences the topics of research on the acquisition of Croatian as L2. Research has mostly dealt with the morphology of nouns and verbs acquired by adult learners, as well as by children. For example, Novak (2002, 2002a) investigated the acquisition of verb morphology by analysing adult learners' implicit and explicit language knowledge and found that verb class frequency and verb item frequency influenced the acquisition of the morphology of verbs. The importance of frequency on verbal morphology acquisition was confirmed by independent research on Hungarian L1 children (Kuvač & Cvikić, 2004).

The acquisition of case systems and declensions in Croatian as L2 was investigated more often. Some researchers focused only on typical errors occuring during the acquisition of cases (Globan, 2002; Novak, 2002b), regardless of the word type (nouns or adjectives) and gender. Others concentrated on a specific category, for example, acquisition of masculine nouns (Cvikić & Kuvač, 2005) by adult learners at the intermediate level. The results showed that some phonological rules, for example the one deleting and inserting an *'a'* (so called *mobile 'a'*), were acquired very early and that they could be applied even to new lexical items. On the other hand, the usage of that rule was restricted only to some forms of the word, that is, it was applied in singular, but not in plural forms of the same nouns. The same topic was investigated more thoroughly in children, speakers of Hungarian and Romani as minority languages in Croatia (Cvikić & Kuvač, 2003; Cvikić et al., 2004; Kuvač & Cvikić, 2004). The research covered only four of fourteen noun forms (Nominative and Genitive in singular and plural) and the results show that there is a clear order concerning the accurate acquisition of those forms: N sg > G sg > N pl > G pl.

Although it is evident that research on Croatian as a second language provides us with important and meaningful results, more systematic research on the topic is still needed. However, that kind of research is limited for various reasons. Some of the main reasons are the difficulty in collecting a large enough sample, and whose subjects are homogenous (similar age, level of language knowledge and same first language). As most of the previously mentioned research was conducted with learners, participants of a short-term intensive course, a longitudinal study was not possible. Also, systematic research requires valid and reliable instruments that the Croatian language still lacks.

Research on vocabulary acquisition for Croatian as a second language

As vocabulary is mostly just a part of a larger study or research on Croatian as L2, there are only a few studies whose focus has been on vocabulary acquisition in Croatian as a second language.

Some researchers dealt with the lexical component in the scope of lexical errors by adult learners. Gulešić (2003) and Jelaska and Hržica (2002) explored lexical errors produced by learners, native speakers of a cognate language: Slovak (Gulešić, 2003) and Serbian (Jelaska and Hržica, 2002). The high degree of similarity between the first and the second language was perceived as a source of lexical errors.

Vocabulary size was one of the components in the research of the acquisition of Croatian by children, speakers of the Hungarian language (Cvikić & Kuvač 2003; Kuvač & Cvikić, 2004) and Romani languages (Cvikić *et al.*, 2004). An investigation of their active and passive vocabulary showed that both groups of L2 speakers had vocabularies of a smaller size than their Croatian L1 peers had at the same age.

There are two works about Croatian as a second language and foreign language that examine vocabulary acquisition only: a paper by Cvikić and Bošnjak (2004) and a study by Cvikić (2004).

Cvikić and Bošnjak (2004) used a corpus of learners' written language at different levels of language knowledge and analysed them according to elements of knowing a word: form, meaning and usage, proposed by Nation (2001: 27). They found different types of errors. A lexical error that leads to misunderstanding can be the result of the transfer of the learner's first language phonological system to Croatian. For example, learners of Spanish L1 transfer their phonological system to Croatian, so that they use [b] and [v] one instead another; that is, *brat* 'brother' is pronounced and written as *vrat* 'neck'. Phonological transfer can lead to morphological errors as well (for example, *liječnice* 'female doctors' and *liječnici* 'male doctors'). At the level of word meaning, learners of Croatian as L2 have difficulties with the acquisition of those words which lexicalise the meaning that is not lexicalised in their first language, for example, *umivati se* 'to wash one's face', *obuvati se* 'to put shoes on'. Instead of those verbs with more specific meaning, learners use verbs with broader, more general meaning, for example, *prati* 'to wash' instead of *umivati se* 'to wash one's face'. The same strategy was reported by Blum and Levenson (1978), according to Laufer-Dvorkin (1991). Regarding the usage of words, difficulties with the usage of culture bound lexemes were found.

But Cvikić and Bošnjak showed that a great deal of lexical errors in Croatian L2 were errors in production of word forms, especially those which contain 'Croatian letters'. The Croatian language has 31 phonemes written with 30 graphemes (Težak & Babić, 2001). Some of the graphemes differ only in diacritics, but they represent different phonemes: č-c, ć-c, š-s, ž-z. Misspelling, that is, omission of the diacritics, may result with a lexical error that affect communication, producing communication breaks and misunderstanding (*koza* 'goat' and *koža* 'skin', *sto* 'hundred' and *što* 'what'). The speakers of English L1 often confuse Croatian *e* [e] with English *e* [i]. Both -i and -e in Croatian function as the endings of different cases of the same noun (*sestre* G pl. 'of a sister' and *sestri* D pl. 'to a sister'). Learners of Croatian as a second language are often faced with the difficult task of linking different tokens to the same type. Due to various morphophonological rules (Težak & Babić, 2001), the inflected form of the word is sometimes so different from the citation form that it is even hard to recognise it as the same word (*posla* G sg. 'of a work' and *posao* 'work'; *dolasci* 'arrivals' and *dolazak* 'an arrival').

Cvikić (2004) investigated vocabulary size in Croatian as a second language on the basis of a receptive translation test, with the test items at five frequency bounds. The vocabulary test, made for the purpose of that very research, was proved to be a reliable instrument to differentiate between beginner and intermediate levels of Croatian knowledge (Cvikić, 2004).

Intralexical factors in vocabulary acquisition

Vocabulary acquisition in a second language is a complex phenomenon that depends on various linguistic as well as non-linguistic factors. Swan (1997: 161) gives examples of various interlexical factors 'caused by interference of transfer from the mother-tongue'. Beside the interlexical, there are also intralexical factors on the vocabulary acquisition. Those factors can be described with the title of Laufer's paper *'What's in a word that makes it hard or easy'* (Laufer, 1997) where she listed various interlexical factors that play a role in the second language acquisition of various languages. Intralexical factors can be a result of a word form, for example, pronounceability of the word, its orthography, word length, part of speech and morphology. They are also connected with word meaning, for example abstractness of the meaning, idiomacity, polysemy, style and register, and so on. In her work, Laufer (1991, 1997) puts an emphasis on synformy in the acquisition of English as L2. Synformy is defined as 'the phenomenon of form similarity between words' which can be caused by etymology or by accident (Laufer-Dvorkin, 1991: 43). The author differentiates three types of synforms:

- synphones (words similar in their sound, for example, *live* and *leave*);
- syngraphs (words similar in their script, for example, *excerpt* and *expert*); and
- synmorphs (words similar in their forms, for example, *comprehensible* and *comprehensive*).

Two (or more) words that are synforms share some general characteristics: they belong to the same word class; they have the same (or similar) number of syllables, they have the same stress and they share most of their phonemes. According to these general characteristics, as well as the pattern of synformic confusion (omission, addition or substitution) Laufer-Dvorkin (1991: 47) differentiates 10 categories of synformy in English. She proved that synformy in general induces error in vocabulary learning and concluded that 'synmorphs belong to the developmental type (of errors), while synphones belong to the interlingual one' (Laufer-Dvorkin, 1991: 173).

Intralexical factors in vocabulary acquisition in Croatian as L2

As previously mentioned, Croatian as a second and foreign language is learned by a relatively small number of people, sometimes only a few of them with the same first language. Further more, learners of Croatian as L2 are sometimes native speakers of languages that do not have contrastive descriptions with Croatian (for example Korean, Japanese, Chinese, and so on) and in all that respect it is very difficult to investigate the interlanguage factors in vocabulary acquisition in Croatian. The interlexical factors affect all learners, regardless of their first language and their sources might be found in the features of the Croatian language itself. Therefore, investigating the intralexical factors in vocabulary acquisition in Croatian as L2 has created more research interest.

Cvikić and Bošnjak's research (2004) provided evidence for some intralexical factors in Croatian, for example, orthography. Words with letters specific to Croatian were very often misspelt and therefore considered more difficult for the learners of Croatian, even in the case of very common words. Another factor proved by Cvikić and Bošnjak is the factor of inflexional complexity. Due to the morphological homonymy, some inflexional forms were considered to be citation forms of a different word (*susjeda* G pl. 'of a male neighbor' and *susjeda* N sg. 'female neighbor'). Cvikić's study (2004) gives more evidence for the intralexical factors in Croatian. But, since the subjects in that study were all speakers of English L1, it was not always possible to decide whether the factors were interlexical or intralexical.

Research

Aim

In order to investigate intralexical factors influencing vocabulary acquisition in Croatian, as well as to determine the linguistic source of these factors, groups of learners with different first languages should be tested.

The main hypotheses are:

(1) If the same type of lexical errors is presented in all groups of learners, independent of their L1, the source of an error is intralexical.
(2) If some types of lexical errors are more frequent than others, the reasons could be features of the Croatian language.

Subjects

For the purpose of Cvikić's study (2004), a large corpus was collected by administering a vocabulary test to the learners of Croatian as L2 during an intensive course in 2002, 2003 and 2004 ($N = 85$). In order to avoid any possible influence of their stay in Croatia on their vocabulary, all subjects were tested on the very first meeting, just after their arrival to Croatia, as Meara (2005) pointed out that even a short period of intensive exposure to an L2 environment can influence second language vocabulary.

In Cvikić's aforementioned study, only one small part ($N = 26$) of the data was analysed. Data from the same corpus was chosen to be analysed for the purpose of this paper. It was decided to analyse the answers of two groups of learners:

- Learners of Croatian, speakers of English L1 ($N = 26$).
- Learners of Croatian, speakers of Italian L1 ($N = 6$).

The reason for choosing speakers of these two languages was the number of subjects and their vocabulary knowledge. Speakers of other languages were either at the beginner's level, with no previous knowledge of Croatian, or the sample was too small (one or two learners with the same language).

The average number of correct answers was similar in both groups (English L1 $x = 32$, Italian L1 $x = 28$), which proves that learners in both groups were at the same level of lexical knowledge. All subjects were of a similar age – student population.

Research instrument

A vocabulary test of Croatian as a second language was created by Cvikić for the purpose of the study. The aim of that study was to investigate the effect that word frequency has on vocabulary acquisition in Croatian. The created test comprises items at five frequency bounds (1k–5k), 20 items at each bound – 100 items in total.

The form of the test was a translation test. Informants had to translate Croatian words to their first language, which means that the test measured their receptive vocabulary knowledge. The test items were chosen randomly and the researcher did not have any information about informant's previous knowledge of these words. The reason for choosing the translation test was twofold (Cvikić, 2004): first, the translation test can provide more reliable results than a simple yes-no test, where it is not possible to check the actual understanding of a word.

Secondly, qualitative analysis of the incorrect answers might provide further insight into a learners' interlanguage.

Test administration

The test was administered so that every answer/translation was checked by dictionaries, as well as by bilingual speakers of Italian-Croatian and English-Croatian. If the translation equivalent was found in at least one of the sources, it was considered to be correct. In order to investigate the source of incorrect answers, all of them were translated back to Croatian. It was assumed that comparison of two Croatian words (a source word and a Croatian translation of the test answer) would enable detection between interlexical and intralexical factors.

Results and Discussion

Figures 9.1 and 9.2 show the percentage of correct answers in both groups. The percentage of correct answers was similar, 61% by English L1 speakers, 68% by Italian L1 speakers. It seems that the group of English L1 speakers felt more comfortable giving the answers as they left no test item unanswered. The group of Italian L1 speakers left 16 test items without an answer.

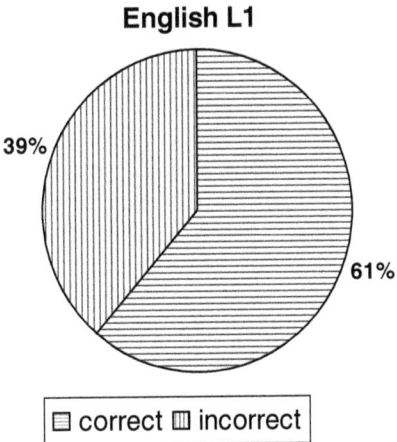

Figure 9.1. Relation between correct and incorrect test answers (English L1 subjects).

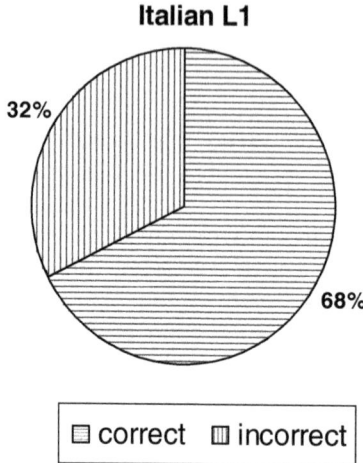

Figure 9.2. Relation between correct and incorrect test answers (Italian L1 subjects).

Qualitative analysis of all the correct answers was conducted in order to investigate all types of errors. For most incorrect answers, it was easy to define a type, even to make conclusions about the cause of the error. However, this was not the case for all of them. As some incorrect answers were found only from one learner or from several learners with the same first language, it was not possible to decide whether the factor that induced the error was interlexical on intralexical.

To examine and verify the intralexical source of some incorrect answers, an additional analysis was conducted. The Croatian translation of the answers given by two groups was compared (for example, target word *netko* 'somebody', given translations: *nobody* [Eng], *nesuno* [It], both *nitko* in Croatian). It was assumed that the presence of the same lexical error (incorrect answers) in both groups of learners was reliable evidence that the incorrect answers had been caused by the influence of intralexical factors on vocabulary acquisition, and not by interlexical or non-linguistic factors. For 21 test items, the learners from both groups gave identical (incorrect) answers and for one test item two incorrect answers were found proven by both groups.

The total number of 21 identical incorrect answers shared between both groups of learners might not seem so relevant, but all the research constraints should be taken into consideration, that is, small group of subjects, no previous information about their language/lexical knowledge, non-standardised testing instrument, and so on. Therefore, the result of 21 test items with identical incorrect answers is considered to be relevant, as well as proof of intralexical factors that influence vocabulary acquisition.

Factors that caused incorrect answers: Type of errors

In general, all the incorrect answers can be divided into four groups:

(1) Incorrect answers caused by phonological similarity of Croatian words.
(2) Incorrect answers caused by morphological features of Croatian words.
(3) Incorrect answers caused by similarity in meaning.
(4) Incorrect answers with no connection between a source word and a target word.

All types of incorrect answers were found in both groups of learners, as well as in the group of shared identical incorrect answers (Table 9.1 shows all shared incorrect answers).

In order to explain different types of incorrect answers in more detail, some examples are going to be presented. Whenever possible, all the examples will be provided from identical incorrect answers produced by both groups of learners. Exceptionally, if in the corpus of identical incorrect answers there is only one example of a particular error, more examples will be provided from the corpus of incorrect answers produced by one of the groups of learners.

Incorrect answers caused by phonological similarity of Croatian words

The group of incorrect answers caused by phonological similarity can be divided into two subgroups. The first subgroup consist of words that make *a minimal pair*, two words that differ only in one phoneme (for example *netko* 'somebody' – *nitko* 'nobody'). The second subgroup consists of other *synphones*, phonologically similar words. According to the patterns of symphonic confusion, different types of synphones were found. For example, synphones identical in all phonemes but one (*jako* 'strongly' – *lako* 'easily'; *jako* 'strongly' – *iako* 'even though'), synphones which differ in more than one vowel (*prisiliti* 'to force' – *preseliti* 'to move'; *vuna* 'wool' – *vani* 'outside'), and synphones that differs in one syllable (*nazvan* 'named' – *izvan* 'outside'). Even though the words *jako* and *lako* differ only in one phoneme, due to their different accent, they

Table 9.1 Identical incorrect answers (shared by both groups of learners)

Cause of incorrect answers	Factor	
Morphological features	Wrong word class	*Izvan* prep. 'out' – *vani* adv.'outside'
		Desni adj 'right' – *desno* adv 'right'
		žedan 'thirsty' – *žeđ* 'thirst'
		Kratko 'shortly' – *kratak* 'short'
		Mala f. adj. 'little' – *malo* adv. 'little'
		Stisnut 'squeezed' – *stisnuti* 'to squeeze'
	Deceptive transparency	*jednom* 'once' – *jedan* 'one' + *-om* 'I sg'
		zelenilo 'greenery' – *pozelenjeti* 'to turn green' po + zelen + je + ti
		ptičji 'bird's' – *ptice* 'birds'
		ptičji 'bird's' – *ptičice* 'little birds'

Importance of Language Features for Vocubulary Acquisition 157

	Symphony	
Phonological similarity		*netko* 'anybody' – *nitko* 'nobody'
		množenje 'multiplication' – *množina* 'plural'
	String of phonemes	*sitan* 'small' – *sit* 'full'
		namjeravati 'to intend' – *mjera* 'measure'
		prijem 'reception' – *prije* 'before'
Similarity in meaning		*dočekati* perf. 'to wait' – *čekati* impf. 'to wait'
		tablica 'table' – *ploča* 'board'
		stepenica 'a stair' – *ljestve* 'ledders'
		rušiti 'to demolish' – *uništiti* 'to destroy'
		prevrtati 'overthrow' – *vrtjeti* 'to turn'
No connection		*izjaviti* 'to state' – *zvati* 'to call'
		sačuvati 'to save' – *čuti* 'to hear'

are not perceived as a minimal pair in the Croatian language. Minimal pairs in Croatian differ not only by one phoneme, but both words in a pair are supposed to have the same accent (Barić et al., 1997).

All the listed examples have the general characteristics of synformy: similar phoneme inventory, same (or similar) number of syllables and mostly belong to the same part of speech. They are also created by substitution (*netko-nitko, jako-lako*) and omission (*nazvan-izvan*) of the word elements. Even though symphonic errors are caused by the features of L2, some examples from the corpus support the connection with the first language as well. Namely, the synphones *jako – iako* were found only in English L1 speakers, as the pair *jako – lako* was found only at Italian L1 speakers. Since there is no study about synformy in Croatian yet, these research results could serve as a starting point for it.

Incorrect answers caused by morphological features of the Croatian language

Among all four groups of incorrect answers, the one caused by morphological features of Croatian words is the richest in examples.

wrong word class

A very large subgroup of errors was the one caused by the choice of the wrong word class. Almost all possible combinations between different classes of content words were found:

(1) A noun was substituted with a verb: *znanje* 'knowledge' – *znati* 'know'
(2) A noun was substituted with an adjective: *žeđ* 'thirst' – *žedan* 'thirsty'
(3) An adjective was substituted with a noun: *lud* 'crazy' – *ludost* 'craziness'
(4) An adverb was substituted with a noun: *namjerno* 'purposely' – *namjera* 'purpose'
(5) An adverb was substituted with an adjective: *jako* 'very' – *jak* 'strong'
(6) A verb was substituted with an adjective: *stisnuti* 'to squeeze' – *stisnut* 'squeezed'

Since Croatian is a flective language, word form is an important element of vocabulary knowledge and the relation between morphology and semantics in vocabulary acquisition on Croatian as L2 should be investigated in more depth. Cvikić (2004) pointed out that the research on vocabulary acquisition based on word families, instead of single words, might not be the best approach for flective languages. On the basis of research conducted, she showed (Cvikić, 2004: 64) the bigger burden on the learner's grammatical knowledge if three nouns are to be replaced with their verbal counterparts. Namely, the knowledge of the three nouns (*znanje* 'knowledge', *zelenilo* 'greenery', *objašnjenje* 'explanation') consist of a knowledge of the same paradigmatic pattern, since their verbal counterparts (*znati* 'to know', *zelenjeti* 'to green', *objasniti* 'to explain') belong to the different verb classes, have different paradigms and require different grammatical and syntactical knowledge. Investigation of the relation between word meanings and word forms in a Slavic language as a second language could give more insight into the structure of mental lexicon in a second language.

deceptive transparency

When learning a second language, knowledge of the meaning of the root and affixes can be a facilitating factor in revealing the meaning of a new word. But that is not always the case. Sometimes, the meaning of a word may seem transparent through its parts, but this transparency may lead to the wrong assumptions. This phenomenon is known as *deceptive transparency* (Laufer, 1997). Examples of deceptive transparency were also found in the investigated corpus. For example, in the word *listopad* (October) two roots were recognized: *list* (leaf) and *pad* (the stem of the verb *padati* 'to fall') and it was translated as *leaf falls*. The verb *prevrtati* 'to turn' was translated with 'to garden' due to the learner's assumption that the meaning is derived from *vrt* 'garden' plus verbal prefix *pre-* and suffixes *-a, -ti*.

string of phonemes perceived as a morpheme

The corpus provides examples of a special case of deceptive transparency. Sometimes, a simple string of phoneme was perceived as a morpheme or a derivational part of a word. The adverb *lukav* 'sly' was translated with *luka* 'harbor' and *luk* 'onion', even though it is not related to any of these two words. Within the word's phoneme inventory, learners had just recognised the string to which they were able to assign the meaning: *l-u-k-a-v* and *l-u-k-a-v*. The same happened in a translation of *siromah* 'poor' with *sir* 'cheese' or when *jakost* 'strength' was translated with *kost* 'bone'.

incorrect answers caused by similarity in meaning

In a group of words with similar meanings, some of the meanings were really close and the context where one could be used instead another could be anticipated (for example *prevrtati* 'to overthrow' – *vrtjeti* 'to turn'). Since none of these words were confirmed as the translational equivalents by bilingual speakers or dictionaries, they were considered to be the incorrect answers.

Incorrect answers with no connection between words
In some cases, it was not possible to define the source of an error. Even though, in some of these examples, it was possible to find a very loose connection between the tested word and the given translation, the assumption about the source of the error was not strong enough to list these examples in any of the previous groups. For example, the word *sačuvati* 'to save' was translated with *čuti* 'to hear'. Although the second word was made from the first word phoneme inventory, the differences were too large for the words to be considered synphones.

Connection between intralexical factors and language features

Given the small number of subjects and the small number of identical incorrect answers, the quantitative analysis of the different types of incorrect answers was not conducted. However, it is obvious that some types of errors are more frequent than others from the number of examples within the particular categories of (shared) identical incorrect answers (see Table 9.2).

Table 9.2 shows that the most frequent incorrect answers where those caused by the morphological features of the words, followed by errors produced due to the similarity in meaning of different words. Although the prevalence of this type of incorrect answers should be proven by more extensive and controlled research, it is assumed that the results given are caused by the type of test and specific language features. The reason why the informants answered with words that are similar in meaning with the target word and not with the correct translation equivalent might be due to the type of test administered. The translation test, with isolated words, did not provide the informants with any context that could have helped them in retrieving the correct meaning of the

Table 9.2 Frequency of different types of identical incorrect answers

Cause of incorrect answers	Number of faults
Morphological features	10
Phonological similarity	5
Similarity in meaning	5
No connection between words	2

target words. The high-frequency of errors caused by morphology, especially those where informants used the wrong word class, show that, in vocabulary acquisition, Croatian L2 learners pay more attentions to the meaning than to the form of the word. This result might motivate more research on the structure of the second language mental lexicon in Slavic languages.

Deceptive transparency shows that learners of Croatian as a second language are able to recognise various suffixes, which means that they are aware of derivational features of the words. Upon the learners' ability to perceive a string of phonemes as a morpheme in a word, it might be concluded that the learners are aware of orthographical rules in the Croatian language as well. Where does that awareness come from? It is supposed to come from the language structure itself. Namely, Croatian is a flective language, a language with a very rich inflectional as well as derivational morphology. The most frequent word formation is derivation and the affix inventory is extensive. It is estimated that, in Croatian, there are 771 suffixes and 77 prefixes (Babić, 2002). There is also a high degree of derivational synonymy and polysemy. Derivational synonymy describes the existence of different suffixes that have the same meaning, for example. *-ac, -ak, -telj* can all mean 'agent of an action'. Derivational polysemy means that one suffix can have more than one meaning, for example, *-ica* has the meaning 'small thing' as well as 'agent of an action of feminine gender'. Here it will not be discussed whether the latter is derivational polysemy (Barić et al., 1997: 306) or derivational homonymy (Babić et al., 1997 listed suffixes according to their form and meaning, not just a form). From the SLA point of view, both can be correct, it depends on how such suffixes are perceived by learners of a second language: as two different suffixes sharing the same form (homonymy) or one suffix with two different meanings (polysemy).

The second important feature of the Croatian language is a high degree of transparency between pronunciation and orthography. Croatian is considered to be a language with almost 1:1 ratio between pronunciation and orthography, which means that every phoneme is almost always written with the same grapheme and that the same grapheme is almost always pronounced in the same way, with the same sound. Although there are some restrictions (see Babić et al., 1996), the transparency is still very high. Also, double letters are not used in Croatian and, in general, there are no silent letters either. These features allow the learners to perceive the string of letters as a string of phonemes, to make a morpheme out of them and assign a meaning to it.

Implication of the Research

The present study is a start in the research of vocabulary acquisition in Croatian as a second language. The conclusions of the influential features of the Croatian language on vocabulary acquisition are still tentative. In order to prove it and to discover its importance and role in the acquisition of Croatian vocabulary, more systematic research has to be done, both in Croatian as a second language, as well as in Croatian as a first.

However, the research showed that the translation test can provide us with more information than just the knowledge of a particular word. The usage of a translation test can give us insight into L1–L2 word mapping and, by a comparison of answers given by learners of different L1, it is possible to investigate the source of the factors that affects second language vocabulary acquisition. Despite all its limitations, the results of the research conducted proved that some of the errors produced in a process of vocabulary acquisition are independent of the learner's first language, and are therefore considered to be intralexical.

The results of the research also suggest that the influence of language specific features on vocabulary acquisition is one of its most important factors and therefore worthy of researching. The strength of these features, as well as their relation with other processes in L2 vocabulary acquisition, is still a treasure waiting to be discovered. The results of all research, including those presented, are another step to furthering our knowledge of vocabulary acquisition in a second language and to motivate us to design new research and research instruments. More information and knowledge about the connection and influence of universal language features and language specific features on vocabulary acquisition will lead us to better understanding the complex processes of vocabulary acquisition in a second language. Once the secret to vocabulary acquisition in a second language is unlocked, it will be possible to predict learners' difficulties and design more successful syllabi and teaching materials.

References

Babić, S. (2002) *Tvorba riječi u hrvatskome književnom jeziku* [*Word Formation in Croatian Standard Language*]. Zagreb: HAZU i Nakladni zavod Globus.

Babić, S., Finka, Z. and Moguš, M. (1996[4]) *Hrvatski Pravopis* [*Ortography of the Croatian language*]. Zagreb: Školska knjiga.

Barić, E., Lončarić, M., Malić, D., Pavešić, S., Peti, M., Zečević, V. and Znika, M. (1997) *Hrvatska Gramatika* [*Croatian Grammar*]. Zagreb: Školska knjiga.

Blum, S. and Levenson, E.A. (1978) Universals in Lexicon simplification. *Language Learning* 28, 399–416.

Cvikić, L. (2004) Rječnik u drugome jeziku: vrste leksičkoga znanja i njihovo mjerenje s osvrtom na hrvatski [Vocabulary in second language: vocabulary knowledge and its assessment with reference to Croatian as L2]. Unpublished paper, Faculty of Philosophy, University of Zagreb.
Cvikić, L. and Bošnjak, M. (2004) Pogled u obilježja i probleme učenja riječi u hrvatskome kao nematerinskome jeziku [Insight in the features and problems of vocabulary learning in Croatian as second and foreign language]. In D. Stolac, N. Ivanetić, and B. Pritchard, (eds) *Suvremena kretanja u nastavi jezika Zbornik HDPL* (pp. 111–121). Zagreb-Rijeka: Graftrade.
Cvikić, L. and Jelaska, Z. (2005) Istraživanja hrvatskoga kao drugoga i stranoga jezika [Research on Croatian as a second and foreign language]. In Z. Jelaska, V. Blagus, M. Bošnjak, L. Cvikić, G. Hržica, I. Kusin, J. Novak-Milić and N. Opačić (eds) *Hrvatski kao drugi i strani jezik* (pp. 127–136). Zagreb: Hrvatska sveučilišna naklada.
Cvikić, L. and Kuvač, J. (2003) Orši neljepo piše. Poteškoće djece, mađarskih govornika, u učenju hrvatskoga jezika [Difficulties in children, Hungarian speakers, in Croatian language learning]. In I. Vodopija (ed.) *Zbornik sa stručno-znanstvenoga skupa Dijete i jezik* (pp. 55–66). Osijek: Sveučiliste J. J. Strossmayera i Visoka učiteljska škola.
Cvikić, L. and Kuvač, J. (2005) The acquisition of Croatian masculine noun morphology in Croatian as second language. In *Proceedings from VII. International Conference of Language Examination, Applied and Medicinal Linguistics*. Dunaújváros (in press).
Cvikić, L., Kuvač, J. and Dobravac, G. (2004) The acquisition of Croatian language for speakers of Roma languages. *14th EUROSLA Book of Abstracts*. San Sebastian, 70.
Globan, N. (2002) Odstupanja u početome učenju hrvatskoga kao stranoga jezika [Errors in learning Croatian as L2 at beginners level], Diploma paper, Faculty of Philosophy University of Zagreb.
Gulešić, M. (2003) Srodnost dvaju jezičnih sustava prednost ili/i nedostatak u usvajanju jezika [Affinity between Two linguistic systems – an advantage or/ and a disadvantage in foreign language acquisition]. In D. Stolac, N. Ivanetić and B. Pritchard (eds) *Psiholingvistika i kognitivna znanost u hrvatskoj primijenjenoj lingvistici* (pp. 289–302) Zagreb – Rijeka: Graftrade.
Haastrup, K. and Henriksen, B. (2001) The interrelationship between vocabulary acquisition theory and general SLA research. In S.H. Foster-Cohen and A. Nizegorodcev (eds) *EUROSLA Yearbook: Volume 1* (pp. 69–78). Amsterdam: John Benjamins Publishing Company.
Institut za hrvatski jezik i jezikoslovlje (2005) On WWW at: http://www.ihjj.hr/o-hr-jeziku.htm
Jelaska, Z. (2003) Hrvatski i višejezičnost [Croatian and plurilinguism]. In D. Pavličević Franić and M. Kovačević (eds) *Komunikacijska kompetencija u višejezičnoj sredini II* (pp. 106–126). Jastrebarsko/Zagreb: Naklada Slap i Sveučilište u Zagrebu.
Jelaska, Z. (2005) Hrvatski u višejezičnosti [Croatian in plurilingusm]. In Z. Jelaska, V. Blagus, M. Bošnjak, L. Cvikić, G. Hržica, I. Kusin, J. Novak-Milic and N. Opačić (eds) *Hrvatski kao drugi i strani jezik* (pp. 277–286). Zagreb: Hrvatska sveučilišna naklada.

Jelaska, Z. and Hržica, G. (2002) Poteškoće u učenju srodnih jezika: prevodjenje sa srpskoga na hrvatski [Learning of Cognate Languages: Translating Serbian into Croatian]. *Jezik* 3 (49) 91-104.

Jelaska, Z. and Kusin, I. (2005) Usustavljivanje naziva [Systematization of terminology] In Z. Jelaska, V. Blagus, M. Bošnjak, L. Cvikić, G. Hržica, I. Kusin, J. Novak-Milić and N. Opačić (eds) *Hrvatski kao drugi i strani jezik* (pp. 49-64). Zagreb: Hrvatska sveučilišna naklada.

Kuvač, J. and Cvikić, L. (2004.) Hungarian kids and Croatian language. *Papers from 6th International Conference of Language Examination and Applied and Medicinal Linguistics*, 140-148.

Laufer, B. (1991) Some properties of the foreign language learner's lexicon as evidenced by lexical confusions. *IRAL: International Review of Applied Linguistics in Language Teaching*, 29(4).

Laufer, B. (1997) What's in a word that makes it hard or easy? Intralexical factors affecting the difficulty of vocabulary acquisition? In N. Schmitt and M. McCarthy (eds) *Vocabulary: Description, Acquisition and Pedagogy* (pp. 140-155). Cambridge: Cambridge University Press.

Laufer, B. (1997) The lexical plight in second language reading: Words you don't know, words you think you know and words you can't guess. In J. Coady and T. Huckin (eds) *Second Language Vocabulary Acquisition: A Rationale for Pedagogy* (pp. 20-34). Cambridge: Cambridge University Press.

Laufer-Dvorkin, B. (1991) *Similar Lexical Forms in Interlanguage*. Tuebingen: Gunter Narr Verlag.

Laufer, B. and Nation, P. (1999) A vocabulary- size test of controlled productive ability. *Language Testing* 16 (1), 33-51.

McCarty, M. and Carter, R. (1997) Written and spoken vocabulary. In N. Schmitt and M. McCarthy (eds) *Vocabulary: Description, Acquisition and Pedagogy* (pp. 20-40). Cambridge: Cambridge University Press.

Meara, P. (1997) Towards a new approach to modelling vocabulary acquisition. In N. Schmitt and M. McCarthy (eds) *Vocabulary: Description, Acquisition and Pedagogy* (pp. 109-122). Cambridge: Cambridge University Press.

Meara, P. (2005) Reactivating dormant vocabulary. In S.H. Foster-Cohen, M. del Pilar Garcia-Mayo and J. Cenoz (eds) *EUROSLA Yearbook: Volume 5*. (pp. 269-280). Amsterdam: John Benjamins Publishing Company.

Meara, P. and Hilton, H. (2005) Vocabulary Acquisition Research Group Archive VARGA: On WWW at: http://www.swan.ac.uk/cals/calsres/varga/

Melka, F. (1997) Receptive vs. productive aspects of vocabulary. In N. Schmitt and M. McCarthy (eds) *Vocabulary: Description, Acquisition and Pedagogy*. Cambridge: Cambridge University Press.

Mondria, J.-A. and Wiersma, B. (2004) Receptive, productive, and receptive + productive L2 vocabulary learning: What difference does it make? In P. Bogaards and B. Laufer (eds) *Vocabulary in a Second Language* (pp. 79-101). Amsterdam/Philadelphia: John Benjamins.

Nation, I.S.P. and Waring, R. (1997) Vocabulary size, text coverage and word lists. In Schmitt N. and M. McCarthy (eds) *Vocabulary: Description, Acquisition and Pedagogy* (pp. 6-20). Cambridge: Cambridge University Press.

Nation, I.S.P. (2001) *Learning Vocabulary in Another Language*. Cambridge: Cambridge University Press.

Novak, J. (2002) Učenje i usvajanje osnovnih glagolskih oblika u hrvatskome kao stranome i drugome jeziku [The acquisition of basic verbal forms in Croatian as a second and foreign language]. MA thesis, Faculty of Philosophy University of Zagreb.

Novak, J. (2002a) Učenje glagolskih oblika u hrvatskome kao stranome jeziku [The acquisition of verbal forms in Croatian as a foreign language]. *Suvremena lingvistika* 53–54, 1–2, 85–101.

Novak, J. (2002b) Neke morfoloske pogreške 'stranaca' kod učenja hrvatskoga kao drugoga ili stranoga jezika [Some morphological errors in Croatian as a second or foreign language]. In N. Ivanetić, B. Pritchard and D. Stolac (eds) *Primijenjena Lingvistika u Hrvatskoj – Izazovi na početku XXI. Stoljeća* (pp. 373–401). Zagreb-Rijeka: Graftrade.

Read, J. (2000) *Assessing Vocabulary*. Cambridge: Cambridge University Press.

Schmitt, N. (1997) Vocabulary learning strategies. In N. Schmitt and M. McCarthy (eds) *Vocabulary: Description, Acquisition and Pedagogy* (pp. 199–228). Cambridge: Cambridge University Press.

Schmitt, N. and McCarthy, M. (1997) (eds) *Vocabulary: Description, Acquisition and Pedagogy*. Cambridge: Cambridge University Press.

Singleton, D. (2000) *Language and the Lexicon*. London: Arnold.

Singleton, D. (1999) *Exploring the Second Language Mental Lexicon*. Cambridge: Cambridge University Press.

Swan, M. (1997) The influence of a mother tongue on second language vocabulary acquisition and use. In N. Schmitt and M. McCarthy (eds) *Vocabulary: Description, Acquisition and Pedagogy* (pp. 156–181). Cambridge: Cambridge University Press.

Težak, S. and Babić, S. (2001) *Gramatika Hrvatskoga Jezika* [Grammar of the Croatian language]. Zagreb: Školska knjiga.

Chapter 10
Analysing L2 Lexical Processes Via C Test

ZSOLT LENGYEL, JUDIT NAVRACSICS and ANIKÓ SZILÁGYI

This study analyses some issues concerning word class identification in L2 lexical processes, based on data collected with the help of the cloze procedure. In the experiment, native speakers of Hungarian were expected to reconstruct English and German texts with varying deletion frequencies.

General Features of the Experiment

Young adult native speakers of Hungarian participated in the experiment (see section titled 'The Hungarian experiment: data analysis and results') carried out as an examination task of the Pannon Language Examination System. Pannon Language Examination measures three levels (B1, B2 and C1) of the language command of the Common European Framework. The examinations consist of a written and an oral part. One of the tasks of the written examination is a gap filling task, that is, the reconstruction of a text prepared according to the cloze procedure. The differences between the levels are reached partly with the differences in the difficulty of texts, partly with the deletion frequency. Every eighth, seventh and sixth words were omitted at levels B1, B2 and C1, respectively. Only authentic texts were used in the test.

Language Typological Remarks

Before we analyse the results of the experiment, it is necessary to make a few language typological (morphological and syntactic) remarks concerning the differences between the agglutinating Hungarian and the inflecting English and German languages.

(1) Hungarian is an agglutinating language with a rich system of suffixes that create an organic unit with the stem in every word class: *házban* (ház + ban: *in house* [house in], *in dem Haus* [Haus in]).

(2) Due to its agglutinating nature, there is a dominance of synthetic structures in Hungarian: *szeretlek* (szeret + l + ek; *love + you + I*, *liebe + dich + ich*). The majority of tense, aspect and modal meanings are also similarly expressed; the synthetic nature characterises each word class.

(3) There might be significant differences, even in the case of word classes, that can be considered as identical. There are definite and indefinite articles in English, Hungarian and German. The more important semantic and pragmatic features are approximately identical (topic – comment, and so on). However, the Hungarian article can acquire an inflection (in this, it is similar to German) but does not refer to the gender of the noun (whereby it is similar to English), because there is no grammatical gender in Hungarian.

(4) From the perspective of language typology, two types of word order can be differentiated: adjunct before head (object before verb, adjective before noun, genitive before noun, postposition) and head before adjunct (object after verb, adjective after noun, genitive after noun, preposition), that is, there are head-final and head-initial languages. The above-mentioned arrangement is not valid without exception, though. English is a rather (German to a lesser degree) head-initial language, while Hungarian is rather head-final. Based on the sequence of the head and the modified elements in the structure of the phrase, a distinction between right and left branching can be made. English and German branch more to the left while Hungarian is a somewhat right-branching language.

(5) English is a configurative language, while Hungarian is less so. Therefore, in Hungarian local and in English sequential (holistic) decisions can be made in the process of sentence comprehension, as Hungarian suffixes directly refer to the syntactic function of the noun, whereas in English, the syntactic function can often only be decided on the basis of a sequence consisting of several words. Configurative languages have a rather fixed word order; they use empty pronouns (*It rains; Es regnet*). In this respect, German takes up an intermediary position with many more restrictions on word order than Hungarian.

Cloze Procedure

Cloze procedure was worked out by Taylor (1953), who originally created it as a device for measuring the readability of a text. Its starting point is one of the propositions of Gestalt psychology: a familiar but not fully completed pattern can be perceived and interpreted as a whole. There are three basic factors involved in the completion of the missing parts. One of them relates to Osgood's disposition theory, according to which human beings endeavour to attain perception in a holistic way. The other two propose that on the one hand, our conceptions and, on the other, our encyclopaedic knowledge allow for the completion of linguistically incomplete patterns, that is, the reconstruction of the whole context. According to connectionism, the ability to establish a context means the recognition of the changing frequency with which the given language pattern is attached to a greater linguistic combination or scheme.

The essence of the cloze procedure is that words are deleted from the given written/oral text with a given regular frequency. The subjects of the experiment are expected to fill in the gaps with the most suitable word (the list of words is sometimes, but not always, provided). The cloze procedure differs from sentence-level gap-filling insomuch that it measures the ability to apply contextual information, which means that it necessitates not only grammatical but also semantic, pragmatic and text linguistic abilities.

Aborn *et al.* (1959) examined the effect of various characteristics of the context (length, distribution, structure and word class) and their findings suggest that word class greatly influences predictability: function words (articles, prepositions, and so on) are easier to guess than adjectives; pronouns are easier to guess than nouns. The (increasing) order of the predictability of word classes among native speakers of English is as follows: adjective, noun, adverb, verb, pronoun and function word. Predictability is in inverse relation to the size of the word class. The more members a word class possesses, the more difficult it is to guess a certain element and vice versa. A bilateral context has an advantage over a unilateral one. If the context (that is, the length of the sentence) is increased, it is generally a helping factor, though not always. There are no great differences between the results in a deletion ratio of 11–25 words, but a deletion frequency of 5–10 words results in serious differences.

Salzinger *et al.* (1962) examined the effect of various deletion ratios among words of the same word class. Their results indicate that the semantic and grammatical factors can, in certain cases, be more easily separated than in others. The grammatically accurate fill-ins (identical word class) are more often correct than the ones that are accurate both grammatically and semantically (identical word class and lexical identity), which suggests that the subjects attend more to grammatical restrictions than to semantic ones.

Fillenbaum *et al.* (1963) examined the role of grammar and semantics in predictability, using texts of varying deletion frequencies (2–6). The increase of the deletion rate results in a larger number of grammatically and semantically accurate fill-ins, but the increase is not proportional (there is a jump of between 2 and 3). The values of correct word class are higher than those of correct word class and correct lexical item, so grammatical identification is easier than the semantic one. Adjectives are easy to identify as a word class, but the access of a particular member of this class is difficult. The grammatical and semantic identification of pronouns and function words is better than that of nouns and verbs. Being a very heterogeneous word class, adverbs are difficult to recognise independently of the deletion rate. Nouns, pronouns, conjunctions and prepositions are easiest to identify. There is little difference in the correct guess of word classes with identical syntactic functions (for example, nouns and pronouns) from a grammatical point of view. However, from the semantic point of view, the correct guess appears to be more difficult in relation to pronouns. The predictability of elements within word classes is variable: there are nouns, verbs, and so on, that are more or less easy to guess. Thus, to guess a word class is not an absolute value, as the very same word might behave differently, depending on the deletion frequency.

As for each word class, there is an optimal microcontext which increases the probability of correct guessing. This microcontext is the relative frequency of the sequential dependencies with which a word class can occur with other words. If, for example, the deleted element is a noun, predictability will be high if the directly preceding element is an adjective. In many languages, it is easy to guess that the deleted element is an adjective if the element is between an article and a noun. The optimal microcontext is characterised by maximum grammatical restrictions: thus identification is easy. Optimal microcontext is different according to word class.

The grammatical restrictions of the context are dependent on the formal sequential features of the immediate linguistic environment. Their recognition gives little help with the selection of the specific element of the class (semantic restriction). The specific element is more sensitive to the wider context (topic, semantic content of near or distant words, and number of elements of the given class). Function words are hardly dependent on the topic: they are more dependent on their immediate environment, and thus they are relatively easy to recognise.

Burke and Schiavetti (1975) compared isolated sentences and coherent texts, but found no significant differences regarding correct guessing: consequently, context has a moderate cumulative impact. In both situations, a context of 6–10 words was found to be the maximum of predictability. Alderson (1979) examined the effect of deletion frequency in texts with varying difficulty. He came to the conclusion that the degree of difficulty largely influenced the predictability of words even with the same deletion frequency.

From the 1970s onwards, the cloze procedure was used to measure foreign language command. According to Oller (1980), the results gained in the cloze procedure correlate highly with other test results. However, the cloze test is, on the one hand, more sensitive but, on the other, it also reflects pragmatic knowledge. The cloze procedure was also applied among aphasics (Fillenbaum & Jones, 1962).

The Hungarian Experiment: Data Analysis and Results

The subjects were 18 to 30-year-old native speakers of Hungarian. Table 10.1. shows the number of participants at each level.

The participants were motivated, since the task was the completion of a language examination test that may have resulted in various benefits for them. No pre-test was used to assess the candidates' foreign language knowledge: being aware of the requirements of each level, the candidates decided which level they wanted to enter for. The participants were familiar with the character of the task: at level B1 every eighth, at B2 every seventh and at C1 every sixth word was deleted – a total of 20 deleted words in each case. The length of the texts was determined by the product of the deletion frequency (eighth, seventh and sixth) and the 20 deletions. The text difficulty increased from level to level. The participants were given 30 minutes to complete the task. The words to be filled in were listed in alphabetical order.

Table 10.1 The number of participants at different levels

	B1	B2	C1	Total
English	375	1284	125	1784
German	191	551	26	768

Predictability is a multifactoral process involving syntactic operations, grammar, semantics and pragmatics of the narrower and broader context, turn-taking and the communication caesura, and so on. Our experiment is the first to analyse the English and German text comprehension of native speakers of Hungarian based on the cloze procedure: therefore, our analysis is restricted to the predictability of word classes. First the English, then the German data will be presented, followed by a data comparison. Linguistic examples will only be provided in cases that significantly worsen or improve the predictability of the particular word class (the word to be guessed is typed in bold, followed by the percentage of correct guesses in parantheses).

Results of the English texts

Level B1 (N = 375 participants)

Nouns ($N = 28$): 55.90%. The left-branching structure is difficult: *fighting* **sailor** (25.58) *England has ever known*. In Hungarian the use of just a Christian name for historical figures is unusual: **Horatio** (44) *was treated kindly*.

Verbs ($N = 17$): 56.68%. Irregular forms are difficult: *spoke, learnt, began, found, became, thought*. The recognition of the Past Perfect is difficult for Hungarians in itself, as there is no compound way of expressing a past activity in Hungarian. From the point of view of Hungarian thinking, it is considered to be a discontinuous morpheme. It gets even more complicated once an additional word is inserted within the structure: *mother had always* **wanted** (39%).

Modal Verbs ($N = 14$): 47.82%. If the verb phrase contains no reference to the accusative meaning, it results in more difficult identification: *She* **was** (19%) *helping a family*. Another difficulty is unusual word order in Hungarian: **Are** (35.65%) *all teachers very poor*.

Adjectives ($N = 20$): 58.23%. Adjectives seem to be easier to identify as elements of predicative structures than attributes.

Adverbs ($N = 9$): 60.75%. Due to the subject-verb order, in Hungarian, adverbs cannot succeed verbs: *she went* **back** (30%) *home*.

Pronouns ($N = 25$): 64.79%. Personal pronouns are the easiest to guess.

Prepositions ($N = 15$): 51.07%. Prepositions *in, of, with* and *to* are easy to guess in their 'usual' references (direction, time, and so on) as opposed to **around** (20%). In longer and left-branching sentences, prepositions are difficult to guess. Idiomatic expressions that differ in form in the two languages are also difficult: **in** (19%) *the end* (would be *on the end* in Hungarian).

Articles (*N* = 15): 68.51%. Articles introducing Noun Phrase groups are easy: **a** (81%) *little girl*. Unlike in English, transitivity is morphologically marked in the Hungarian verb, thus it is more difficult if the reference to the transitive meaning in English is 'missing': *mother took* **the** *(40%) little girl*.

Conjunctions (*N* = 8): 60.64%. The conjunction expressing co-ordination (*and*) is easy while the conditional conjunction (*if*) is more difficult.

Level B2 (N = 1284 participants)

Nouns (*N* = 33): 74.10%. A word conveying special information at the beginning of the text (first occurrence) causes difficulty.

Verbs (*N* = 11): 80.18%. Irregular past causes no difficulty at level B2; the lower identification value can be attributed to lexico-semantic reasons (*combines, specified, treated*).

Modal Verbs (*N* = 10): 82.71%.

Adjectives (*N* = 16): 56.61%. Lexical identification is difficult in long sentences: *The size may be* **intimidating** *(65.77%) but it is an exciting and* **manageable** *(19.38%) destination – and is emerging as a* **favoured** *(42.26%) location for the British traveller*.

Adverbs (*N* = 10): 60.16%. Lexical identification is difficult in long sentences: **Between** *(87,05%) them, Elizabeth and the Cecils handled* **Parliament** *(19%) carefully and tactfully and Parliament was* **now** *(6.61%) very strong and influential*.

Pronouns (*N* = 15): 61.71%. Anaphoric reference is difficult: *And then* **it** *(14.28%) hit me*, as well as those structures in which no pronoun is used in Hungarian: *However, she knew* **she** *(19%) had to win Parliament's co-operation*.

Preposition (*N* = 16): 65.33%. Rarely used meanings can cause difficulties: *Elizabeth was,* **by** *(27.54%) nature*.

Articles (*N* = 20): 73.80%. Articles are easy to recognise when they lead in nominal groups: *and* **the** *(89.69%) football is not bad*.

Conjunctions (*N* = 3): 70.32%. Co-ordinating conjunctions are easier, while conjunctions expressing logical functions (*because*) are more difficult.

Level C1 (N = 125 participants)

Nouns (*N* = 67): 73.10%. Long sentences are also difficult at C1 level: *The crude awfulness of* **the** *(55.81%) Ossuaire reminds visitors that Verdun was* **was** *(88.37%) not simply a battle of* **extermination** *(25.58%) but, even as it was* **fought** *(11.62%) was recognised as the emotional* **battle** *(9.3%) for the*

survival of France. Left-branching structures can also provide difficulties: **people** (31.42%) *at high risk of Type 2 diabetes*.
Verbs (*N* = 25): 79.89%.
Modal Verbs (*N* = 20): 85.77%. In Hungarian, the predicate is singular even in the case of a number larger than one: *48 million people – 7.8% of the population –* **are** *(31.42%) living with it*.
Adjectives (*N* = 37): 71.33%.
Adverbs (*N* = 26): 71.14%. Some adverbs that belong to the Verb-preposition in English function as postpositions belonging to the noun in Hungarian. It creates confusion for the learner: *the fog coming* **off** *(10%) the river; they went* **over** *(10%) the edge*. Left-branching is difficult: *30 million people* **worldwide** *(17.14%); you wouldn't* **need** *(100%) to expend so much energy* **just** *(16.66%) keeping warm*.
Pronouns (*N* = 18): 79.95%.
Prepositions (*N* = 39): 76.49%.
Articles (*N* = 20): 83.92%.
Conjunctions (*N* = 21): 80.81%.
The identification rates of content and function words.
Although the deletion frequency decreases from level to level, correct identification increases from level to level (Figure 10.1). The difference between levels B1 and B2 is caused by the identification of content words (nouns, verbs and modals), between B2 and C1 in the identification of function words (pronouns, prepositions, articles and conjunctions).

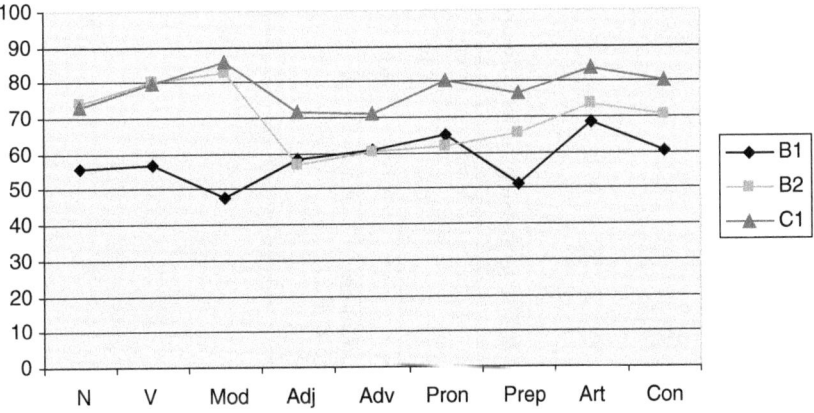

Figure 10.1 The identification rates of content and function words.

Table 10.2 The increasing order of word class identification

	Mod	Prep	N	V	Adj	Con	Adv	Pron	Art
B1	Adj	Adv	Pron	Prep	Con	Art	N	V	Mod
B2	Adv	Adj	N	Prep	V	Pron	Con	Art	Mod
C1	Adj	N	Adv	V	Pron	Function word			
Native speakers (Aborn et al., 1959)									

The increasing order of the word class identification
The difference between the highest and lowest identification rates are 20.69% at B1, 26.1% at B2 and 14.63% at C1 level (Table 10.2). At B1 level, function words yielded a better result: thus, in the case of beginners, grammatical knowledge exceeds lexical knowledge. It is explained by the fact that in English, the number of lexical items exceeds that of grammatical entities. Consequently, in a given period of learning, from fewer grammatical entities more can be acquired than from the more numerous semantic items. At level B2, the identification of content words is better. It can be suggested that in the achievement of intermediate level language proficiency, the acquisition of content words follows the geometrical sum, while that of function words relates to the arithmetical sum. The smallest difference occurs at level C1 (14.63%), which meets our expectations, proving that semantic and grammatical knowledge become more and more balanced. The low identification values of adjectives and adverbs suggest that advanced-level language proficiency more and more resembles the knowledge of native speakers (adjectives and adverbs are the word classes most difficult to recognise for native speakers of English). With the improvement of language proficiency, the accuracy of identification approaches more and more that of native speakers.

Results of the German texts

Level B1 (N = 191 participants)

Nouns ($N = 35$): 50.4%. The identical morphological and syntactic environment aids in identification: *einige Hefte,* **Schminksachen** (90%), *leere Tüten.* Identification is weak in idioms: *auf alle* **Fälle** (17%). Left-branching also yields weak results: *mit* **Ausstellungen** (20%) *aktueller Künstler.*

Verbs ($N = 11$): 62.1%. The best results could be seen with subject-verb word order, which is similar to Hungarian. Identification is low if the verb is at the end of the sentence: *die ich mit einer netten, spanischen Studienkollegin* **teile** (25%) the verb *werden* is used as a main verb: *Ich will später einmal genauso gut* **werden** (33%), and *sein* is used as a copula: *Eine besondere Rarität* **ist** (40%) (there is no verbal predicate in the Hungarian equivalent of this sentence).

Modal Verbs ($N = 1$): 31.5%.

Adjectives ($N = 7$): 55.6%. Identification as part of coordinated constituents is high: *die größte und* **schönste** (86%): the preceding adjective and the conjunction have a high predictive power.

Adverbs ($N = 7$): 44.7%. Identifying the structure *geht jeder Vierte* **regelmäßig** (11%) *an die Uni* yielded the weakest results, the structure **Selten** (50%) *habe ich* yielded the best results due to its emphatic position.

Pronouns ($N = 10$): 57.2%. The identification of *ich* with the same function as in Hungarian is the highest (92.6%). The identification of reflexive and relative pronouns causes difficulties: *bereite ich* **mir** (35%); *einer Wohnung,* **die** (13%) *ich*.

Prepositions ($N = 14$): 55.5%. Geographical names without articles are easy to guess: **aus** (88%) *Brasilien;* **in** (88%) *Dresden* because Hungarian and German show a full structural identity. The idiomatic **zum** (89%) *Beispiel* is also successfully identified.

Articles ($N = 10$): 49.9%. Definite articles are easier to guess than indefinite articles: *auf* **der** (68%) *Welt*. Indefinite articles occur in noun-pronoun groups with a branching different than in Hungarian: **eines** (19%) *der größten Universitätsmuseen; die Schüler* **einer** (24%) *zweisprachigen Klasse* and this may be the cause of the differences in guessing the two types of articles.

Conjunctions ($N = 8$): 62.2%. It is easiest to guess the word *und* (77.75%) connecting coordinated phrases: *seit vielen Jahrhunderten* **und** (46%) *überall auf der Erde*.

Level B2 (N = 551 participants)

Nouns ($N = 41$): 67.7%. Genitive is structurally different from Hungarian, and is therefore difficult: *der begehrte Preis der* **Fernuniversität** (38%); attributive structures including more than one elements are also difficult: *auf der dem* **Regen** (32%) *abgewandten Seite*.

Verbs ($N = 12$): 72.2%. At level B2, the word order does not influence the identification of verbs while discourse-level problems do: so, for example, predicates with different tenses within a sentence: *sind die Filmautoren rund um den Globus gereist und* **präsentieren** (45%); or grammatico-semantic entities different from Hungarian may cause difficulties: *Tauchtipps, Wissenswertes über Land und Leute, Naturschutz* **sind** (14%) *Themen* (there is no plural copula in Hungarian).

Model Verbs ($N = 5$): 68.6%.

Adjectives ($N = 16$): 67.9%. Adjectives with an attributive function are easy to guess; suffixes help this process: *mit* **kaltem** (88%) *Leitungswasser*. Adjectives with a predicative function are difficult to guess: *ist* **möglich** (41%), and the identification of adjectives lacking syntactic support in comparative and superlative forms is even weaker: *am* **besten** (49%); *der* **leichtere** (59%) *Weg*.

Adverbs (*N* = 11): 50.3%. It is easy to guess the constituents of frequent, lexicalised structures: *ein* **Jahr** *(69%)* **lang**; whereas others are more difficult to retrieve: *kann* **nur** *(38%) derjenige*.

Pronouns (*N* = 8): 65.3%. The identification of personal pronouns with a lexico-grammatical function similar to Hungarian is good: **Er** (93%) *würde gern*. The identification of the indefinite pronoun *man* depends on the syntactic position: it is easier to guess in subordination than in a relative clause: *dass* **man** *(71%) es kaum überblicken kann*; or *die* **man** *(64%) schwerelos erkunden kann*. The identification of possessive pronouns unknown in Hungarian is difficult: *bei* **seinem** *(27%) Verlauf*.

Prepositions (*N* = 26): 58.9%. It is easier to guess prepositions with a concrete (local) meaning than those with a more abstract meaning: **in** (82%) *der Welt*; **An** (86%) *fast jeder Ecke*; or *versteht sich* **als** (46%). The identification of semantically similar but lexically different idioms is weak: **zum** (25%) *größten Teil*.

Articles (*N* = 8): 73.4%. Identifying an article at the beginning of a sentence is the easiest: **Der** (94%) *Körper kann ansonsten*.

Conjunctions (*N* = 5): 82%. The identification of conjunctions at the beginning of sentences or clauses is the easiest: *Besonders wichtig ist,* **dass** (100%) *man*; the retrieval of *und* connecting clauses is weaker: *Geschichten* **und** *(77%) Geheimnisse*.

C1 (N = 26 participants)

Nouns (*N* = 54): 69.5%. It is difficult to guess nouns in noun-pronoun groups that are structurally highly different from Hungarian: *man wollte nicht der* **Gewalt** *(33%) weichen*; and nouns at the end of determiner groups: *mit der Gesellschaftstruktur, Kommunikationstheorie und der* **Erforschung** *(17%) der Lebensbedingungen*. The guessing of nouns in more or less lexicalised structures is successful: *zwischen* **Ost** *(90%) und West; in diesem* **Jahr** *(83%)*. It is easy to guess names in headlines: *der ermordeten Außenministerin Anna* **Lindh** *(100%) gedacht*. The degree of familiarity is an influencing factor: *wird* **Heiner** *(90%) Müller im sächsischen Eppendorf*; **Habermas** *(50%) erhält die Ehrung als zweiter Deutscher*.

Verbs (*N* = 20): 66.1%. There is no difference in guessing tenses, however, it is difficult to retrieve the verb *werden* as main verb: *Er ist unter anderem bereits Träger . . .* **geworden** *(17%)*; the identification of subjunctive forms is good: *da die Polizei dazu nicht bereit gewesen* **sei** *(83%)*.

Modal Verbs (*N* = 9): 81.3%.

Adjectives (*N* = 14): 51.5%. Adjectives are easier to guess as attributes of the subject than as attributes of prepositional phrases: *ein* **wirksames** *(67%) Heilmittel*; or *im* **materiellen** *(17%) und geistigen Sinne*.

Adverbs ($N = 9$): 52.5%. The worst results could be seen in front of nouns without articles: *noch* **fast** (0%) *Preisstabilität in Deutschland herrschte*; and in appositional positions: *zum technischen Fortschritt von* **heute** (17%) as these structures are unknown in Hungarian.

Pronouns ($N = 7$): 63.3%. The correct guess of personal pronouns (in different cases) is better than those of reflexive pronouns: *sieht* **es** (100%) *seit 2001 … aus; einer von* **ihnen** (83%) *sagte*; or *befasste* **sich** (33%) *während seiner Laufbahn*.

Prepositions ($N = 20$): 50.3%. It is easy to guess prepositions with concrete meanings: *abends* **im** (100%) *Dunkeln nach Hause kommen*. A longer distance from the noun results in weak identification: **für** (0%) *die eigenen vier Wände geworben*.

Articles ($N = 21$): 64.5%. The correct retrieval of indefinite articles (70.8%) is better than that of definite articles (58.2%). The retrieval of articles in genitive structures is the weakest: *die Inflation* **der** (0%) *letzten Jahre; als* **einer** (33%) *der einflussreichsten Deutschen*. Identification is good in lexicalised structures: *in* **den** (100%) *nächsten Jahren*.

Conjunctions ($N = 8$): 61%. It is easier to guess conjunctions if they connect constituents: *Banken* **und** (100%) *Konjunkturforscher*; than if they connect clauses: *wird oft unterschätzt* **und** (67%) *ist demnach*.

The identification rates of content and functions words

The lowest identification rates are reached at level B1 (Figure 10.2), despite the lower deletion frequency, with the exception of adverbs,

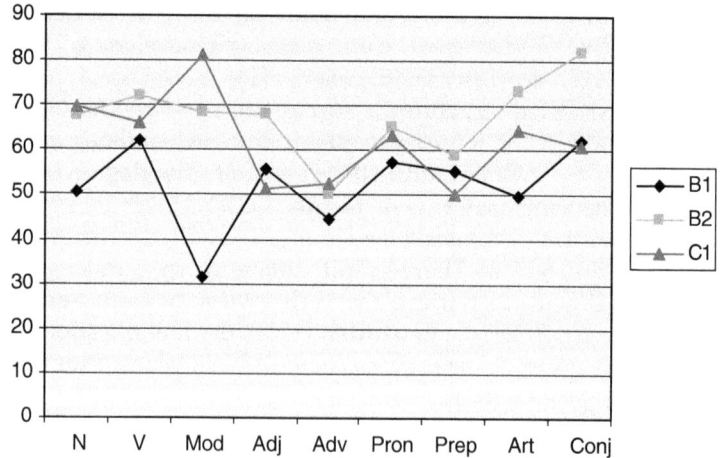

Figure 10.2 The identification rates of content and function words.

pronouns and prepositions. In the case of adverbs, there are no big differences between the three levels. In the cases of pronouns and prepositions the highest results are reached by candidates at Level B2.

At level B1, the correct retrieval of each word class falls into the 50–60% zone, with the exception of modals and adverbs: there is no major difference between the identification of function or content words. This balance – with an increase to 60–75% – characterises level B2 (except for the lowest adverbs and the highest conjunctions). At level C1, the identification of content words is better than that of function words (except for the low rates of adjectives and adverbs). The identification rates recur at the two lower levels, indicating that German tends to distribute grammatical 'load' more proportionally and native speakers of Hungarian are sensitive to this.

The identification rates at levels B2 and C1 are either very similar (nouns, adverbs and pronouns), or level B2 candidates reach better results (verbs, adjectives, prepositions, articles and conjunctions). Two explanations might be given for this fact: candidates may have misjudged their language proficiency and therefore reached a worse result in more difficult texts with higher deletion frequency (that is, candidates' misjudgement of required knowledge); the other explanation may have a more linguistic reason: the German language itself creates a disproportionately more difficult situation in a more difficult text with higher deletion frequency even in the case of better language proficiency.

In accordance with our prior expectations, smaller or greater differences between levels B1 and B2 can be observed, but always in favour of level B2. It is higher in the case of nouns, modals, articles and conjunctions and smaller in the case of verbs, adjectives, adverbs, pronouns and prepositions.

The increasing order of word class identification

The difference between the highest and lowest identification rates is 30.7% at level B1 (Table 10.3), 31.7% at B2 and 31% at C1. At level B2, the increase is proportionate from adverbs to (50.3%) articles (73.4%), whereas conjunctions seem to yield outstanding results (82%). At level

Table 10.3 The increasing order of word class identifications

B1	Mod	Adv	Art	N	Prep	Adj	Pron	V	Con
B2	Adv	Prep	Pron	N	Adj	Mod	V	Art	Con
C1	Prep	Adj	Adv	Con	Pron	Art	V	N	Mod

C1, the increase is proportionate from prepositions (50.3%) to nouns (69.5%), and modals (81.3%) yield outstanding results. If we exclude the extreme values, the difference is 23.1% and 19.2% at levels B2 and C1, respectively. At level B1, if we ignore the last result (conjunctions 62.2%), it does not change the arrangement since the preceding candidate reached verbs 62.1%. As our common experience dictates, the difference in the correct identification of word classes slightly decreases with the improvement in language proficiency due to balanced language command.

Taking all three levels into consideration, the identification of some word classes is easier whereas that of others it is more difficult. Conjunctions can be easily guessed within both noun-pronoun and verb-pronoun, between preposition-subject; thus linguistic (structural) caesura helps identification. Adverbs are the most difficult to guess. They have no syntactic-morphological markers and there are only a few sequential (order) restrictions that might predict their obligatory appearance. Preposition and adjectives – although at varying degrees for each level – are word classes difficult to guess, though formal morphological, sometimes sequential (order) markers promote correct identification. Language typological considerations might serve as an explanation, especially in the case of prepositions: the discontinuous morpheme is not used in Hungarian. Verbs, nouns, articles and pronouns yielded average or good identification results.

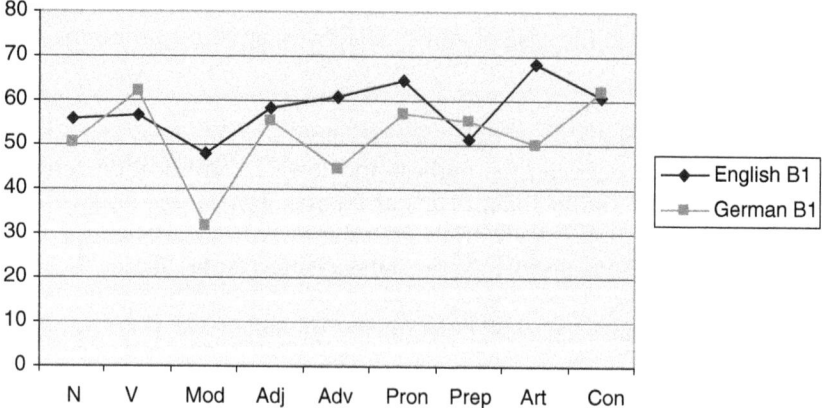

Figure 10.3 A comparison of the identification of English and German word classes (B1).

The mean identification order is as follows: Con, V, Art, N, Pron, Mod, Adj, Prep, Adv.

A comparison of the identification of English and German word classes at each level

Level B1

There is a significant difference between modals, adverbs and articles: they are more difficult in German than in English (Figure 10.3).

Level B2

Compared to the previous level, the differences seem to decrease. German modals and adverbs are still more difficult than the English ones (Figure 10.4).

Level C1

The identification rates in the English tests are higher for each word class: sometimes to a larger, sometimes to a smaller extent (Figure 10.5).

The order of identification

In summary, the (increasing) order of identification for the two languages is: Adv, Prep, Adj, N, Pron, Mod, V, Art, Con (Table 10.4).

Summary

Foreign language (English and German in this instance) lexical processes of native speakers of Hungarian were analysed via the C-test,

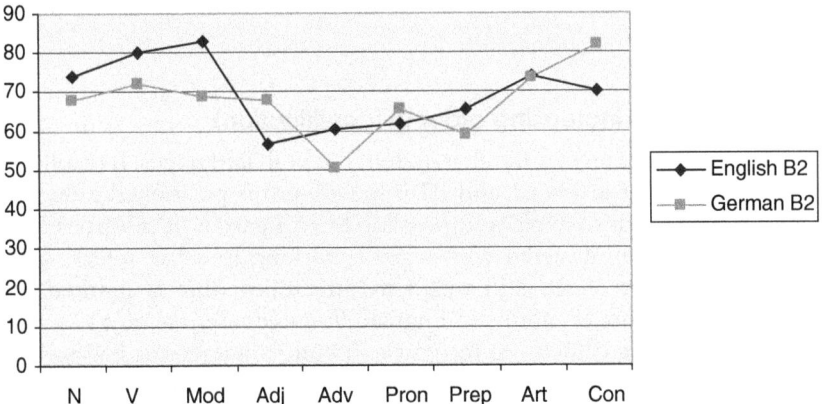

Figure 10.4 A comparison of the identification of English and German word classes (B2).

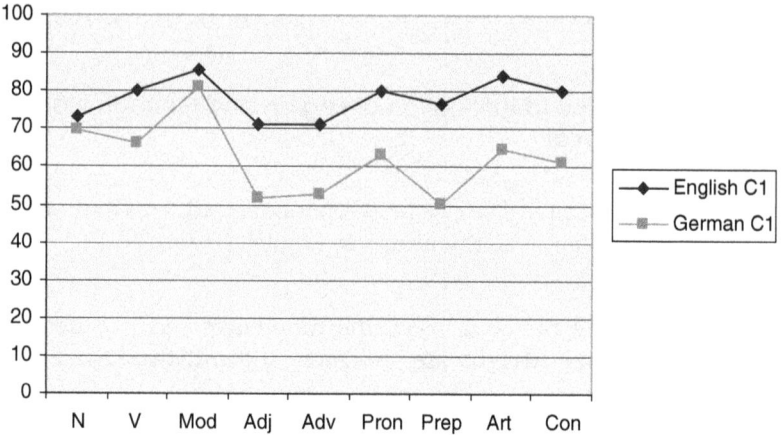

Figure 10.5 A comparison of the identification of English and German word classes (C1).

focussing on word class identification. The results were expected to improve despite the decrease in deletion frequency. Considering the data of other areas of performance, the improvement was not expected to be linear. Among aphasics, despite the loss of, for example: nouns, certain nominal groups (for example, the names of the days of the week) might remain intact; and it is frequently observed in child language that children are able to utter a certain sound in one word, although they are unable to utter it in another word.

Word classes (in increasing order of identification)

Adverbs are the most difficult to identify in both languages. It results in difficulties both at levels B1 and B2 if the adverb is positioned after the verb – a word order which is impossible in Hungarian. It disappears at level C1. However, adverbs with a path marking function referring to nouns rather than verbs still result in difficulties (this is marked on verbs in Hungarian, on nouns in English: *they went over the edge*.)

Prepositions are difficult to recognise in both languages. It is easier to guess prepositions with more general spatial and temporal meanings, whereas more abstract meanings are difficult, even at level B2. Idiomatic phrases differing from the first language are difficult, especially for beginners: *in the end, auf alle Fälle*. Prepositions located far from the noun can

Analysing L2 Lexical Processes Via C Test

Table 10.4 The order of identification at all levels in both languages

English B1	Mod	Prep	N	V	Adj	Con	Adv	Pron	Art
German B1	Mod	Adv	Art	N	Prep	Adj	Pron	V	Con
English B2	Adj	Adv	Pron	Prep	Con	Art	N	V	Mod
German B2	Adv	Prep	Pron	N	Adj	Mod	V	Art	Con
English C1	Adv	Adj	N	Prep	V	Pron	Con	Art	Mod
German C1	Prep	Adj	Adv	Con	Pron	Art	V	N	Mod

even cause difficulties at level C1 in German (in Hungarian this position is a discontinuous morpheme).

Adjectives are difficult to identify in both languages, but the reasons for difficulties are different. In English texts, the identification of adjectives is easier in a predicative than in an attributive function. In German texts, the situation is the opposite; due to the fact that the morphological identification of adjectives in German attributive function (owing to suffixation) is easier than its identification in predicative function.

Nouns yield medium difficulties. In left-branching structures (within both noun-pronoun and noun-verb groups) it is difficult to identify at level B1 and B2, as Hungarian is more characterised by right-branching structures. The mistakes due to differences in branching disappear at level C1, but can occur in longer sentences, as the latter require simultaneous storage of more transitional data in the buffer memory.

Pronouns have partly grammatical, partly semantic references and, probably due to this fact, belong to the word classes presenting medium difficulties. Personal pronouns with a semantic content are easier to guess, while semantically 'empty' (*es, it*) pronouns and those with an anaphoric reference function are more difficult to identify. German (possessive, reflexive) pronouns can even cause difficulties at level B2.

Modal verbs seem to present medium identification difficulties. It is a relatively underused word class in Hungarian: therefore, for beginners, it is difficult to identify both in German and English. Learners with intermediate and good language proficiency have only some grammatical difficulties (congruency agreement and copula).

Verbs are easy to identify (owing to their relatively universal argument structure). Although the difficulties posed by English and German are nearly identical in the case of nouns, the verbal system behaves in a different way. At level B1, irregular forms cause difficulties in English and word order (end position) causes difficulties in German. On the one hand, there is no irregular past tense (*spoke*), but on the other, there is no *Ich will ... werden, He had ... wanted* type discontinuous morpheme in Hungarian. These difficulties decrease and disappear at level B2. The Hungarian verb refers to the direct object argument morphologically as well; the absence of this marking makes identification more difficult at level B2, sometimes even at higher language proficiency.

Articles are the opening member of noun-pronoun is easier to recognise in both languages. However, in German it can be difficult even at level C1, in attributive structures in which it is positioned farther from the noun.

Conjunctions are easy to identify in both languages. It is easiest to recognise the conjunctive meaning.

Universal versus language specific features in L2 lexical processes

In foreign language lexical processes, the ontological status of word classes is quickly established (universal feature). It could be observed in our experiment insomuch that, with the improvement of language proficiency, the identification rate of word classes approaches more and more that of native speakers.

Sequential operations (influenced by word order) and lexical identification processes (branching, the distance of constituents) proved to be more difficult. In such cases strong first language (language specific) tendencies were observed.

Idiosyncratic foreign language proficiency is a dynamic system. Its changes are not proportional and cannot always be described in algorithms. They are governed by universal language operations to varying degrees. Certain partial systems quickly exhibit the characteristics of L2, while other partial systems do not or take a longer period to acquire such features (language practice, experience in oral communication, maturation).

References

Aborn, M., Rubinstein, H. and Sterling, T.D. (1959) Sources of contextual constraint upon words in sentences. *Journal of Experimental Psychology* 57.

Alderson, J.C. (1979) The Cloze procedure and proficiency in English as a foreign language. *TESOL Quarterly* 13(2), 219–227.

Burke, J.P., Schiavetti, N. (1975) Effects of cumulative context and guessing methods on estimates of transitional probability in speech. *Language and Speech* 18, 299–311.

Fillenbaum, S. and Jones, L.V. (1962) An application of cloze technique to the study of aphasic speech. *Journal of Abnormal and Social Psychology* 65, 183–189.

Fillenbaum, S., Jones, L.V. and Rapoport, A. (1963) The predictability of words and their grammatical classes as a function of rate of deletion from a speech transcript. *Journal of Verbal Learning and Verbal Behavior* 2, 186–194.

Oller, J. (1980) Communicative competence: Can it be tested? In R. Scarcella and S. Krashen (eds) *Research in Second Language Acquisition*. Rowley, Massachusetts: Newbury House.

Salzinger, K., Portnoy, S., and Feldman, R.S. (1962) The effect of order of approximation to the statistical approximation to English on the emission of verbal responses. *Journal of Experimental Psychology* 64, 52–57.

Taylor, W.L. (1953) Cloze procedure: A new tool for measuring readability. *Journal ism Quarterly* 30, 415–433.

Index

Authors

Aarts, B. 119
Aborn, M. 168
Aitchison, J. 89
Alderson, J. 170
Altenberg, B. 119
Appel, R. 17
Arnaud, P.J.L. 108

B. Fejes, K. 121
Babić, S. 149, 161
Bachman, L.F. 103
Baker, L.A. 86
Balló, L. 21
Bánréti, Z. 84
Bárdos, J. 61, 66
Barić, E. 158, 161
Beauvillain, C. 4
Beöthy, E. 136
Besner, D. 84, 86, 91
Bialystok, E. 17
Birdsong, D. 57
Bley-Vroman, R. 5
Blum, S. 149
Bond, Z.S. 60
Borer, H. 139, 140
Bošnjak, M. 149, 151
Brones, I. 3
Brown, R. 136
Bruck, M. 55
Burke, J. 170
Bybee, J. 5

Caramazza, A. 3
Carter, R. 146
Changeux, J-P. 39
Chee, M. 18
Cieślicka, A. 9
Clark, E.V. 60, 61, 136
Clark, H.H. 60, 61
Cobb, T. 121
Cole, R.A. 63
Cook, V. 3, 4, 9, 20
Corballis, M.C. 39

Coxhead, A. 119
Cristoffanini, P. 4
Csapó, B. 128
Cvikić, L. 147, 148, 149, 150, 151, 152, 158

d'Arcais, G. 85, 91
De Bleser, R. 19
De Bot, K. 6, 7
De Groot, A. 8, 9, 19, 33
De Houwer, A. 133, 134, 135, 136
Dehaene, S. 40
Deuchar, M. 133, 136
Dijkstra, T. 3, 4
Doró, K. 121
Dušková, L. 6

Ellis, R. 64, 65, 91
Elman, J. L. 85, 91
Emmorey, K. 5

Fabbro, F. 5, 6, 18, 40
Farkas, J. 83, 84
Fillenbaum, S. 169, 170
Fillmore, C.J. 84
Fodor, J. 5
Forster, K. I. 61
Franceschini, R. 3, 5
Francis, N. 45, 58
Fromkin, V.A. 5, 86

Garfield, J. 5
Garman, M. 61, 63
Garnes, S. 60
Gaskell, M. 4
Gass, S.M. 63, 64, 65, 80
Gathercole, S.E. 47
Genesee, F. 55
Gjerlow, K. 5
Globan, N. 147
Goldblum, M. 6
Gósy, M. 17, 19, 42, 60, 61, 63, 68, 69, 73, 74, 78, 85, 86, 89
Grainger, J. 4

Index

Granger, S. 119
Green, D. 7, 20
Grosjean, F. 6, 21, 143
Gulešić, M. 148

Haastrup, K. 146
Hamp-Lyons, L. 103
Hapsburg, D. von 55
Hatch, E.M. 64
Henriksen, B. 118, 146
Herdina, P. 3
Heredia, R. 19
Hernandez, A. 18
Herwig, A. 11
Hilton, H. 146
Hržica, G. 148

Illes, J. 18

Jackson, H. 20
Jacobs, H.R. 104, 105
Jagusztinné, U.K. 21
Jakimik, J. 63
Jelaska, Z. 147, 148
Jessner, U. 3
Jiang, N. 9
Joannopoulou, M. 3
John-Steiner, V. 136
Johnston, J.C. 84, 86, 91
Jones, L. 170

Kellerman, E. 6
Keresztes, Cs. 83, 84, 91
Kilborn, K. 40, 58
Kim, K. 19
Kirsner, K. 8
Klatt, D.H. 63
Klaudy, K. 87
Kniezsa, V. 83, 84
Kontra, M. 83, 84
Kouritzin, S. 7
Krashen, S. 65, 66
Kraus, N. 40
Kroll, J. 9, 19
Krueger, M. 4
Kusin, I. 147
Kuvač, J. 147, 148

Lamb, S. 17
Lanza, E. 133, 134, 135
Laufer, B. 101, 102, 108, 109, 110, 111, 112, 114, 118, 119, 146, 150, 159
Laufer-Dvorkin, B. 149, 150, 151
Lengyel, Zs. 60, 66, 85, 137

Leśniewska, J. 113
Levelt, W. 85, 91
Levenson, E.A. 149
Linnarud, M. 108, 109
Little, D. 3, 9, 10, 11
Luce, P.A. 63

Mack, M. 52
MacWhinney, B. 5, 136, 137, 143
Marslen-Wilson, W. 84
Massaro, D.W. 61, 63
Matthewson, L. 143, 144
McCarthy, M. 146
Meara, P. 3, 114, 146, 152
Meisel, J. 21, 134, 135, 142, 143
Melka, F. 118, 146
Meyer, C. 119
Molis, M. 57
Mondria, J.-A. 146
Moss, H. 4
Muysken, P. 17
Myers-Scotton, C. 7

Nation, I.S.P. 146
Nation, P. 101, 102, 109, 110, 111, 114, 118, 119, 122, 146, 149
Navarra, J. 40
Navracsics, J. 83
Neville, H. 18
Nihalani, N.K. 108
Novak, J. 147

Ó Laoire, M. 11
Obler, K. 5
Odlin, T. 64, 65, 83
Oller, J. 170

Pallier, C. 40
Palmer, A.S. 103
Paradis, M. 6, 7, 18, 45
Parke, T. 58
Perfetti, C. 85
Peterson, E. 83
Pinker, S. 138
Pisoni, D.B. 61, 63
Praninskas, J. 119

Quay, S. 133, 136

Read, J. 102, 103, 104, 106, 108, 109, 146
Renouf, A. 108
Ringbom, H. 6
Rohrbacher, B. 139, 140
Romaine, S. 135, 143

Salzinger, K. 168
Sawusch, J.R. 61
Schaeffer, J. 143, 144
Schelletter, C. 58
Schiavetti, N. 170
Schmid, M. 7, 8
Schmitt, N. 146
Schreuder, R. 6, 7, 85, 91
Selinker, L. 63, 64, 65, 80
Service, E. 6
Simon, O. 66, 72
Simpson, G. 4
Sinclair, J. 108
Singer, M. 62
Singleton, D. 3, 5, 6, 9, 10, 11, 19, 55, 57, 63, 83, 92, 117, 146
Skehan, P. 61, 65
Slobin, D. 136
Smith, F. 5, 86
Soufra, M. 12
Stemberger, J. 5
Stewart, E. 19
Swan, M. 113, 150
Swinney, D. 4

Tabossi, P. 4
Taeschner, T. 133
Taylor, W. 168
Težak, S. 149
Thomason, S. 83

Thorn, A.S. 47
Tokowicz, N. 9
Tribble, C. 104, 105, 106

Ullmann, M. 18
Ure, J.N. 106

Vančoné Kremmer, I. 72, 79
Viberg, Å. 119
Volterra, V. 133

Waller, T. 108
Walter, C. 113
Waring, R. 118, 146
Weber-Fox, C. 18
Weinreich, U. 8
West, M. 111, 119
Wheeler, D. 85
Whitaker, H. 6
White, L. 60, 63, 64, 65
Wiersma, B. 146
Wilson, D. 5
Witalisz, E. 101, 107, 110, 113, 115
Wolter, B. 3
Woutersen, M. 9

Yeni-Komshian, G.H. 62, 63

Zé Amvela, E. 20

Subjects

accuracy 78, 106, 115, 175,
acoustic perception 43, 46, 50-52, 61-63, 68, 71, 78
acquisition (L1 and L2) 18-19, 33-34, 39-42, 44, 47, 55, 57-58, 60-67, 75, 77, 79-80, 133-139, 143-144, 146-152, 154-155, 158, 161-162, 175
adjective 21-23, 26-28, 30-33, 113-114, 148, 158, 167-169, 171-180, 184
adverbs 22-23, 26-27, 169, 171-173, 175-182
affixes 159, 161
agglutinating language 167
agreement errors 139
allomorphic realisation 141
allophonic variation 137
analogizing 5-6
analytic rating 103
anaphoric reference 172, 184
antonyms 11, 20, 26-27, 29-32
aphasia 6
aphasics 170, 182

article 47, 86, 88-91, 137, 139-140, 142-143, 167-169, 172-173, 176-181, 184
association 20-21, 62-63, 69, 71-75, 85, 118
associative memory 20, 26
attitude 8
auxiliary 125, 136, 141-142
awareness 55, 64-65, 67, 75-76, 78, 87, 91, 135, 161

backwardness 48, 57
basal ganglia 17-18
bicultural 143
bilingual 4, 8-9, 17-21, 23, 27-29, 32-34, 39-43, 45-51, 53-58, 72, 133-135, 141, 143-144, 147, 153, 160
bilingual lexicon 17, 34, 39
bilingual speech processing 19
bottom-up processing 61-63, 79
brain activation 18
brain-imaging 5
buffer memory 184

Index

cerebral cortical organization 18
closed-class 18, 138
cloze procedure 166, 168, 170-171
code-switching 6-7, 85, 134
cognates 8-9, 11, 114
cognitive development 139
cognitive maturity 136
coinages 11
collocations 12, 26-27, 30-31, 34, 104, 119
Common European Framework 166
common storage 34
communication caesura 171
Complete Lexical Tutor 121
compound bilingualism 8-9
comprehension 43-49, 52, 53-58, 60-63, 65, 69, 171
conceptual representation 19, 20, 33
conceptual store 19
concrete words 8
configurative language 167
conjunctions 169, 172-173, 176-180, 185
connectionism 168
connectivity 3, 4, 8, 13
contact induced features 83-84, 86-90, 92
content words 106, 122-123, 158, 173, 175, 179
context 4, 33, 61, 65, 71, 76, 78, 85-86, 89, 91, 117-118, 138, 142, 159-160, 168-170
Contrastive Analysis Hypothesis 6
conversion 11
co-ordinate bilingualism 8-9
co-ordination 23, 172,
cortical activation 19
Croatian 21, 147-152, 158, 161-162
cross-linguistic 6, 7, 23, 26, 32, 40, 64-65, 80, 86, 143
cross-linguistic influence 6, 64-65, 80, 86
C-test 10, 118, 181

deceptive transparency 159, 161
declarative memory 17, 33,
decoding errors 64, 67
decoding process 60-64, 66-69, 71, 74-77, 80
deletion frequency 166, 168-170, 173, 178-179, 182
derivation 30-31, 137, 159, 161
Determiner Phrase (DP) 140, 143
discontinuous morpheme 136, 171, 180, 184
discourse community 88
dominant language 19, 39-42, 45, 47, 57-58
dual-store 19

early bilinguals 27-28, 33
encyclopaedic knowledge 61, 69, 168

English 5-7, 9, 11-12, 21, 41-49, 51-58, 66-70, 72-79, 83-84, 86-92, 101, 103, 105, 107, 109-111, 113, 119-120, 123-125, 128, 133-134, 136-143, 149-153, 158, 166-168, 170-173, 175, 180-184

frequency 3, 43, 68, 101-102, 106-120, 122, 124-125, 127, 136-137, 147, 150, 152, 160
frequency bands 107, 110-112, 119, 121-122, 124
Full Competence Hypothesis 139
function words 106, 123, 137, 168-170, 173, 175, 178-179
functional units 39

German 6-8, 10-11, 21, 84, 91, 147, 166-167, 170-171, 175-176, 179-184
Gestalt psychology 168
GMP test package 42, 62, 67-68
GMPeng 42, 67-70, 72-77, 79
grammatical gender 167
grammatical restrictions 169
graphemes 149

head-final languages 167
head-initial languages 167
high-frequency 117-128, 161
holistic rating 103, 108-109, 115
homonymy 151, 161
Hungarian 20-23, 27, 32, 41-50, 52-54, 56, 66-79, 83-84, 86-91, 120-121, 123-128, 133-134, 136, 138-143, 147-148, 166-167, 170-173, 175-182, 184
Hungarian–English bilinguals 41-42, 133
hyperonyms 23
hyponyms 20, 23-26, 29-32

individual differences 41, 45, 55, 67, 71, 75
infinitives 21-22, 26, 28, 31, 33,
Inflection Phrase (IP) 139, 143
Integration Continuum 9
interaction 3-4, 9, 41, 60-61, 76, 125
interference 84, 87-89, 92, 150
interlexical factors 150-151
interpretation 61-63, 68-69, 86, 115, 134
intralexical factors 150-151, 153-155, 160
introspective data 10, 12
irregular forms 138, 171, 184
Italian L1 152-154, 158

L1 speech perception and comprehension abilities 60, 66, 69, 72-73, 75, 77-80
L1 vocabulary/lexicon 117-118

L1 influence on L2 perception and comprehension 65
L2 learner 5, 40, 43, 55-56, 58, 64, 66, 108, 119, 128, 161
L2 speech perception and comprehension abilities 60, 66, 69, 72-75, 77-80
L2 teaching 57-58
L2 vocabulary/lexicon 117-118, 162
language contact 83, 86, 92
language examination 166, 170
language loss 6, 7
language proficiency 19, 42, 120, 175, 179-180, 184-185
language typological 166, 180
late bilinguals 20-21, 23, 27-29, 32-33
left-branching 167, 171, 173, 184
lexical access 47, 60, 63, 66, 68-69, 71, 73, 75-76, 80, 86, 92
lexical density 106, 108
lexical development 117
lexical equivalents 23, 26, 29, 32-33
lexical errors 112, 148-149, 151, 154-155, 160, 162
lexical frequency profile 101-102, 107, 109, 111, 114, 119
lexical individuality 109
lexical richness 106-108, 111
lexical sophistication 101, 106, 114
lexical statistics 106, 109, 113
lexical variation 106, 108
linguistic borrowing 83
links 23-26, 28, 33-34
low-frequency 106, 113, 115, 117-128

mark scheme 103-104
maturational factor 57
meaning 4, 8, 18-21, 23, 25-27, 29, 32-34, 44-45, 48, 61-62, 69, 74, 79-80, 84-85, 88, 102, 105, 108-109, 118-119, 125, 127-128, 136-139, 141, 148-150, 155, 157, 159-161, 167, 171-172, 177-178, 182, 185
measuring the readability 168
medical text 83, 86, 92
mental lexicon 3-5, 8-9, 12, 17, 19-20, 25, 39, 73, 84-85, 88, 91-92, 139, 146, 159, 161
mental representation 17, 25, 143
meronyms 20, 29, 32
microcontext 169
migration 7-8
minimal pair 155, 158
modified word/rule theory 138
modularity 5
morphemes 133, 136-137, 159, 161, 171, 180, 184
morphophonological rules 136, 149

morphosyntactic development 135
multicompetence 3-4

native speakers 73, 108, 119-120, 128, 148, 151, 166, 168, 170-171, 175, 179, 181, 185
native students 121-128
neighbours across languages 4
neuroimaging studies 19
non-native students 123-128
nouns 21-23, 25-26, 28-30, 32-33, 84, 112, 114, 119-120, 140-141, 143, 147-149, 158-159, 167-169, 171-173, 176-180, 182, 184

open-class 18
orthography 150-151, 161
overuse 119-120, 125

paradigmatic links 26
paradigmatic relations 23
parallel activation 4, 6-7, 12
pedagogical implications 66-67, 80
perceptual basis 39, 62, 78
perceptual mechanism 41
phoneme identification 47
phonemes 40, 62, 85, 149-150, 155, 157, 159-161
phonetic perception 43, 46, 50, 54, 58
phonological awareness 55
phonological rules 136, 148-149
phonological similarity 155, 160
phonological system 6, 149
plasticity of the brain 40
predictability 168-171
prime word 21-22, 25-28, 32-33
procedural memory 17, 34
processing time 52
productive lexicon 112, 114-115
pronouns 22-23, 28, 33, 167-169, 171-173, 176-180, 184
proofreading 83, 86-88
psychotypology 6, 9-13

qualitative assessment 103, 106

reading 42, 58, 66, 83, 85-86
receptive vocabulary knowledge 152
response 10, 20-29, 32-34, 44-46, 49-51, 53, 102
right branching 167, 184
Romani 148

semantic memory 17
semantic representation 17, 61
semantic similarity 19

sentence comprehension 44-45, 47-48, 52, 54, 69, 72, 74, 167
Serbian 21, 148
serial subprocess 43-44, 46-47, 50-51
single-store 19
Slavic 159, 161
Slovak 21, 72, 148
speech perception 39-45, 47, 52, 54-55, 57-58, 62-63, 71, 75, 77-79
speech processing 19, 34, 39-42, 47, 52, 57, 60-63, 75
storage 18-20, 23, 25, 32-34, 39, 184
strategies 11, 18, 40, 57-58, 76-77, 79-80, 114, 146
subordinative bilingualism 8-9
super-ordination 23, 25
synformy 150, 158
syngraphs 150
synmorphs 150
synonyms 11, 20, 23, 26, 29, 31-32, 107, 118, 127, 161
synphones 150-151, 155, 158, 160
syntagmatic links 23, 28, 34
syntagmatic relations 22-23, 28
synthetic structures 167

text comprehension 43-44, 47-51, 58, 62, 69, 71-74, 76, 78-79, 171
top-down processing 61-62, 74, 76, 79-80

topic – comment 167
translation 11, 19, 84, 88, 118, 150, 152-153, 159-160, 162
turn-taking 171
type-token ratio 108

universal argument structure 184
Universal Grammar 143-144

verbs 7, 21-23, 26-28, 30, 33, 119-120, 122, 138, 147, 149, 168-169, 171-173, 175-177
VocabProfile 121-123
vocabulary acquisition 146, 148-152, 154, 161-162
vocabulary assessment 101-104, 115, 146
vocabulary size 66, 115, 117-118, 148, 150
vocabulary test 109, 118, 121, 150, 152
vowel harmony 138

word association 20, 62, 69, 71-75, 118
word class 17, 19-23, 26-29, 32-33, 150, 158, 161, 166-169, 171, 175, 179, 180-182, 184-185
word families 106, 109, 111-112, 114, 119, 122, 158
word order 86, 138, 167, 171, 175-176, 182, 184-185
word recognition 85-86, 91-92
word retrieval 20, 23-24, 32-33, 138

For Product Safety Concerns and Information please contact our EU Authorised Representative:

Easy Access System Europe

Mustamäe tee 50

10621 Tallinn

Estonia

gpsr.requests@easproject.com

www.ingramcontent.com/pod-product-compliance
Ingram Content Group UK Ltd.
Pitfield, Milton Keynes, MK11 3LW, UK
UKHW022217250326
4937IPUK00005B/32